REDEEMING
THE DREAM

REDEEMING THE DREAM

The Case for
Marriage Equality

David Boies

AND

Theodore B. Olson

VIKING

VIKING
Published by the Penguin Group
Penguin Group (USA) LLC
375 Hudson Street
New York, New York 10014

USA | Canada | UK | Ireland | Australia | New Zealand | India | South Africa | China
penguin.com
A Penguin Random House Company

First published by Viking Penguin, a member of Penguin Group (USA) LLC, 2014

LIBRARY OF CONGRESS CATALOGING-IN-PUBLICATION DATA
Boies, David, author.
Redeeming the dream : the case for marriage equality / David Boies, Theodore B. Olson.
pages cm
Includes index.
ISBN 978-0-670-01596-2 (hardback)
1. Hollingsworth, Dennis, 1967—Trials, litigation, etc.   2. Perry, Kristin—Trials, litigation, etc.
3. Same-sex marriage—Law and legislation—United States—Cases.   4. Gay couples—Legal status, laws, etc.—United States—Cases.   5. Lawyers—United States—Biography.
6. United States. Defense of Marriage Act.   7. California. Proposition 8 (2008)
I. Olson, Theodore B., author.   II. Title.
KF228.H645B65 2014
346.7940168—dc23   2014007170

Printed in the United States of America
1   3   5   7   9   10   8   6   4   2

Designed by Nancy Resnick

To my wife, Mary Boies,
whose love and great mind are always there when I need them,
which is always,
and
to my daughter Caryl Boies,
whose courage, love, and dedication to justice inspire me every day.

—DB

To Lady Booth Olson,
my loving wife, partner, collaborator, and muse
and
to my mother, Yvonne Bevry Olson,
who instilled in me a passion for learning, reading, and writing.

—TBO

Contents

Preface

A few words about the origin of our collaboration and why we have written this book.

Our joint enterprise to challenge and overturn California's Proposition 8 had its origins in the most unlikely of contexts. In the fall of 2000, we found ourselves polar opposites in one of the most dramatic, intense, and hard-fought legal and political contests in our nation's history as Democrat Al Gore and Republican George W. Bush, candidates for president, battled over who would receive Florida's electoral college votes and election victory. Although a few presidential elections wind up being landslides, most are spirited and close contests and are not decided until election day. In 2000, though, even election day was not the end of the line: Legal battles and political turmoil would unfold for another five weeks before the outcome was finally decided.

The electoral college system allows each state to select "electors" based upon the size of its congressional delegation. And because most states choose electors on a winner-take-all basis, large popular vote margins in heavily populated states can be offset by considerably smaller margins for the opposing candidate in less populated states. Thus a candidate with less than a majority of the popular vote in a presidential election, or even with fewer popular votes than an opponent, can win a presidential election. Prior to 2000, three persons were elected president while losing the popular vote: John Quincy Adams in 1824, Rutherford Hayes in 1876, and Benjamin Harrison in 1888. It happened again in

2000, but the final result that year became known only after a bitter fight for the electoral votes of Florida, which were ultimately awarded to Texas governor George W. Bush over Vice President Al Gore as a result of a decision of the U.S. Supreme Court on December 12.

The electoral college system, a peculiarly American invention, has its supporters and detractors. On the one hand, it encourages campaigning in less populous states; on the other, it can lead candidates largely to ignore the voters in populous states like California, Texas, and New York when one or the other of the candidates has a lock on the vote. But because it is engraved in the Constitution, it is not likely to go away anytime soon.

While scores, if not hundreds, of lawyers were involved in the legal skirmishes that took place in federal courts and the courts of Florida, the two of us were the principal opposing Supreme Court advocates who squared off against each other at the Court's oral argument on December 11, 2000, when the matter came to a climax.

The controversy stemmed from the razor-thin closeness of the Florida popular vote. The winner would receive Florida's twenty-five electoral college votes and the election. The lead switched back and forth on the night of election day, with Bush seeming to hold a very slight edge as the initial counting was ending. At one point Gore conceded, and then withdrew his concession. Legal battles began even as dawn approached Florida on the following morning. While Bush clung to and fought to preserve his slight lead, controversies arose immediately as officials struggled over how to deal with the now infamous "butterfly" ballot, as well as veteran and absentee ballots, and the manner in which punch-card ballots were to be tabulated. Recounts were demanded, started, opposed, stopped, started again, and stopped again. The Florida Supreme Court ultimately rendered three decisions on various aspects of the recount process and the deadlines for counting votes, and the U.S. Supreme Court twice heard arguments and rendered opinions overturning the Florida Supreme Court (the first of which was argued for Bush by Ted but argued for Gore not by David but by another member of the Gore legal team).

With the numerous rulings by the courts and Florida election officials, new recount totals, and conflicting tabulations, the possible outcome seemed to change daily. The Bush lead kept shrinking with each new count. The world was transfixed by the avalanche of lawsuits and competing explanations and arguments by the campaign spokespersons and their lawyers. David led the Gore legal team and appeared frequently on television, explaining and defending the Gore position. Ted was performing similar duties for Bush, in court and in the public arena.

The day-to-day drama of the recount controversy has been depicted in exhaustive detail—including in David's own book *Courting Justice* and in the popular HBO television film *Recount*—and will undoubtedly be written about again and again. We will, for now, leave that to others. For the two of us, it all came down to our appearance before the Supreme Court of the United States on December 11. With the election of the forty-third president of the United States hanging in the balance, all of us were exhausted and sleep-deprived after five weeks of nonstop work. Had it gone on another day, it is far from clear that any of us would have remained standing.

Outside, on that Monday in December, the Supreme Court was surrounded by satellite trucks, cameras, reporters from all over the world, competing protestors with handmade posters and manufactured signs, tourists, and the simply curious. Inside, the courtroom was packed with leaders of the respective campaigns, members of Congress, journalists, dignitaries and celebrities, lucky members of the public who had managed to score a ticket, law clerks, and lawyers, lawyers everywhere.

In the moments before a Supreme Court argument, opposing counsel meet with the Supreme Court clerk, mostly to make sure everyone knows the ground rules and to receive last-minute guidance from the clerk concerning any changes in procedure. That meeting typically takes place in the lawyers' lounge, adjacent both to the courtroom and to a small office reserved for the solicitor general. On this day the lounge had been reserved as an overflow room where spectators could hear an audio broadcast of the argument, so the meeting took place in the clerk's office.

The Court's clerk, William K. Suter (who retired in 2013), formerly the acting judge advocate general of the army, is a tall, distinguished man, with the erect bearing that befits a retired army general. Elegantly dressed in the customary morning suit worn by certain Court officials and representatives of the solicitor general's office, he went over the protocol with us, mindful, as everyone was, that this was an historic occasion, like few others in the Court's history. He explained the day's procedures and tried to put us at ease with a few light comments about the Court and his office, which was decorated with an autographed photograph of himself and Private First Class Elvis Presley, who had trained with him at Fort Hood in 1958. It was a noble effort, but nothing was going to put either of us at ease with the presidency at stake and the whole world watching. We then entered the courtroom and took our positions on opposite sides of the podium facing the justices, who entered shortly thereafter. The tense but respectful and professional argument ensued.

In his oral arguments, David urged the Court to allow the statewide manual recount of votes ordered by the Florida Supreme Court. He argued that state officials should make every effort to decipher individual ballots so they might "count every vote." Ted's position was that the Supreme Court should uphold the properly granted certification of a Bush victory by the Florida secretary of state. He argued that the recount ordered by the state court amounted to a "major restructuring of the Florida Election Code" with "evolving" standards varying "from county to county" that would be "different throughout sixty-four different counties."

Although the suspense seemed to last forever, especially for those of us who had been in the trenches—this included all our colleagues and many reporters—the conclusion came just thirty-six hours later. At around 10 P.M. on December 12, the clerk's office called the competing lawyers and announced the Court's decision, as copies were handed out to exhausted, confused, frazzled, and windblown reporters standing on the courthouse steps, who began to try to explain the decision to their respective broadcast audiences. The recount was stopped, and the election was finally declared over—Bush was the winner.

Vice President Gore delivered a gracious but heavy-hearted concession speech the next evening. The nation, and the world, began the process of moving on.

It was out of that historic controversy that our friendship developed and ripened. When Ted was nominated by President Bush in February 2001 to be solicitor general, the government's advocate in the Supreme Court, a partisan confirmation battle ensued. Emotions from the close election were still running high, and Democratic senators, still smarting from the Supreme Court decision, were decidedly cool to the idea of putting Ted in the position of the nation's top Supreme Court lawyer. David, however, lent Ted his support, including a personal appeal to Senator Edward M. Kennedy, with whom he had a close relationship.

When Ted was finally (narrowly) confirmed by the Senate, David and his wife, Mary, attended his swearing-in at the Justice Department. Later that year David and Mary offered comfort to Ted when his wife, Barbara, was murdered by terrorists on September 11 when the plane she was on, American Airlines Flight 77, was hijacked and flown into the Pentagon. Later that fall, at a formal dinner in Washington attended by two thousand or so Washingtonians, Ted was the presenter when David received an award for his inspirational accomplishments in overcoming a learning disability. A prolonged standing ovation was accorded the two of us—an emotional outpouring of appreciation for the fact that two former adversaries could come together with respect and affection for each other in a city emotionally exhausted and wounded by the close election, the 9/11 attacks, and a frightening and deadly anthrax incident soon afterward.

As time went by we began to spend more time together socially. While we differed on many political issues, we found we had much in common, including our respect for and dedication to the law, and our love of fine wine. David and Mary were present in Napa Valley in 2006 when Ted married his wife, Lady. The four of us enjoyed bicycling in Italy, France, Croatia, and Ireland together with friends in the succeeding years.

We frequently discussed seeking opportunities to work together on a case one day, although we occasionally found ourselves yet again on opposite sides of the courtroom. Ironically, in one case, Ted, the conservative, wound up representing labor—the NFL Players Association—while David, the liberal, represented management—the

NFL and team owners. In another we were on opposing sides in a high-stakes battle between owners of Argentinian bonds.

It wasn't until 2009 that our chance finally to team up arose in our former home state of California.

———

Proposition 8 was a watershed event of sorts in California's—and America's—history. Just about everything major that happens in California, from the Gold Rush, to the Reagan revolution, to the property tax revolt, reverberates nationally. When it isn't mocking or satirizing California, the rest of the country adopts, adapts, mimics, emulates, or envies what happens there.

Unfortunately California, a progressive state in many respects, with a frontier and welcoming attitude, also has a regrettable history of inequality and discrimination. This includes the institutionalized mistreatment of Chinese immigrants who helped build the state; the internment of Japanese Americans (albeit directed by the federal government) in camps in California during World War II; racial discrimination against and ghettoization of African Americans, leading to urban riots during the 1960s and 1970s; and a statewide ballot proposition in the mid-1960s to repeal fair housing laws. The last was ultimately overturned by a 5–4 Supreme Court decision.

But California has also become a remarkably diverse society, rich in multiple subcultures from Asia, distinctive Latino populations, blacks, Armenians, and innumerable other nationalities and ethnicities. California's Supreme Court was the nation's first, in 1948, to strike down laws prohibiting interracial marriage, beating the U.S. Supreme Court to that milestone by nineteen years. In 2008 the California Supreme Court was also one of the first to strike down a state law limiting marriage to the union of a man and a woman.

Although we were both born in Illinois, within six months of each other, our parents brought us to California at an early age (David to Southern California, Ted to the Bay Area). We grew up in families that taught us to appreciate the differences between individuals in our society and to believe in principles of equality, to respect the views and backgrounds of others, and to be sensitive to the rights of our fellow citizens. We were both educated in California public schools and California colleges, and so the state's racial, ethnic, and cultural melting pot became part of our DNA. Honoring the differences between individuals and understanding their perspectives, as well as a certain libertarianism, were qualities we took almost for granted as Californians.

It thus came as a surprise, even a shock, to both of us, as it did to many others who consider themselves Californians, when, six months after the California Supreme Court issued its decision upholding the right of gays and lesbians to marry, California voters took that right away by a popularly enacted amendment to the state's constitution. The incongruity of this measure, Proposition 8, seemed even more pronounced given that the vote that passed it took place the same day that an African American man, the product of an interracial marriage, was elected president of the United States, with the overwhelming support of California voters. What was going on?

We both felt deeply that Proposition 8 was wrong and fundamentally at odds with our vision of America, and with our understanding of California and Californians. As we describe in these pages, we vowed to do everything we could to reverse this immensely unfortunate and strikingly un-Californian, and ultimately un-American, decision. Throughout our effort we kept in mind the Reverend Martin Luther King Jr.'s famous *Letter from Birmingham City Jail*, in which he responded to pastors and others who had urged him to proceed slowly in the pursuit of equal rights because they feared a backlash. He wrote that "for years now I have heard the word 'Wait!' It rings in the ear of every Negro with piercing familiarity. This 'Wait' has almost always meant 'Never.'" King made a similar point in his famous "I Have a Dream" speech when he declared, "This is no time to engage in the luxury of cooling off or to take the tranquilizing drug of gradualism. . . . Now is the time to make justice a reality for all of God's children." We believed that Reverend King's vision for America included equality for all, and that our efforts could help redeem the dream for those whose lives, loves, and aspirations had been diminished and demeaned by Proposition 8.

————

This book will tell the story of how we joined to fight to overturn Proposition 8 in the courts and to do everything in our power to change public attitudes and address fears regarding our gay and lesbian brothers and sisters that had led to this harmful, depressing, and, in our eyes, tragic development. We feel that it is exceedingly important to share why we believe this endeavor was a critical step in the process of changing not only California but, we hope, America and the world. And to invite our fellow citizens to share our experiences in undertaking this challenge.

At the end of this segment of our journey—though we certainly do not intend that the story finish there—we succeeded in overturning Proposition 8. Thousands of gays and lesbians have married and formed families in California, and attitudes and public opinion have changed dramatically throughout this nation. Numerous states have subsequently enacted laws allowing gays and lesbians to marry, and many courts have acted where legislatures and citizens have not. The country has evolved swiftly and decisively in the direction of marriage equality and against various forms of discrimination on the basis of sexual orientation. Our effort and the efforts of the scores of people who helped and supported us have contributed, we hope, to the beginning of the end of this last major bastion of institutionalized discrimination in America. We wrote this book to explain our process, our thinking, and our education, and, we hope, to persuade more and more Americans to join us in achieving the ultimate goals that brought us together in this case.

David Boies
Theodore B. Olson
New York City and Washington, D.C., 2014

ONE

Proposition 8

Although the 2008 presidential election produced an historic victory for his candidate, Barack Obama, Rob Reiner was so depressed in the days afterward that he didn't feel like getting out of bed. He was deeply pained by the fact that at the very moment the country had elected the first African American president, a majority of the voters in his state had enacted Proposition 8, which denied marriage rights to gay men and lesbian women. *If Californians couldn't get this right,* he thought, *who could?*

After brooding for days, Reiner finally roused himself for lunch with his wife, Michele, at a favorite haunt, the Polo Lounge at the Beverly Hills Hotel. An award-winning actor, director, and producer, Reiner was bound to run into friends who had supported his many political causes and would cheer him up. But to ensure that he would be in sympathetic company, he asked Chad Griffin and Kristina Schake to join them. Partners in a public relations firm, Griffin and Schake had worked hard to defeat Proposition 8 in a "Vote No" campaign that was funded mainly by Hollywood and Silicon Valley. Chad was a political wunderkind who had signed on to the first Clinton presidential campaign instead of going to college and wound up as the youngest member of the White House staff at the age of nineteen. Chad had first met Rob when he was assigned to assist on Reiner's 1995 film *The American President.* White House friends had talked him into returning to school to get a degree. After graduation he went to work for Reiner's charitable foundation, and a deep personal friendship developed. Reiner regarded Griffin as a son.

During the lunch, Proposition 8 dominated the conversation. Like mourners at a wake, Griffin, Schake, and the Reiners poured out their shock, grief, and dismay at the outcome of the vote. Only six months earlier, in May 2008, the California Supreme Court, by a vote of 4–3, had determined that denying gay and lesbian Californians the right to marry the person of their choice—regardless of their sex—would violate the state constitution's guarantee to all its citizens of equal protection under its laws. California had thus become only the second state, after Massachusetts, to legalize marriage between persons of the same sex. That case, titled *In re Marriage Cases,* was the culmination of a long process that had begun in 2000 with the passage of Proposition 22, a statewide ballot measure that restricted marriage to opposite-sex couples. In 2004 San Francisco mayor Gavin Newsom effectively defied that law by unilaterally authorizing the San Francisco county clerk to issue marriage licenses to gay and lesbian couples. Thousands had flocked to City Hall to wed, and pictures of the joyous couples were transmitted all over the world. The celebrations were brought to a halt when the courts ruled that Mayor Newsom had no authority on his own to alter the state's marriage laws, that marriage was a statewide issue, not a matter for local discretion. That ruling was in turn challenged in the litigation that resulted in the May 2008 *In re Marriage Cases* decision pronouncing, as a matter of the California constitution, that marriage between persons of the same sex was a constitutional right. The decision explained that California's domestic partnership law—a law that gave gays and lesbians virtually all the same legal rights as married persons except for the right to call themselves married—was not an adequate substitute for the institution of marriage but bestowed instead a form of second-class citizenship.

The opponents of same-sex marriage had anticipated the outcome of the state supreme court decision by gathering signatures for Proposition 8 and taking the steps to put a constitutional amendment to reverse it on the November ballot. Thanks to massive amounts of funds and manpower from, among others, the Catholic, Baptist, and

Mormon faiths, Proposition 8 was approved by 52 percent to 48 percent.

After the vote, the leaders of the groups that had opposed Proposition 8 were reluctant to bring a federal (as opposed to a state) constitutional challenge to the measure, fearful that a federal court loss, perhaps in the U.S. Supreme Court, would set back for decades the rights of gays and lesbians not only in California but across the country. Instead they initiated proceedings in the California Supreme Court, arguing that Proposition 8, which was labeled an amendment to the California constitution, was itself in violation of that constitution. It was not actually an amendment, they argued, but a revision of the constitution, which required submission to and approval by the California legislature as well as the voters. Hence, they claimed, the November 8 voter approval was insufficient and the proposition was invalid. (The lawsuit made other claims, but the "revision" argument was the most prominent.) Most legal experts were skeptical that Proposition 8 could be overturned with a California constitutional challenge. Proposition 8 was labeled and marketed as an amendment, and there seemed little prospect that the California Supreme Court would rule otherwise.

Thus, at the time of their Polo Lounge lunch, Rob and Michele Reiner and their colleagues were convinced that Proposition 8 would survive a procedural challenge under the California constitution and that the only hope for marriage equality in California was a federal constitutional case. They were also concerned that such a suit was inevitable, given the tens of thousands of gay Californians who yearned to be married. But they were worried that such a case would be brought by a lawyer inexperienced, unprepared, or otherwise ill-equipped for bringing a case that might well go to the Supreme Court of the United States. There were countless lawyers in California who might file such a suit. Unless the plaintiffs themselves had the right background, history, and determination, and were spearheaded by experienced, respected constitutional lawyers, that case, they believed, was also destined to fail. The question was obvious, immediate, and urgent: What to do?

As the lunch wound down, Michele Reiner looked up from the table to see a familiar face. A talented event coordinator and fund-raiser, Kate Moulene was a professional "connector" whose work included linking the rich, famous, and powerful to important and worthy causes. A brilliant networker, she knew more prominent and success-ful people on a first-name basis than most people meet in a lifetime. Like the Reiner lunch group, she had been opposed to Proposition 8 and was dismayed by the outcome of the voting. Kate stopped by the Reiners' table and chatted with the group about how best to proceed in opposing the measure. Listening to their concerns, she suggested someone who she thought might offer the best insight on the subject, a Washington lawyer named Ted Olson.

"He used to be my brother-in-law," explained Kate. "He and my sister divorced, but we all stayed friends. He's brilliant. He's approach-able. And I think he'll help you."

Chad, Kristina, Michele, and Rob were flabbergasted. A passionate liberal with a long memory, Rob had come to view Ted Olson as "the devil" during *Bush v. Gore*. Rob had been a strong supporter of Al Gore, and had actually been in the vice president's residence the night of the Supreme Court decision. Also, as solicitor general, Ted had been one of the people responsible for policies that, Rob believed, had brought misery to so many Americans during the George W. Bush administration. Given that it was Bush who had backed an amend-ment to the U.S. Constitution that would have banned same-sex mar-riage across America, how, Rob wondered, could Ted Olson possibly be helpful in support of marriage equality?

Kate had expected Rob's response and explained that Ted was open-minded and, in her experience, had manifested an abiding con-cern for equality and fairness. He was sensitive to the rights of mi-norities and was outraged whenever he discovered that someone had been bullied. As Kate described Ted as "caring and compassionate," she remembered, without mentioning it, that when her mother was being treated for cancer, Ted had written to her every day. Returning to practical considerations, she pointed out that Ted's experience might just tip the balance at the Supreme Court, where the justices seemed evenly divided on many controversial issues. "Besides," added

Kate, "if you are going to do this in the federal courts, I don't think there's anyone who has won more historic Supreme Court cases."

While Rob, who had been inspired by seeing his parents join the civil rights movement in the 1960s, had no intention of giving up on the marriage equality fight, he wasn't quite ready to consider recruiting someone like Ted Olson as an ally. Olson may have been smart and successful—heaven knows, he had prevailed in *Bush v. Gore*—but he was a political *enemy*. Michele, if anything, was even more stunned by the idea of joining forces with Olson for a challenge to Proposition 8. "Are you brain-dead?" Kate recalls her saying.

As she left the Polo Lounge and drove home, Kate thought she had made her point effectively but was convinced that she had failed to persuade her friends. In fact, they had been so unreceptive that she feared they had forgotten that she was on their side. Then her cell phone rang. It was Rob, and as she would recall it, he said something like, "I know you are not really stupid, so tell me again, why would Ted take this case?" She repeated her points about Ted's core values and added, "He can really make a good argument on anything. I recall from time to time asking him to explain some conservative position that I could not comprehend, and even though I'm like a Che Guevara liberal, he helped me actually appreciate why conservatives think the way they do on a lot of things."

Rob trusted Kate not only as a friend but as an ally and intermediary. His natural creativity kicked in, and he let himself imagine what might happen if Kate were right. In the role of champion of same-sex marriage, Ted would be a wonderful example of casting against type, and sometimes the unexpected worked quite effectively. "Okay," said Reiner. "We could take a shot." He said he would put Chad in charge of the outreach and send him to Washington to take Ted's temperature and evaluate his willingness, sincerity, and level of commitment.

After she got home and checked on her five kids, Kate dialed Washington. When Ted came on the line she couldn't resist teasing him about the GOP's loss in the presidential election, but then got down to business. "I'm going to assume that you think Prop 8 passing was a mistake," she said confidently.

Ted told her that she was correct. He believed that discrimination against our citizens based on aspects of their identity—race, gender, sexual orientation, who they are as persons—was wrong, and the use of a constitutional amendment to make it the law, in any state, seemed beyond the pale. Kate told him about the Polo Lounge discussion and Rob's later phone call. Rob's fame, which began when he played Michael "Meathead" Stivic on the groundbreaking 1970s TV show *All in the Family* and was consolidated when he became a highly regarded director, meant that she didn't have to explain who he was. However, she did make a point of mentioning Reiner's political affiliation, and his dedication to the cause. Ted knew Rob not only as a talented creative person, but also as someone who put his heart, energy, and financial resources into the things he believed in. Ted respected that. "Rob is serious," Kate concluded, "and he's in it for the long haul."

It would indeed be a long haul. As Ted confirmed, any legal challenge to the amendment would likely start in a state or federal trial court but had a very good chance of moving all the way to the U.S. Supreme Court. He mentioned that the people who had put Proposition 8 on the ballot were also well aware of this, that he had been approached, very indirectly and informally, about helping on that side. But Ted had never felt comfortable with efforts to stigmatize, isolate, or label gays and lesbians. He leaned toward a free-market, low-tax, less-government, libertarian brand of politics that allowed individual Americans as much freedom as possible. From that perspective he viewed with skepticism restrictions on personal freedoms.

"I turned them down," said Ted. "And you can tell Chad he can call me. I'm interested."

TWO

Why I Took the Case

Theodore B. Olson

I t is not unusual in Washington offices to find at least one "vanity wall" decorated with an array of framed photographs featuring the occupant's smiling face with dignitaries, celebrities, officeholders, and diplomats. My office has several photographs of my wife and family members and two signed photographs of the two presidents I have served, Ronald Reagan and George W. Bush. Most visitors to my office give those photographs a passing glance, but almost everyone is intrigued by the framed circle of white goose-feather quills, assembled by my wife, Lady Booth Olson. They come from the U.S. Supreme Court, where by tradition lawyers receive one as a memento each time they appear for an argument. My collection, which now exceeds sixty, comes not just from my tenure as solicitor general in the George W. Bush administration; over thirty represent cases for clients in my practice as a partner of the Gibson, Dunn & Crutcher law firm.

My early career involved all kinds of litigation matters: product liability and medical malpractice defense, antitrust, securities, entertainment and commercial disputes. But I was particularly drawn to constitutional law, having been privileged to represent the media—the *Los Angeles Times,* NBC, *Los Angeles* magazine—in battles regarding gag orders, libel suits, and subpoenas to reporters. In representing outdoor advertisers—known to most people as billboards—I asserted property rights and First Amendment claims against cities, states, and the federal government seeking to remove advertising signs, often without compensation. One of the cases, *Metromedia Inc. v. City of San Diego,* wound up in the Supreme Court in 1981. Although I didn't argue that one in the high court—by then I had entered public service—it did increase my appetite for complex appellate and constitutional work. In the years since, I've handled constitutional cases on behalf of clients that included international corporations, banks, communications conglomerates, students who challenged racial preferences in law school admissions, the states of Virginia, New York, and Kansas, the U.S. Chamber of Commerce, the American Bar Association, and Presidents Reagan and George W. Bush. I've represented individuals as varied as convicted spy Jonathan Pollard, journalist Timothy Phelps, Hawaiian rancher Freddy Rice, and Los Angeles police officer Stacey Koon.

Like most of us, I could never have predicted the course of my life. Born in the Midwest, I was raised in California in a solidly middle-class family. My father was an engineer with United Airlines, and my mother, who grew up on a dairy farm in Wisconsin, became a teacher after her five children were well launched. I never met a lawyer until I was in college and published a cartoon in the student newspaper that so offended a professor that he threatened to sue me. I met with an attorney who helped communicate to the aggrieved academic the meaning of and protection for satire under the First Amendment. But this incident, and four years of extensive experience speaking and debating on my college forensic team, heightened my interest in the law as a career. More inspiration came from Clarence Darrow's autobiography, *Attorney for the Damned,* and Louis Nizer's *My Life in Court,* both of which make a compelling case for a life in the law.

My parents instilled in me a belief in the American dream and the value of hard work. I also became interested in politics and began working for Republican candidates in 1960. I served as president of my law school's Republican group, which was a lonely position at the Berkeley campus of the University of California in 1964 during the Johnson/Goldwater presidential election. After graduating from law school I joined the Los Angeles office of Gibson, Dunn & Crutcher. I sought out a partner there, William French Smith, who was widely known in legal, business, and Republican circles, and offered to be his spear carrier, speechwriter, gofer—whatever he could use. That turned out to be a fortunate relationship. Smith was among those who convinced Ronald Reagan to run for governor of California, and Reagan became a client of our firm. When he ran for president, we were both active in his campaigns. And when Smith became President Ronald Reagan's first attorney general, the president named me to be assistant attorney general in charge of the Office of Legal Counsel. I was, in essence, the president's and the attorney general's lawyer, the primary lawyer charged with providing legal advice to the president and the executive branch.

The position as head of OLC (previously held by William Rehnquist in the Nixon administration and Antonin Scalia in the Ford administration) in the Reagan administration put me in the middle of controversies such as the air traffic controllers' strike and executive privilege. When President Reagan left office, I represented him throughout the Iran-Contra investigation. Years later I represented George W. Bush in the *Bush v. Gore* litigation, which culminated in the two Supreme Court decisions that resolved the 2000 election controversies and put Governor Bush in the White House.

Although I didn't tell Kate Moulene at the time, and probably did not fully realize it myself, I think that I had made up my mind to accept the opportunity to take on Proposition 8, if it were offered to me, by the time I hung up the phone after speaking with her. I had been shocked by the California voters' decision to enact Proposition 8. It seemed wrong, gratuitously hurtful to gays and lesbians, and wholly inconsistent with my views as to what California—and America—is all about.

Had he been aware of my frame of mind, Chad Griffin wouldn't have been so nervous on the day in late November 2008 when he flew to Washington to meet me in my office.

Chad has said that he had never before imagined visiting the Gibson Dunn law offices in Washington, D.C., on Connecticut Avenue. He saw our firm as identified with conservative causes. He could hardly have known that most of our practice had nothing to do with politics, and that our lawyers were reasonably evenly divided between Republicans and Democrats and had handled politically controversial cases on all points on the political spectrum.

As Chad entered my office he noticed the framed photographs of me with Presidents Reagan and Bush but drew some comfort from the quill pens, the experience they represented, and from the fact that I knew the Supreme Court well. Still, I was the one he blamed, almost personally, for the Supreme Court decisions that made George W. Bush president over Al Gore in 2000. Since he had worked in the Clinton-Gore administration, Chad had been heartbroken by the outcome of *Bush v. Gore.* Also, he blamed President Bush and political wizard Karl Rove for recent anti–gay marriage ballot referendum campaigns that had tapped into the fear and prejudices of certain "values" voters to increase turnout. In 2004 these referenda were passed in each of the eleven states where they were proposed. The intense interest in the same-sex marriage issue might have increased turnout for Bush in key states, and that may have given him the margin that ensured a second term. In Chad's mind, none of it would have happened but for my victory in the court struggle over the 2000 election.

In fact, the responsibility for the Supreme Court's decisions in 2000 rested with the justices alone. My advocacy for the Bush-Cheney team had been to present the most compelling arguments to support my client. David did the same for Vice President Gore. The justices made the decisions. Likewise, Chad couldn't have known that although I was responsible for supporting the administration's position in the Court, when the White House had sought my opinion on a constitutional amendment to define marriage as exclusively heterosexual, I responded that I thought it was a bad idea. As I recall, I said, "I wouldn't vote for it and I am quite sure it would never get the votes required to pass."

As Chad asked me about matters of law and fact surrounding marriage equality, he realized that I was more conversant with the issues than he had anticipated, and sympathetic. He began to relax and later explained that it was then that he began to consider that I might be the right person to make a federal case against Proposition 8. The irony of a former intimate of the Clinton White House teaming up with someone who had been an outspoken Clinton critic piqued his interest. More important, he sensed that if I threw my weight behind the cause, I might influence at least some fellow conservatives or moderates. At minimum, my presence in the case would spark media interest, which would be an important part of persuading the public that the cause was just.

For my part, I found Chad to be both intensely bright and far more direct and candid than most of the people you meet in political circles. Although more than thirty years and a lifetime of experience separated us, I was impressed by his passion, intensity, sincerity, and strength of purpose. He also seemed realistic. He knew that a challenge to Proposition 8 would almost certainly end up at the U.S. Supreme Court. The risk—that a loss there would set back the cause of equality nationwide—had inhibited other lawyers who had considered the issue. The reward, however, would be profound. A victory, even if confined to California, would restore what the voters had taken away. A more sweeping decision, upending all the laws in the country that discriminated against same-sex couples, would make tens of millions of people, and their loving relationships, equal in the eyes of the law.

The implications of marriage equality were both broad and deep. A foundational relationship in personal, social, cultural, and legal terms, marriage determines an individual's status with regard to Social Security, property rights, inheritance claims, health insurance coverage, and parental rights. These are only a few of the areas where spouses enjoy special rights, privileges, and responsibilities. On the federal level alone, more than a thousand statutes and regulations touch on marriage as a defining legal and social bond. Any change in the definition of who might or might not be legally wed would help overturn long-standing prejudices about sexual orientation, gender, and relationships.

For decades the courts had been moving gradually toward a point where a decision favoring marriage equality seemed possible. One crucial landmark had been the famous *Loving v. Virginia* decision of 1967, which held that no couple could be denied the right to marry on the basis of the race of their chosen spouse. After *Loving*, which underscored the fundamental importance of marriage in many aspects of our culture, came the 1996 case of *Romer v. Evans*, which found that

Colorado had no "rational basis" for acting to limit legal protections accorded to lesbians and gays. Finally, in 2003 the Court held in *Lawrence v. Texas* that antisodomy laws used to criminalize same-sex relationships were unconstitutional. Taken together, these precedents provided powerful support for the next step—full marriage equality.

The Supreme Court record and related constitutional principles were present in my mind as I talked with Chad, but in this first encounter, much of our conversation was personal. Chad's life story would fill a book by itself.

Chad spoke powerfully about the emotional and psychological burdens of growing up gay in the American South of the 1980s, an experience that heightened his understanding of the toll that anxiety over one's sexual identity can take on young people, inspired his passion for justice, and provided him the energy and drive to pursue the goal of equality for gays and lesbians everywhere. He was raised in Arkadelphia, Arkansas (population 10,000), during the time when Bill Clinton was governor of that state. Arkadelphia was steeped in the traditions of the Southern Baptist Convention and small-town America. Education was the family business: His mother taught elementary school, and his father was a district superintendent. "The golden rule was the most important lesson they taught me," he told me. "It was that and the idea that if you saw something wrong you were supposed to do something about it. Don't just sit there. Get involved."

As Chad explained it, Arkansas was the kind of place where, even as late as the 1990s (he graduated from high school in 1991), it was possible to believe you didn't know a single gay person. He understood this because he didn't even acknowledge his own identity as a gay man until he was well into his twenties. "No one talked about these issues where I grew up," he recalled. "I really did think that I had never known a gay person. I didn't even know that *I* was a gay person."

He then raised a fact that I had only vaguely understood: the high suicide rate among teenagers struggling with their sexual identity. Reliable studies have shown that gay and lesbian teens are more than twice as likely as their heterosexual peers to say that they have attempted suicide. They are also subject to higher rates of bullying.

Historically the rejection and hostility that lesbian and gay kids feel flow from deep sources of fear and prejudice that were codified as moral imperatives in religion and law. Just as the Constitution justified racism by condoning slavery and counting blacks as just three-fifths of whites, thousands of laws effectively supported, even endorsed, the oppression of gay men and lesbian women. Although certain individuals across the country resisted this discrimination, inferiority and "differentness" were deeply ingrained in the law. Fortunately, when equality is enforced, it has demonstrably beneficial effects. Teens who say they live in less hostile communities and supportive families do better in every measure of well-being, from mental health to resistance to drug use. This suggests that while life can be challenging for young lesbian and gay people, we make it better every time we move, as individuals and as a society, to break down prejudice and increase equality.

Before we ended our meeting, I made certain that Chad understood the demands of a Proposition 8 challenge. First, the process would be a marathon, not a sprint, and it could take five years or more. Actually, it would be more like those obstacle endurance races that more and more Americans are joining these days. Second, while Gibson Dunn would donate substantial time and resources to the fight, the actual cost would likely run into the millions of dollars, and the Griffin/Reiner group would have to prepare to meet the financial burden. It was very important that any effort like this involve broad support—personal and financial buy-ins—not just a lawyers' venture. Finally, the project would require some responsible, levelheaded people—gay and lesbian couples—who were being denied their rights under Prop 8 and could withstand all the pressures they would face as plaintiffs. These individuals would be the public faces of the case, subject to press scrutiny and intense questioning at trial. They would have to be capable of grace under enormous pressure, and they would have to be committed to staying together throughout it all. "We need real, legitimate human beings who really want to be married," I stressed.

Chad later told me that he returned to Los Angeles believing I was the right lawyer to lead the effort against Prop 8. He expected resistance from others in the equal-rights community, but he thought that once they met me they would change their minds. A meeting at the Reiners' house would be a starting point. If I could win over the passionate, committed, demanding, irascible Rob and Michele, others would fall into place.

When I went home that day after my meeting with Chad I talked it over with my wife, Lady, who greeted the prospect of this civil rights challenge with real enthusiasm. She too had been raised in a family that could not tolerate prejudice. But as a lawyer and self-described "legal geek," Lady recognized immediately the difficulties the case presented. Chief among them was the matter of asking the courts to overturn a legally valid—if constitutionally flawed—plebiscite. In the American system we tend to favor direct democracy whenever possible. This means that the voice of the people, expressed in a referendum, usually prevails. But like me, Lady believed that marriage equality was a truly just cause, and this case could be the opportunity of a lifetime to bring justice to millions of people. In her mind, bringing a case against Proposition 8 would give meaning and value to our careers in a way that made meaningful contributions to many, many lives.

The Reiners are very down-to-earth people. They are neither young nor glamorous, and they don't come with an entourage. You can't be around them without becoming imbued with their passion, energy, and enthusiasm. Rob and Michele expressed no discernible skepticism about me when we met at the doorstep of their Brentwood, California, home; indeed, I was welcomed with literally open arms. Chad was present, as was Kate Moulene, and also two Academy Award winners, producer Bruce Cohen and writer Dustin Lance Black. Bruce, a big player in the gay and lesbian rights movement, had married his longtime partner, Gabriel Catone, during the brief period in 2008 when same-sex marriages were legal in California. An extremely effective fund-raiser for liberal causes and candidates, he had also founded one of the first organizations in Los Angeles—a group called Out There—to support gay men and lesbian women in the film industry. Lance was widely regarded as one of the most influential young men in Hollywood. He won an Academy Award for his screenplay for the movie *Milk,* which tells the story of San Francisco's first openly gay member of the board of supervisors Harvey Milk, who was murdered by a fellow supervisor.

Energetic, outgoing, and somewhat larger than life, Rob blurted out that he still found it a bit mind-boggling that "Ted Olson is at my house!" He delivered this line with his iconic and infectious big, warm smile. When the conversation turned serious he explained that he didn't have a direct stake in marriage equality. "We don't have a gay child, so about all you can say is we're in the 'gay-adjacent' community," as he put it. However, Rob said, he was very serious about politics and social policy, especially when it came to civil rights. In this particular case he was also motivated by his love for Chad, and his belief that "this was something we could realistically hope to accomplish." He was unwilling to accept that the fight for equality had ended on election night 2008 with the other side holding the prize.

When the conversation turned to me, I acknowledged that if I filed the initial lawsuit to overturn Proposition 8, many in the gay and lesbian community were not going to believe I was doing it for the right reason. There was, after all, nothing new in the idea of asking the federal courts to settle the marriage equality question. LGBT lawyers had been arguing the pros and cons of this approach for more than a decade and had formed an informal consensus that it was just too risky. If someone with my conservative background and reputation now brought such a case, it might well be perceived as an underhanded maneuver or trick. Those who didn't know me might think I was hoping to lose, effectively facilitating a judicial decision upholding a ban on same-sex marriage and setting back the cause for generations to come. The notion that I might be acting as some sort of legal double agent was both paranoid and slanderous—I don't take cases to lose—but we would have to deal with that kind of reaction.

As I explained to the group, "When Californians enacted Proposition 8, I was saddened. It struck me as mean-spirited and gratuitously cruel." To this day I do not understand, and recoil against, antipathy or hostility toward gay, lesbian, or transgender individuals. I am convinced that with few exceptions we have very little or no control over our sexual orientation. It is a characteristic that is an inherent part of who we are when we are born and as we develop sexually. From what I sense, and from what I have learned, there is nothing we can do to change that part of ourselves, and attempts to do so are both ineffective and often quite harmful. As someone put it to me, "Did you choose to be heterosexual?" The answer was, and is, "No." Just as I would not envision myself in an intimate same-sex relationship, I would certainly not expect a gay man or woman to find fulfillment in an opposite-sex relationship.

The Prop 8 case also appealed to me, I explained, because diversity—however overused a term—is one of America's most attractive characteristics. As a people, we have many more qualities in common than those that divide us. By and large we share the same aspirations, needs, fears, and hopes. We're taught from an early age that we are all Americans, linked by the fundamental promise expressed most vividly and unforgettably in the Declaration of Independence that "all men are created equal." However different we may look or behave on the surface, we are equally entitled to our nation's promise of freedom and happiness.

Sexual orientation, I told the group, seems to me very much in the same category as race, nationality, or gender. We not only accept and respect such differences in this country, but that acceptance is something that distinguishes us. President Reagan was fond of saying that one can go to Japan but not become Japanese, or go to Norway and not become Norwegian. But people can come to America from anywhere and everywhere and become truly American. It has been said that America is an idea, a promise, a dream. Although our country has at times been tragically deficient in living up to those aspirations, they have always been our collective national commitment.

I had not been able to conceive of a reason why our gay brothers and sisters, neighbors, friends, and coworkers were not equally entitled to enjoy the relationships and institutions recognized by our laws or created by our governments, and equally entitled as well to the pursuit of happiness. We would all agree, even if the Supreme Court had not repeatedly told us as much, that marriage is a fundamental right and a basic cultural value in our society. It is a building block of our neighborhoods and our economy, an expression of liberty, and a right of privacy and association. Gays and lesbians crave the right to be married, in the same way and for the same reasons as other citizens do. Why should we expect them to be different from the rest of us? And what right do we have to say that the woman next door who is attracted to another woman cannot marry the person she loves? Who are we to say that their love is inferior, unacceptable, and, worst of all, against the law? That seemed to me wrong, without rational purpose, harmful, exclusionary, demeaning, and un-American.

To my thinking, I explained, the fact that heterosexual sex could result in children did not refute any of this. Marriage is not now and never has been restricted to achieving that outcome. We know and accept that some married people are unable or unwilling to have children, or are uninterested in doing so. Yet their marriages are just as important to them in their sexual relationship, their spirituality, and their need for love, affection, and security. Children are of course an important consideration for those who wish to be married, but marriage is a great deal more than that. And children are being brought into this world and quite happily raised by gays and lesbians.

I had once been asked—very indirectly and not officially—whether I would be willing to defend a Colorado enactment that overturned laws that protected gays and lesbians from discrimination. I did not like what that measure was doing to Coloradans and so I declined. After Proposition 8 was passed, I received a call—I do not even remember from whom—inquiring about my interest in possibly helping with the legal defense of the measure. I said I would not want to be on that side of the case, fighting to deprive citizens of California of the right to marry the people they loved.

When first approached about taking on the challenge to Proposition 8, therefore, I had already decided that I did not like the law and the fence it put around gay people. I did not think that the right to marriage should or could constitutionally be withheld from homosexuals. And I could only begin to imagine the hurt, pain, anguish, isolation, and alienation that is created when that relationship is denied to two loving individuals. It struck me then, and strikes me now, as wrong, morally and legally, and contrary to the spirit that I was taught growing up in California.

That I was a conservative was, I explained that day, not the slightest bit inconsistent with my undertaking to overturn Proposition 8. Marriage is a coming together of two loving individuals to create a family, to seek stability, to work together, to share hopes and dreams, to build an economic unit, to provide mutual support, to help form a community. What could be more conservative than that?

Over the course of my career I had come to have enormous respect for our Constitution and our commitment to the rule of law. A lawyer has a responsibility to step forward when those rights are withheld from our citizens. I thought that I could contribute to vindicating the rights of those whose equality was diminished and whose place in our society was demeaned by Proposition 8. I was not willing to look those individuals in the eye and tell them to search elsewhere for help. So, I told my listeners, I would take the case if I was sure that we could do it right and if I thought we could win.

I went on to describe the main concerns we would have to resolve. A federal lawsuit, I explained, "is never a small undertaking, and in my experience a lot of people do not understand what a big deal it actually is. They believe in a cause. They want to get involved, but they don't understand what will be required of them." More specifically, I noted that not only would it be a long and expensive process, as I had warned Chad, but it would be hard going every step of the way, with many potential setbacks. It would also be emotionally draining, as we could all expect to be attacked and criticized, even by our friends. (For some of us, of course, especially by our friends.)

Although I didn't reveal it at the time, I had already experienced some blowback around the issue. In confidential conversations with trusted friends on the right I had received a few harsh reactions to the mere possibility that I would choose to challenge Proposition 8. Some felt that the will of the people, expressed in the election, was inviolate. Others objected to marriage equality on moral or religious grounds. Some were particularly disturbed that I would lend my skill and stature to an effort to "add a new right to the Constitution."

Most disappointing to me was that so many people failed to see how marriage equality was a truly conservative ideal, based on bedrock values such as liberty, freedom, and equality. On a moral level, marriage was about forming a binding, committed, and stable relationship. In this light, lesbians and gays should be hailed for wanting to enter into the institution. As a legal matter, it seemed obvious that no citizen should be forced to accept second-class status because of immutable characteristics such as race, color, or sexual orientation. And when it came to social policy, there was no legitimate basis that I could perceive to support discrimination against gays and lesbians who sought to marry and have children, or to make them some sort of outcasts.

All these points were discussed at the Reiners' home, as lunch was followed by coffee and then more coffee. Trust was established, commitments formed, and it became clear that a team was taking shape. The conversation then shifted to strategy.

The timing of the lawsuit would depend in part on the outcome of the Proposition 8 challenges that were already before the California Supreme Court. Eventually consolidated into a single case titled *Strauss v. Horton,* this action would take about six months to resolve. Since few informed observers believed the court would overturn Prop 8 on state constitutional grounds, a federal challenge could be mounted as soon as the state court made its decision. During the period in which the state court case was being decided, I could start work with a small team to begin researching and drafting a complaint. All of this would be done quietly—under the radar, as the cliché goes—so that we could enhance the likelihood that we would be the first to file and get ahead of anyone else who might have the same idea about bringing a federal suit. Our desire to file as soon as possible wasn't merely a matter of competitiveness or pride, although both were certainly factors. More important was the concern that other lawsuits would only confuse matters without contributing any meaningful benefits. It was all too easy to imagine the process breaking down as competing attorneys and activists argued over particular decisions and brought long-standing disputes and rivalries into the process. It would be far more effective, I believed, to move nimbly and efficiently and without the excess baggage of partisanship, or multiple chefs in the kitchen.

The full scope of the task we would face would depend on the way various courts might respond to the case. One judge might be willing to act on the basis of briefs, motions, and pleadings from lawyers; another might want to conduct a full-blown trial to resolve a host of issues related to the status of gay and lesbian Americans. In the decades-long history of struggle over equal rights for gay men and lesbians, no court had ever received testimony and considered evidence to address on a comprehensive, thorough basis the fundamental questions about the nature of homosexuality, society's attempts to regulate relationships, the impact of official discrimination against same-sex couples, and the welfare of children in families headed by same-sex couples. A judge who chose this route would, in effect, put prejudice on trial.

Besides the legal initiative, our side would also need to undertake substantial public relations and fund-raising efforts. Money would be needed for the expense of the litigation, which would require thousands of lawyer hours, perhaps expert witnesses, and various support services. Public relations would be important to deal with the press and potential criticism from the lesbian and gay rights establishment, and to communicate our message regarding marriage and discrimination to the wider public. Fortunately Rob, Chad, and Michele had significant experience putting together the kind of organization required for this job. In the 1990s they had conducted a successful campaign for a referendum called Proposition 10, which raised taxes on tobacco to fund a host of services for children aged five and younger. Prop 10 translated Rob's abiding interest in child development into action on behalf of kids and established him as an effective public advocate. By 2008, First 5 California, as the agency that Prop 10 created was called, had funded almost $1 billion in child health, nutrition, and education programs serving more than three million kids.

For the marriage equality battle we would create a new organization, to be called the American Foundation for Equal Rights (AFER), that would become a hub of activity in support of the case. As the sponsor for the litigation, AFER would lead the fund-raising drive and build public support for the cause. Along the way the new organization would energize people who had not previously been involved on the assumption that the established lesbian and gay rights groups would make progress on their own. Finally, and most important, AFER would help to identify the individuals—two couples, as it turned out—who would put their names on the Prop 8 challenge.

Ideally our named plaintiffs would be articulate, resilient, patient, and calm under pressure. The press and our legal opponents would probe every aspect of their lives, from their family histories to their school records. No one enjoys being the subject of such questioning and investigation. In this case it would also likely involve many questions—reasonable and unreasonable—about sexual identity and intimate relationships. This sort of scrutiny could easily provoke anger, resentment, and resistance, and our plaintiffs would have to handle it with openness and confidence.

The last bit of business discussed at the Reiner home was the ultimate makeup of the legal team. My firm, Gibson, Dunn & Crutcher, was a large and sophisticated firm with offices in Los Angeles, San Francisco, Washington, D.C., New York, and major international cities. We would have to count on significant firm resources to bring this case and manage it properly. Before making a binding agreement to take the case, I would have to consult our chairman and managing partner, Ken Doran. As a matter of policy Gibson Dunn often undertook projects that promised to deliver more public good than profit, and because this one certainly fit that bill, I was fairly confident that the firm would welcome the opportunity to undertake this challenge.

But while Gibson Dunn possessed the firepower, expertise, and resources to wage the battle that lay ahead, I mentioned that I would be looking for another lead lawyer with nationally recognized credentials to balance my conservative reputation. Everyone agreed that finding that person should be high on our agenda.

Before taking the final step of formalizing an agreement to take the case, I consulted Lady again, whose judgment and instincts I respect and value, as well as my daughter, Christine, and my son, Ken, to determine how they would feel about the controversy the case might spawn. I also spoke to a few of Gibson Dunn's partners with whom I have close relationships. I find that it is almost invariably prudent to run important personal decisions by a few selected friends. We should each, in his own way, have a personal council of elders—a board of directors, a collection of a few individuals available individually or collectively with whom to consult on important decisions. Making decisions in isolation seldom produces the best results. And that body of wise people should include persons who think differently from us or have different backgrounds. We all too often consult only with people who give us the answer we want to hear (or the answer that they *think* we want to hear).

As I had when I first discussed the possibility of joining the effort, I encountered a few contrary voices. I was told that I would disappoint some colleagues and friends, and was warned that in some quarters I might pay a steep personal and professional price. But the overwhelming reaction, especially among family members and close friends, was supportive and encouraging. In the end I had no doubt that the right thing to do was to take on this case and support the right to love, happiness, and equality sought by gay people. I have never regretted the decision.

One essential ingredient to our legal team and strategy remained open. I was all too keenly aware of my reputation as a conservative, having served in high-level positions in two Republican administrations, as private counsel to Ronald Reagan and George W. Bush, and often being identified with Republican and/or conservative causes. I was concerned that my motives and commitment to the cause of marriage equality would be questioned in some quarters. That would be a damaging distraction. Credibility is very important in cases like this. And it would not be helpful for this case to be seen through a political or partisan lens.

Everyone on the team agreed that in light of these concerns, it would be important, indeed critical, to have the help and partnership of a respected legal figure at the other end of the political spectrum to provide balance to the image of the case and, not incidentally, heighten the visibility of the effort.

We gave early consideration to recruiting a prominent Democratic gay lawyer, possibly a lesbian, to provide political and sexual orientation balance as well, perhaps, as gender balance. But obstacles presented themselves with respect to each of the candidates initially considered.

The process of finding the ideal lawyer for the role we had in mind took several weeks while we were locating the right plaintiffs, fine-tuning our strategy, and preparing the case. But the epiphany, when it came, struck all of us as a perfect solution. During a Saturday conference call in May to discuss strategy, I suggested my *Bush v. Gore* opponent, and by then friend, David Boies. California's motto, "Eureka" ("We have found it"), leapt to mind.

David had handled appeals, including the Supreme Court, but was best known nationally as an outstanding and extraordinarily successful trial lawyer. I had done trial work, but was better known as an appellate lawyer. It seemed perfect. Democrat, Republican. *Bush v. Gore*. Trial lawyer, appellate lawyer. We were both about the same age, had both been born in Illinois, raised in California and educated in its public schools, and had become partners in major law firms. I knew David was passionate about civil rights. He had energy, drive, charisma. He was sensational on camera. He was married, as I was, to a charming, talented, creative, and indefatigable lawyer who had great ideas and superb judgment. We both loved California and its people, not to mention its wine.

David did not disappoint. In a single phone call, he accepted the challenge, signing on without hesitation and with enthusiasm. Our partnership was formed.

THREE

Why I Took the Case

David Boies

When Ted Olson called me in the spring of 2009 to ask whether I would be interested in bringing a federal lawsuit challenging California's Proposition 8 as unconstitutional, I immediately said yes. As I told my wife, Mary, that afternoon, it was the easiest decision of my professional life. Ted and I had been looking for a case to do together for several years. But it was also the case itself that made the decision so easy.

The movement to end antigay discrimination is the defining civil rights issue of the first half of the twenty-first century. In the late eighteenth century the "we" in the "we the people" with which our Constitution begins was essentially limited to white male property owners. The history of our country's slow but continuing march toward fulfilling the promise of our founding principles has been a history of gradually expanding the circle of who is included in "we the people."

My father, a high school teacher of American history, had taught me by word and example that we were all in fact equal, endowed by our creator, as our nation's founders declared in 1776, with the unalienable rights of life, liberty, and the pursuit of happiness. The principle of equality was a lesson confirmed for me on the mixed-race streets of Compton, California, where I lived during the eighth and ninth grades. In the middle 1960s I was a volunteer lawyer with the Lawyers' Committee for Civil Rights in Mississippi, and I continued to bring cases attacking racial discrimination in the 1970s and 1980s while a partner at Cravath, Swaine & Moore. In 1986, to the consternation of a few of my Republican partners and clients, I successfully sued to enjoin the Republican National Committee from targeting minority election districts with "ballot security" or "voter fraud" efforts. In 1997 I left Cravath, and my friend Jonathan Schiller left the equally large Kaye Scholer firm, to form what would become Boies, Schiller & Flexner. We did so with the express goal of being able to undertake cases important to the law and justice.

There remains much to be done to mitigate the effects of past discrimination based on race (as well as on religion and gender), and to eliminate related social discrimination. But at the end of the twentieth century, with limited exceptions based on gender, there was only one group of American citizens that continued to suffer systematic discrimination at the hands of their own government: gay men and lesbians.

That discrimination, like all such discrimination, was both damaging to the indviduals it was directed against and corrosive to the American soul. America is not a nation defined by a common race, religion, ethnicity, land of origin, or even a common language. What binds us together as a nation is a common culture based on the principles of our Declaration of Independence and the democratic government and fundamental rights guaranteed by our Constitution. Prejudice, particularly prejudice sanctioned and enforced by the government, breaks the promise of those documents, undermines our culture, and frays the ties that bind us together as a people.

If you grew up gay or lesbian in America in the second half of the twentieth century, your world was a universe apart from the world that Ted and I enjoyed. In 1952 the American Psychiatric Association listed homosexuality as a sociopathic personality disorder in its official *Diagnostic and Statistical Manual,* and ten years later that same manual described the disorder as resulting from a pathological hidden fear of the opposite sex caused by traumatic parent-child relationships. Today that diagnosis sounds as absurd as the practice in George Washington's time of using leeches to purify the blood, and it is recognized as such by the APA. But the harm that such thinking caused continues in the views of many whose opinions were formed when such attitudes were widely accepted.

The tolerance for diverse sexual orientations that had existed in certain ancient civilizations seemed not only gone but forgotten in twentieth-century America. In the face of government, religious, and academic condemnations of homosexual Americans as criminal, deviant, and dangerous, it was inevitable that LGBT (lesbian, gay, bisexual, and transgender) citizens would be harassed, beaten, and even killed solely due to their sexual orientation. No one will ever know how many gay Americans were attacked before statistics on sexually oriented hate crimes began to be kept, and even today those statistics understate the actual facts because of the reluctance of many victims to report such crimes.

Even when perpetrators of antigay violence were apprehended and prosecuted, bias on the part of judges and juries often resulted in unjustified acquittals or very light sentences. In 1988 a Texas state court judge rejected prosecutors' request to sentence the killer of two gay men to life in prison. As the judge explained, "I don't much care for queers cruising the streets picking up teenage boys." He stated that he "put prostitutes and gays at about the same level" and that "I'd be hard put to give someone life for killing a prostitute."

Violence against LGBT Americans continues today. In March 2007 William Brown Jr. and Joseph Bearden killed twenty-five-year-old Ryan Skipper because they believed he was a "faggot." Brown and Bearden stabbed their victim nineteen times, slit his throat, and dumped the body near Skipper's home. The following year the FBI reported 1,617 crimes based on sexual orientation, including five murders and six forcible rapes. (By comparison the FBI reported for the same year one racially motivated murder and one forcible rape.)

Perhaps most tragic of all are the young LGBT men and women and boys and girls who have been driven to kill themselves because of the pain, insecurity, and doubts about their self-worth caused by their friends', their government's, and often even their family's rejection and condemnation of them. Over the last several decades gay teenagers have been more than twice as likely as their straight counterparts to commit suicide.

Most supporters of antigay discrimination would sincerely deny any tolerance of violence against LGBT Americans and express genuine grief at their suicide rate. But a culture that criminalized and condemned homosexual conduct as immoral and sinful, that taught that same-sex couples are different from their heterosexual neighbors, and that warned that gays represent a threat to children was the root cause of that violence and those suicides.

Like almost all members of my generation, when I was growing up I didn't realize that a number of the people I knew were gay. My generation, like all generations, was made up of a mix of sexual orientations. But the brutal discrimination openly LGBT citizens suffered then caused most of them to conceal their attractions and relationships, making them largely invisible to the rest of us. That relative invisibility served as a partial protection against violence and discrimination, but it was also a double curse: First, forcing gay people to hide their sexual orientation inevitably fostered feelings of alienation and ambivalence about their nature and self-worth. Second, it facilitated the persistence of antigay prejudice.

We tend to overcome the cognitive dissonance of holding a fundamental belief in equality while at the same time discriminating against certain groups by ignoring or denying the fact that those who bear the brunt of our bias are really like us. The further removed people who suffer our prejudices are from our consciousness, the easier it is to preserve that fiction. It is too easy to accept that people we don't know somehow don't want what we want and feel what we feel, and that they may somehow represent a threat to be guarded against. Many of my children's and grandchildren's generations may not understand how in the world we could ever have viewed gay and lesbian citizens that way. But we did.

The march toward LGBT equality began, as virtually all such movements begin, with a few courageous, committed souls. Even during the darkest and most dangerous days of antigay bias, there were gay activists, and a few straight supporters, who began to work to end discrimination. In 1950 a small number of Los Angeles gay men formed the Mattachine Society to promote homosexual rights and acceptance.

Shortly thereafter several San Francisco lesbians formed the Daughters of Bilitis with similar goals.

These groups, and others like them, were small, lacking in financial resources, and shunned by virtually all elected officials. For years they were also largely unsuccessful in making even limited progress. When Ted and I were in high school, President Eisenhower issued an executive order prohibiting the federal government from employing any homosexual person in any capacity. In 1966, after Ted and I had graduated from law school, the Johnson administration rejected the Mattachine Society's request to modify the federal government's absolute bar on employing homosexuals. The Civil Service Commission's rejection of the request asserted that "pertinent considerations here are the revulsion of other employees by homosexual conduct . . . the apprehension caused other employees . . . [and] the unavoidable subjection of the sexual deviate to erotic stimulation."

It is instructive that the same "pertinent considerations" were used in the past to justify exclusions based on race, religion, and even gender.

Nevertheless, like the boy who first exclaimed that the emperor had no clothes, these groups, by asserting the simple truth that gay Americans were just like their straight fellow citizens and entitled to the same rights, began a movement.

By the last quarter of the twentieth century, more and more courageous gay people were risking their jobs, relationships, and even lives to publicly acknowledge their sexual orientation. By enabling the rest of us to see them as they really were, they forced us to recognize that sexual orientation, like race and gender, is a characteristic irrelevant to a person's humanity or worth, and it became increasingly impossible to ignore the evil and irrationality of discriminating against them.

If one moment can be singled out as marking when the march toward LGBT equality began to gain traction, it might be the early morning of June 28, 1969. In the 1950s and 1960s police in cities across the United States, including New York City, regularly raided bars and other establishments that served openly gay patrons. The Stonewall Inn on Christopher Street in the Greenwich Village neighborhood of

Manhattan was such a place. Small, dingy, and reputedly owned by the Genovese crime family, the Stonewall was periodically raided and closed, only to reopen (sometimes later the same day).

Raided bartenders and patrons usually quietly accepted their fate in the face of armed police officers and laws that had been enforced for decades, peacefully dispersing or submitting to arrest. This was what had happened at the Stonewall itself when it was raided earlier that June.

On the evening of Friday, June 27, the police decided to descend on the Stonewall again. When the uniformed officers arrived shortly after one in the morning on June 28, undercover officers were already inside. The raid began as usual with arrests of the bartender and a few patrons and orders to everyone else to go home. This time, however, the patrons arrested did not go quietly, and those told to go home did not.

Years of anger and frustration from repeated mistreatment and humiliation soon erupted in a full-scale riot, with shouts of "Gay Power!" echoing over the sounds of thrown bottles and bricks. Why the eruption occurred then and not earlier or later has no convincing explanation. There were reports that police officers were groping lesbian patrons and hitting with nightsticks people who did not move quickly enough. However, those actions were not unique to June 28.

What is clear is that the event began to change the way society viewed gay Americans, and the way they viewed themselves. Although the police succeeded in dispersing the demonstrations before dawn, the next night the demonstrators reappeared, joined by many more who had gone to bed before the Friday night raid. A year later thousands marched in New York City's first annual Gay Pride parade on the anniversary of the raid. June 1970 saw Gay Pride marchers in Los Angeles and Chicago as well as New York City, and by June 1972 there were Gay Pride marches in more than a dozen major American cities.

At the time of the Stonewall uprising, I lived in the Village at 110 Bleecker Street, a few blocks from the Stonewall, and I was among the many who came to the second day's demonstration. I did not, however, join in the parade the following year, and it would be decades before I did so.

Stonewall was not the first time that gay citizens had fought back against public harassment, but the nature and timing of the Stonewall riots, the attention they garnered, and the subsequent annual celebrations they spawned gave particular importance to the event. Soon thereafter the Gay Liberation Front, the first organization to use "gay" in its name, was formed, soon to be followed by the Gay Activists Alliance. Before the end of 1969, a new newspaper, *Gay*, was started in New York City. Other gay publications, including *Come Out!* and *Gay Power*, later joined *Gay* in serving the city's gay community. In 1970 the Greek letter lambda was adopted as a symbol by the Gay Activists Alliance of New York. In early 1972 Bill Thom filed an application in New York to establish the nonprofit Lambda Legal Defense and Education Fund to combat LGBT discrimination in the courts. The fund was designed to fight for gay American rights the way the NAACP Legal Defense Fund had fought for African American rights.

It is illustrative of the bias of the times that initially Lambda Legal's application was rejected on the ground that promoting gay Americans' rights was "neither benevolent nor charitable," a rejection upheld by New York's lower courts. In 1973 New York's highest court ruled that Lambda's mission was an appropriate cause for a nonprofit organization, and Lambda began a decades-long battle for LGBT equality. (By contrast, the following year the IRS denied 501(c)(3) charitable status to San Francisco's Pride Foundation on the ground that the foundation's purpose of "advancing unqualified and unrestricted promotion of the alleged normalcy of homosexuality" was patently offensive, contrary to public policy, and therefore not charitable.)

In its early days, Lambda, like the race, religion, and gender civil rights organizations that preceded it, lost at least as many cases as it won. But its victories were significant, including its success in enjoining bans on gay organizations at schools and in holding schools responsible for violence and harassment directed at gays on campus. Even its losses drew attention to the evils of LGBT bias.

In 1978 Harvey Milk, a member of the San Francisco Board of Supervisors and one of the first openly gay elected officials, gave a landmark gay civil rights speech. Although Milk was assassinated later that year, his speech and example inspired a generation of gay Americans to begin to demand the equality they deserved. Two years later the Human Rights Campaign Fund was formed as a political action committee to contribute to political candidates who were in favor of ending LGBT discrimination. Over time the HRC expanded its mission to include education and advocacy, and grew into the nation's largest organization supporting LGBT rights.

The hopes that Harvey Milk and others had raised, and the progress that Lambda and other gay rights organizations had been making, seemed to come to an abrupt halt in June 1986 when the U.S. Supreme Court decided *Bowers v. Hardwick,* which upheld as constitutional state laws criminalizing homosexual conduct. Although the decision was five to four, with Justices Harry Blackmun and John Paul Stevens writing eloquent dissents, and although enforcement of such statutes was limited, the implications of the decision were striking. If states could justify criminalizing homosexual conduct, it was a short step to arguing that citizens who engaged in such conduct should be considered moral outcasts. The police raids on gay bars and restaurants that had declined after Stonewall now appeared more justified. State laws prohibiting adoptions by gay couples seemed more reasonable. Even efforts to eliminate LGBT discrimination in employment and housing were suddenly suspect. And why should schools have to permit students to organize to promote conduct upheld as criminal by the highest court in the land? There were answers to all of these questions, but there was no doubt that *Bowers* significantly set back the battle for equal rights.

The battle continued nevertheless, encouraged particularly by the reasoning and passion of Justice Stevens's dissent, and by the knowledge that the LGBT community had come within one vote of striking down all state laws criminalizing homosexual conduct. Then, in the early 1990s, Lambda began work on a case that would lead to the first U.S. Supreme Court decision upholding the constitutional rights of gay Americans.

In the 1980s and early 1990s certain municipal and county governments in Colorado passed local ordinances that prohibited employment and other discrimination based on sexual orientation. In reaction to these relatively modest steps, the voters of Colorado passed a statewide referendum that nullified those ordinances and barred the enactment of future local laws protecting LGBT rights. In 1996 the U.S. Supreme Court in *Romer v. Evans* held the referendum unconstitutional in a six-justice opinion written by Justice Anthony Kennedy. The Court ruled that because there was no legitimate state interest in discriminating against gay Americans, it violated the equal protection clause of the U.S. Constitution for the state to take away protections that had been granted by local governments.

Justice Kennedy's opinion was limited to the question before the Court—whether a state could nullify protections previously granted and bar such protections in the future. It did not expressly decide the extent to which states were required to grant such protections in the first place. Nevertheless, the inescapable implications of *Romer* were as dramatic as the implications of *Bowers*. If there was no legitimate state interest in nullifying protections for LGBT citizens, what could be the justification for a state discriminating against these citizens in the first place? Indeed, if Colorado could not nullify protections against discrimination against homosexual citizens in employment and housing, what was the justification for the *Bowers* holding itself? And what did *Romer* imply for the embryonic movement for marriage equality?

The premises of *Bowers,* and of antigay discrimination generally, were that homosexual conduct was immoral and that society was entitled (indeed, in some people's view, obligated) to condemn and penalize such conduct and the people who engaged, or who were inclined to engage, in it. Those premises were rejected in *Romer,* but how far the rejection would carry the movement for equal rights, particularly the equal right to marry, remained to be seen.

Three years before *Romer* was decided, the Hawaii Supreme Court had held that denying marriage licenses to same-sex couples raised serious equal protection questions under the Hawaii constitution.

However, before any Hawaiian couples were actually allowed to marry, voters passed an amendment to the state constitution that gave the legislature the power to limit marriage to persons of the opposite sex.

At the time *Romer* was decided, cases were pending or being proposed in a number of states based on the reasoning of the Hawaii Supreme Court. All of these cases were based on state constitutions. While the U.S. Constitution contained comparable guarantees, *Bowers,* coupled with the perception that the U.S. Supreme Court was continuing to shift to the right, discouraged anyone from relying on those federal provisions.

Confirmation of at least the national legislature's antipathy to marriage equality was provided the same year *Romer* was decided when Congress passed and President Clinton signed the Defense of Marriage Act (DOMA), which restricted federal recognition of marriage to unions of persons of the opposite sex.

Gay rights activists were divided as to whether to make marriage equality a priority or to concentrate on less controversial issues such as discrimination in employment, education, benefits, and housing. In part this reflected the recognition that sexuality is a particularly sensitive issue that tends to be the last element of a discriminatory regime to be eradicated. It took the Supreme Court thirteen years after its 1954 holding in *Brown v. Board of Education* that segregation was unlawful to hold in *Loving v. Virginia* that state bans on interracial marriages were unconstitutional. Although the vast majority of Americans accepted in the 1950s that government discrimination against African Americans in education, housing, and employment was wrong, when the Supreme Court struck down state bans on interracial marriage in 1967, 64 percent of Americans still opposed such marriages.

Proponents of gradualism in ending antigay discrimination argued that it was best to try to make gains in areas such as employment, education, and even adoption without risking what was seen as an inflammatory reach for gay marriage. The wide support for the absurdly misnamed Defense of Marriage Act gave credence to these views. Even proponents of pushing for marriage equality tended to prefer a state-by-state approach relying on state constitutional provisions rather than going to federal court.

I myself had thought relatively little about marriage equality, let alone about the best way to achieve it, until about five years before Ted's call. I knew in 1986 that *Bowers* was wrong and that the law the Court upheld was more accordant with Salem, Massachusetts, in the 1690s than with the United States of America in the 1980s.

I knew that the gay teachers, lawyers, doctors, clients, and friends whom I had met in twenty years of practicing law were no different than my straight teachers, lawyers, doctors, clients, and friends. I knew that it was wrong to discriminate against gay people in employment or education or housing, that they posed no threat to me or anyone else, that common caricatures were no more realistic reflections of the average gay person than earlier blackface caricatures had been realistic reflections of the average African American. I supported what I thought of as equal rights for gay people, just as two decades before I had supported what I thought of as equal rights for African Americans.

But at the time I thought little about gay marriage. I didn't reject the idea; it simply didn't seem to come up. Perhaps I retained a vestigial subconscious feeling that gay people were not really the same. Perhaps my gay friends did not mention it because it seemed at the time a bridge too far. Perhaps there were other steps in ending antigay discrimination that seemed more important.

Over the next decade and a half, as the LGBT community inched toward equality, the right to marry began to come into focus for me as well as others. Then in 2003, in *Lawrence v. Texas* the U.S. Supreme Court overruled *Bowers* and held state laws criminalizing homosexual conduct unconstitutional.

Even more important than *Lawrence*'s holding was its reasoning. In a majority opinion by Justice Kennedy, the Court held that the due process clause of the Constitution protected "personal decisions relating to marriage, procreation, contraception, family relationships, [and] child rearing" and that "persons in a homosexual relationship may seek autonomy for these purposes, just as heterosexual persons do." The opinion eloquently concluded:

>Times can blind us to certain truths and later generations
>can see that laws once thought necessary and proper in fact
>serve only to oppress. As the Constitution endures, persons in
>every generation can invoke its principles in their own search
>for greater freedom.

In her concurrence, Justice Sandra Day O'Connor emphasized, "Moral disapproval of a group cannot be a legitimate governmental interest under the Equal Protection Clause."

Justice Antonin Scalia in his dissent (joined by Justice Clarence Thomas and then–chief justice William Rehnquist) was candid about *Lawrence*'s significance:

>Today's opinion dismantles the structure of constitutional
>law that has permitted a distinction to be made between hetero-
>sexual and homosexual unions, insofar as formal recognition
>in marriage is concerned. If moral disapprobation of homosex-
>ual conduct is "no legitimate state interest" . . . what justifica-
>tion could there possibly be for denying the benefits of marriage
>to homosexual couples . . . ? Surely not the encouragement of
>procreation, since the sterile and elderly are allowed to marry.

Loving had confirmed that marriage was a fundamental right, and that the Fourteenth Amendment prohibited states from infringing on an individual's right to marry without a sound basis. Now *Lawrence* established that in the eyes of the law homosexual relationships were as valid, and as entitled to constitutional protection, as heterosexual relationships. As Justice Scalia recognized with regret, there was now no justification for "denying the benefits of marriage to homosexual couples." But marriage equality still remained for me largely an abstract legal right until February 2004.

On February 12, 2004, Gavin Newsom, then the mayor of San Francisco, directed the county clerk's office to issue marriage licenses to couples of the same sex. In the days that followed I watched television images of gay couples from around the country and around the world lining up for the chance to marry the person they loved. Seeing their joy, excitement, and anticipation, I was struck, really for the first time, by how important this right was to liberty, dignity, and the pursuit of happiness. "Why in the world," I asked Mary, "would anyone want to prevent someone from doing something that brings them joy, fosters family values, and can't hurt anyone else?"

As I thought about it over the following weeks and months, the right to marry the person you love became more and more important to me. I learned only much later that upon their emancipation, American slaves, who had been forbidden to marry during bondage, rushed to apply for marriage licenses. What I understood then, however, was that marriage not only celebrates, sanctions, and strengthens a relationship; it celebrates, dignifies, and validates people who are allowed to marry. Forbidding certain people from marrying not only deprives them of the benefits of marriage but says to them, and to society at large, that they are inferior, suspect, outsiders. The same message applies whether the ban is based on race, religion, sexual orientation, or other criteria.

When a state labels a group of its citizens as inferior, suspect, and outsiders, it inevitably fuels antagonism that can lead a minority of society to believe they can with impunity, and even with justification, harass, beat, and even kill the "immoral" outsiders. This was as true for LGBT citizens as it earlier had been true for African American citizens.

Progress could be, and was, made in reducing violence against gay people, and discrimination in education, employment, housing, and other areas, without confronting the more inflammatory questions of gay marriage. But precisely because bias against gay marriage with its validation of gay relationships was at the heart of antigay discrimination, until that bias was confronted all progress was fragile. Correspondingly, if marriage equality could be achieved, all other discrimination would collapse.

The case Ted proposed was an opportunity to confront, and hopefully eliminate, the core of antigay bias. In a sense it was not a proposal I was free to immediately accept. The case would, I knew, require a great deal of my time and my firm's resources—time and resources for which I was aware our plaintiffs could not begin to pay. I also knew that the nature of the case would arouse fierce and passionate opposition, and that there would be a fringe that would direct their anger at my family as well as myself. (During *Bush v. Gore* death threats against my youngest son, Alexander, had been called in to his elementary school, and many were made against me.)

Fortunately, when I discussed the case with Mary, my children, and my partners at Boies, Schiller & Flexner, later that day, I found that they were as determined as I was that this was a case we should accept. Although the American Foundation for Equal Rights, which was sponsoring the litigation, had offered a partial payment, Jonathan Schiller, Donald Flexner, and my other partners agreed that we would take the case entirely without a fee.

I soon discovered that many in the gay community, including most of those who had long led the fight for equality, were adamantly opposed to our proposed lawsuit. They did not, of course, oppose our objective, but believed that the time was too soon, that the federal courts were too conservative, that we would lose, and that in losing we risked setting back the movement.

Coming as they did from people who had worked much longer and risked much more in the battle for equal rights than I had, those concerns were entitled to respect. I nevertheless decided it was right to proceed for four reasons.

First, I believed we would win. This was not a case where we were asking the courts to recognize a new right, merely to hold that an established right could not be withheld based on sexual orientation. The combination of *Loving* and *Lawrence,* together with numerous Supreme Court decisions holding unconstitutional state laws barring marriages by imprisoned felons and people who had abused a prior marriage, were compelling. Even as staunch an opponent as Justice Scalia seemed to recognize the inevitability.

Second, both our individual plaintiffs and tens of thousands of couples like them in California wanted to exercise what they and we believed to be their constitutional right to marry. I did not know how to tell them this was not their time, that only future generations could enjoy that right.

Third, I believed that simply bringing this case, and the national discussion it would engender, would advance the cause of equality and public support for it. The opposition to marriage equality did not have arguments that could withstand scrutiny. They had a tautological bumper sticker (MARRIAGE IS BETWEEN A MAN AND A WOMAN) and a religious belief ("God forbids gay marriage") that, however sincerely held, was barred by the First Amendment as a basis for legal decisions. In part because of our reputations (and our "odd couple" relationship that I knew would make good copy), I felt that Ted and I could bring this issue to mainstream America, and I believed that when we did, the common sense and fairness of the American people would do the rest.

Fourth, we believed there was no way that a federal constitutional challenge could be avoided. If we didn't bring this case for these plaintiffs, someone else would do so for other plaintiffs. It was essential that the case that was decided first be prepared, tried, and presented on appeal as perfectly as possible. With our experience, and with the unparalleled resources our two firms offered, we were confident that we could prepare, try, and appeal the case as well as, and probably better than, any alternative team.

A few times between Ted's call and the day we actually filed the complaint, I asked myself whether my desire to accept this case, and to do so with Ted, was causing me to too quickly dismiss the arguments of those who counseled caution. Each time I concluded this was the right case, in the right place, at the right time, and that Ted and I and our team were the right lawyers to bring it.

FOUR

Preparing the Challenge

Thanks to television and the movies, many people imagine that the most compelling legal stories feature a lone attorney, obsessed with a cause, risking career, health, and even life itself to win justice for a worthy client. Solo operators sometimes do achieve results in this Hollywood fashion, but this almost always happens in cases involving a discrete harm or injustice affecting a limited number of people, such as when a determined advocate frees an innocent man, or a public interest lawyer protects a whistleblower.

Larger actions that change the course of history, however, almost always require a team effort. Thurgood Marshall did not prevail in *Brown v. Board of Education* without the help of a large group of lawyers funded by the National Association for the Advancement of Colored People. The famous *Miranda* case, which established the rights of every American detained by the police, involved several lawyers and the resources of the powerful American Civil Liberties Union.

The case against Proposition 8 would require a comparable array of talent, more expertise and resources than any one attorney could possess. At Gibson Dunn, Ted could select, among more than a thousand lawyers, many who had the skill, interest, and temperament required for the case. He turned first to a top partner, Ted Boutrous, who was based in Los Angeles and was one of the country's most accomplished appellate and constitutional law experts. Boutrous in turn would assemble a California-based group from the firm's Los Angeles and San

Francisco offices to begin work on the Prop 8 challenge, and Ted Olson would add two attorneys, Matt McGill and Amir Tayrani, from his Washington office. This small team was to work in secrecy to prevent premature publicity. Their initial assignments included monitoring the state case, *Strauss v. Horton,* beginning the research and drafting of a complaint, and, perhaps most important, working directly with the couples who as plaintiffs would bring the case.

Among the first to join the group Boutrous recruited was Enrique Monagas, a talented young lawyer in Gibson Dunn's San Francisco office. Barely three years out of law school, Enrique had already established a reputation for his energy, his charisma, and his creative, high-quality work. He had published a law journal piece on marriage equality in California and had begun to prove himself as a member of the firm's litigation group. He was also personally acquainted with the issues faced by gay men and lesbians with respect to social and legal equality in twenty-first-century America.

As an adolescent Enrique had settled in Southern California after growing up near various American air bases around the world. His father was an air force officer, and his mother was a schoolteacher. Like many "military brats," Enrique learned to adapt quickly to new people and places. Bright, outgoing, and empathetic, he made friends easily, but as a child he heard his classmates disparage people as "queer" and saw how certain boys were bullied. His success as a cross-country runner and sports editor of his high school newspaper helped him to avoid becoming a target of this kind of prejudice.

"I didn't intentionally try to pass as straight," Enrique recalled, "but I also didn't tell anyone how I really felt." He once heard his mother remark, "If I had a son who was gay, I'd commit suicide." Given such signals, he kept his own sexual identity secret, even though he knew who he was by the time he was ten years old. In adulthood Enrique showed no obvious scars from the antigay prejudice and bigotry he had experienced. But if asked, he would share vivid memories of ugly incidents. During his freshman year in college, while walking through the shopping district in the seaside community of Santa Monica, Enrique gave an excited hug to a friend who suddenly appeared on the sidewalk. A man on the street shouted, "Faggots go home!" Enrique shrank a bit and felt embarrassed, he would later say, "about being pointed out, in public, as 'the gay one.'" In the next moment, though, a woman who happened to be passing by turned to the man who had made the comment and shouted, "How dare you!" She then planted herself protectively, allowing Enrique and his friend to walk away unharmed.

Afterward Enrique struggled to deal with both the verbal assault and the questions raised by his own passive response. He felt trapped in the terrible bind that widespread bigotry can impose on people, a vise that members of oppressed minorities often face. And it's all the more difficult when government and laws reinforce the discrimination or family members are not supportive. Unlike members of racial or ethnic minorities, though, many gays and lesbians are rejected as "different" by family and friends who erroneously believe they have made a choice to be something that society regards as unacceptable.

Fortunately, the process of untangling the web of rejection and self-doubt can lead to growth and discovery. In Enrique's case it included a bit of amateur sleuthing that turned up evidence that his mother's brother had died of AIDS-related cancer. It was at that time that Enrique came out to his family. His brother, sister, and father offered their unequivocal support, and, to his relief, so did his mother. He found great strength in acknowledging the truth, and in his family's response to it.

Enrique assisted the Reiner/AFER group in their search for the couples who might become the plaintiffs. He consulted with them almost daily, counseling them on the qualities that might make for ideal candidates, and briefing them on the matters of law and procedure these couples would need to understand. Among them were:

- They must be mature adults with a strong and deep desire to be married.
- They must be seeking to marry.
- They must be able to handle the rejection of being turned down for a marriage license because of their sexual orientation.

- They must be willing to put their names on the suit.
- They must be prepared for huge amounts of attention from the press and public.
- They must be willing to testify and undergo potentially hostile and withering cross-examination.
- Their relationship must be stable and committed; they would have to remain together for the three to five years the process could require.

Beginning with people they knew personally and recommendations from friends and colleagues, the core AFER activists considered a number of couples who seemed to fit the bill. As they deliberated, though, they kept returning to two. One couple was Paul Katami and Jeffrey Zarrillo. They were a close, committed couple who lived in a small ranch house in Burbank with a pair of French bulldogs named Gracie and Gordy. Paul, thirty-five, was a fitness trainer, and Jeff, thirty-four, worked for a movie theater company. Paul was a native Californian who was born in San Francisco, moved to Los Angeles for college, and stayed to try his hand at acting. Jeff was born and raised in the mostly middle-class town of Brick, New Jersey.

When Jeff came out to them, his mother and navy veteran father told him they "knew already" about his sexual orientation and were glad for his happiness. They welcomed Paul as a son, with the hope that together the two men would make them grandparents. Jeff and Paul responded that they did want to have children, but not unless they were married. Marriage, they said, would make their relationship—and their family—equal to all others.

Jeff and Paul would never have come to AFER's attention but for a campaign commercial aired by the backers of Prop 8. Called "A Gathering Storm," the commercial featured actors portraying a California doctor, a Massachusetts parent, and a member of a New Jersey church, all of them speaking in ominous tones while dark storm clouds scudded across a distant sky. Identifying themselves as a "rainbow coalition of people of every creed and every color . . . coming together in love to protect marriage," the actors spoke lines that implied that marriage between same-sex individuals threatened heterosexual couples and their children. Borrowed from the civil rights activist Jesse Jackson, the term "rainbow coalition" was obviously meant to resonate with black voters. The lightning flashing in the sky suggested heaven's judgment. Altogether, the fearmongering in the ad amounted to a very strange and inadvertently comic message. One writer called it "*Village of the Damned* meets *A Chorus Line*." It was, at bottom, an insulting appeal to ignorance.

Outraged when they saw the ad, Jeff and Paul contacted friends in the TV and film business to work on a parody to refute it that would air on YouTube. Four days later they had a script in hand and were at work in a production studio complete with a so-called green screen that enabled them to put images of a beautiful sunrise behind actors positioned to mimic the original ad. The brilliantly executed "Weathering the Storm" asked how opposite-sex couples and their families could possibly be damaged if loving same-sex couples were given the chance to marry. It included a slide noting, "These are REAL people telling THEIR stories." The parody ad affirmed that marriage equality was "not about laws" but rather "about love," and ended with the words "Not Special Rights. Equal Rights."

"Weathering the Storm" quickly racked up more than 100,000 views. Among the people featured in it were a rabbi, a priest, the parents of a lesbian, and several gay couples. The first couple to appear on camera were Jeff and Paul, who said, "They want to tell us how to live our lives."

In the relatively small community of gay and lesbian rights activists, word quickly spread about the couple in Burbank who had provided the energy, inspiration, and organization behind the video. Kristina Schake contacted them on AFER's behalf and got an extremely enthusiastic response when she mentioned the idea that they could be plaintiffs in a Prop 8 lawsuit. Jeff and Paul were acutely aware of the politics around marriage equality and sensitized to the discrimination practiced against gay men and lesbians. Although they knew people who were active in organizations like the Gay and Lesbian Alliance Against Defamation (GLAAD) and the Human Rights Campaign (HRC), leading public advocacy groups for equality, they were not closely tied to these groups themselves. This was a point in their favor when it came to becoming part of the case, since these very established and very influential organizations were known to be cool, if not outright hostile, to the idea of a federal court challenge to Prop 8. In fact, we learned at some point that AFER was viewed by these groups as an upstart rival and even a threat. Had Jeff and Paul been deeply involved in either HRC or GLAAD they might have felt pressure to stay out of the case. Fortunately, they were eager to be considered as candidates, and after a couple of meetings with members of the legal team and AFER, an agreement was reached: Jeff and Paul would be the Southern California plaintiffs.

Meanwhile, Chad and the Reiners had favorites in mind for the Bay Area. Kris Perry had been hired as executive director of the First 5 California children's program fund in 2005, when Rob Reiner was winding down his work as an unpaid commissioner overseeing the agency. In the years since, the two had run into each other from time to time, and Rob had been impressed by Kris's calm intelligence. In the world of children's advocates and service providers, many people bring more heart than head to their jobs, but Kris brought both. This became clear when she was interviewed for the press release that announced her hiring. Asked to imagine her version of "a perfect world" Kris answered:

> A perfect world is one in which kids hear early and often that they are wonderful and important, so that they have no desire to exclude or demean anyone else, and embrace uniqueness and achieve their greatest potential.

In the same interview she was asked to share her professional motto and replied, "That which gets measured, gets done."

Inspired by the First 5 California mission and informed by a serious sense of purpose, Kris supervised a staff of thirty-five and collaborated with fifty-eight different counties as the agency distributed well over $100 million per year for child health and education programs. Kris was also the one who dealt with the hundreds of politicians who wanted to make sure their constituents got their fair share of services (or perhaps a little more). Taken together, Kris's talents and her personality made her a steady, cool-under-fire person, and her appearance only enhanced this impression. A conservative dresser who wore her hair short and looked at the world through big glasses, she seemed approachable, unshakable, mature, and sensible.

In a world without Proposition 8, Kris would have been married to her partner, Sandy Stier. They had been together since 1997 and had actually gotten married when San Francisco mayor Gavin Newsom ordered the county clerk to issue marriage licenses to same-sex couples in 2004. When those marriages were later voided by the courts, the experience was devastating for Sandy and Kris, but they soon returned to their daily routines in a cozy home on a hillside street not far from the University of California in Berkeley. With four rambunctious boys to raise and demanding full-time jobs (Sandy was a data analyst for Alameda County), they were, like millions of other ordinary American parents, happily busy.

Sandy's background was almost impossibly all-American. Raised on a farm twenty miles outside little Ottumwa, Iowa, she grew up doing farm chores with three siblings. Her devout mother (who actually carried holy water in her purse) raised her children to be Roman Catholics. As a girl Sandy read a book every day during summer vacations and developed a keen interest in the world beyond the farm. After getting an undergraduate degree from the University of Iowa she traveled in Europe, worked in Colorado, and then migrated to the Bay Area. She had previously been married to a man, and the split from her husband had been rough, but that was more than ten years in the past. Like Kris, Sandy said she was ready to take a stand for marriage equality and unconcerned about any scrutiny she might be subject to as a plaintiff. "They're going to find out we're very boring, very ordinary," she said.

The surface ordinariness of the Perry-Stier household was a quality that made them appealing to AFER and the legal team. Just like Paul and Jeff, Kris and Sandy seemed very much like the people you would meet at a neighborhood block party or in the aisle of a suburban supermarket. They were more politically aware than most people, but they were articulate and smart as well as consistently honest, genuine,

and direct. They understood themselves extremely well and were committed to each other. It was hard to imagine that anyone might shake
their resolve or rattle their equanimity.

———

With Sandy, Kris, Jeff, and Paul on board, the Prop 8 challenge had its
plaintiffs, the real, familiar, likable, steady people Ted had described in
his first meeting with Chad. Ted Boutrous then enlisted Gibson Dunn
litigators Chris Dusseault and Theane Evangelis, who would take responsibility for developing the first draft of the complaint we intended
to file to initiate our challenge to Proposition 8. A former clerk to Supreme Court justice Sandra Day O'Connor, Theane began with Gibson
Dunn in October 2007. Much later she would recall, "I printed out
Loving and *Romer* and *Lawrence*. I also got the complaints and the
briefings done in the state cases on same-sex marriage in Iowa, Massachusetts, California, and other states. While I was doing this I said
to myself, *This has got to be the world's greatest job.*"

As a new lawyer in the firm, Theane was awed by her assignment,
not only because it involved a veil of secrecy, but also "because of the
pressure of its being a potentially groundbreaking federal challenge,"
as she would explain. But she had become a lawyer because she hoped
to be involved in cases precisely like this one. She was acutely sensitive
to minority rights and all the social and psychological implications of
discrimination. This interest had only increased during her time with
Justice O'Connor, who, despite being a moderately conservative jurist,
had voted to uphold affirmative action in education and a woman's
right to abortion. For Theane, the chance to play a role in a case that
was concerned with minority rights and was quite likely to end at the
Supreme Court was a dream come true. Chris Dusseault was a bright
young partner, with an engaging, can-do personality, who would be
given a large role in organizing the litigation and seeing to it that the
trains ran on time.

David's firm, with a little more than two hundred lawyers, was considerably smaller than Gibson Dunn; nevertheless, David was soon

swamped with volunteers eager to work on the case. Boies firm partners Robert Silver and Jeremy Goldman recruited two associates, Meredith Dearborn and Josh Schiller, to help them with the complaint and with the planning for discovery that might come.

Fortunately, once past the potential impact of the case, which of course was substantial, the legal questions involved were relatively straightforward. The right to marry had repeatedly been declared, by the courts in cases such as *Loving,* to be a fundamental right for all citizens. And the equal protection guarantee of the Fourteenth Amendment requires equal treatment under the law for all citizens, that is, as the Supreme Court has explained, the protection of equal laws.

These precedents, plus evidence that depriving gays and lesbians of the fundamental right of marriage and equal treatment under California law because of their status as homosexuals served no legitimate interest and harmed gay and lesbian citizens, formed the core of the legal case.

While Theane's draft was being reviewed, edited, and revised by the team, a strategy was developed to ensure to the extent possible that this case would be the first to be filed after the California Supreme Court released its decision in *Strauss v. Horton.* That decision was expected to uphold Proposition 8 against state-law challenges, so the place and timing of the filing of the Proposition 8 lawsuit were important. We wanted to be the first to file—to occupy the field, so to speak—in order to preempt competing challenges that might prove to be distracting or counterproductive. We also had to ensure that the case would be brought in the most favorable venue in the most congenial environment.

After considerable analysis the team decided to file a federal constitutional challenge in a federal court. Federal constitutional challenges may be brought in state courts, but federal courts are more familiar with the federal Constitution. The next decision was to determine which federal court. Two of the plaintiffs, Jeff and Paul, were residing in Los Angeles, so the court there was a possible venue. But another case had been filed in Southern California that, while seemingly going nowhere, was viewed as a possible competing vehicle. The Northern District of California, centered in San Francisco, was the logical alternative. Kris and Sandy lived in Berkeley, and since both Gibson Dunn and Boies Schiller had offices in the Bay Area, the firms' resources could be deployed effectively and efficiently there. And of course, because the contest over marriage equality had first come to a head in San Francisco, it seemed particularly appropriate to start where it had begun. Besides, San Franciscans were clearly sensitive to and sympathetic to gays and lesbians. We would be in a friendly environment. While that was an intangible value, it was not insignificant: The emotional toll the case would take on the plaintiffs was going to be real and sustained, and it would help if they felt they were among friends.

The next question was timing—and our meticulous planning could not have worked out better. The California Supreme Court had heard arguments in March 2009 and a decision was expected in *Strauss v. Horton* sometime in late May or early June. Various gay rights groups had banded together to bring that case, and each group had wanted its own lawyer to have a piece of the argument. Thus four separate lawyers wound up speaking. This kind of fractured presentation is seldom advisable; it makes a unified, cohesive approach virtually impossible. The other side had been represented by one of the most famous lawyers in America, Kenneth Starr. A former federal appeals court judge and former solicitor general, Starr was best known to the public as the "independent counsel" who led the investigation of President Clinton and others in the Whitewater and Monica Lewinsky inquiries. In 2009 he was dean of the Pepperdine School of Law, and subsequently he became president of Baylor University in Texas.

Pro-equality demonstrators had held candlelight vigils in several California cities the night of March 4, 2009, the eve of the *Strauss v. Horton* argument. Los Angeles mayor Antonio Villaraigosa attended one where about two hundred people braved a steady rain to watch six same-sex couples declare their commitment to one another in what were called "recommitment ceremonies."

Strauss v. Horton was argued the next day. Outside, most of the sidewalk demonstrators gathered to show their opposition to Proposition 8, with hundreds holding placards that read EQUALITY NOW and FREEDOM TO MARRY. One young woman stood with tape on her mouth, on which was written the word LOVE. Though fewer in number, the supporters of Prop 8 were present and vocal.

Inside the serene court chamber, seven justices sat under a vaulted ceiling and in front of a Willard Dixon mural called *The Eastern Sierra in Fall,* which depicts the Sierra Nevada mountain range in the glowing light of autumn. Starr had the better of the argument, sounding statesmanlike and reasonable. His task was not as great: He only had to convince the court that Proposition 8 had simply *amended* the California constitution, not revised it, and that the voters alone, without the involvement of the California legislature, could enact the measure and change the result of the California Supreme Court's *In re Marriage Cases,* thus eliminating the right of same-sex couples to marry in California that the court had recognized in that case. From the tenor of the questions asked by the justices, Starr seemed destined to prevail. After all, Proposition 8 had been identified in the ballot materials submitted to voters as an "Initiative Constitutional Amendment." It contained only fourteen words: "Only marriage between a man and a woman is valid or recognized in California." It was hard to see that this constituted a "revision" of the California constitution rather than an amendment.

With an end-of-May deadline (prescribed by law) for the California Supreme Court's decision in mind, Chad and other AFER founders held confidential meetings with many gay and lesbian rights leaders, who expressed widely varied reactions to the idea of a federal suit. Overall they seemed to agree that while a big federal challenge would be exciting, they felt considerable anxiety over the potential for a negative outcome and generally favored a state-by-state campaign to change laws in legislatures or pursuant to constitutional amendments. As Kate Kendell of the National Center for Lesbian Rights would eventually explain to one reporter, "This federal case has the potential to be a total game changer. But it also has the potential to have devastating consequences."

Although we considered seriously the concerns raised by the

activists, we could not overlook the plight of children in gay households who could not understand why their parents could not be married, gay couples who craved the rights and respect accorded to their
neighbors, lesbians living in Mississippi who might never benefit from
a popular vote upholding their rights, and the intolerable specter of an
America that would continue to relegate its gay and lesbian citizens to
second-class status. These factors—plus the virtual certainty that some
lawyer was certain to bring a case anyway, so delay was never a viable
option—persuaded us to go forward in the face of potential criticism
from groups and individuals we respected, to trust our instincts and
carefully considered judgments, and to believe in the power of the
courts and the Constitution. The *Perry* case would be filed. (Initially
called *Perry v. Schwarzenegger,* the case name became *Perry v. Brown*
after California changed governors, and ultimately *Hollingsworth v.
Perry* in the U.S. Supreme Court.) The battle would begin.

———

On Wednesday, May 20, Jeff and Paul went to the Los Angeles county
clerk's office in Beverly Hills, where they filled out the paperwork to
apply for a marriage license. They had to apply, and be rejected, in
order to establish that they had been harmed directly, immediately,
and personally by Proposition 8. On Thursday, May 21, Enrique accompanied Kris and Sandy as they went through the same exercise in
Alameda County. The office worker who received their application
didn't want to be the one to reject it. She summoned a supervisor who
read a statement that had been expressly written for this purpose. It
stated that although Proposition 8 barred the clerk from issuing same-
sex couples marriage licenses, if and when the law was changed, applicants who still wanted to marry should return. As this was
happening Enrique thought to himself, *This is the first step toward
marriage equality. It happened today. Right now.*

Like Paul and Jeff, Kris and Sandy had known that their request
would be rejected, but it was deeply humiliating and painful nonetheless. No one should have to stand at a counter and listen to a civil servant

explain that he or she isn't entitled to equal treatment and fundamental rights simply because the person he or she loves doesn't have the right combination of chromosomes. Enrique recognized what the women were feeling and tried to reassure them, stressing that they had taken one important step toward an historic goal. He didn't say that the next steps wouldn't also bring stress and pain, but he did tell them that he believed they were up to the task.

With the predicate rejections accomplished, we waited for a decision from the California Supreme Court. On Friday, May 22, the court issued a press release announcing that the *Strauss* ruling would come on Tuesday, May 26, after the long Memorial Day weekend. With the ruling imminent, Chad Griffin and Bruce Cohen quietly approached some of the leading figures in major gay and lesbian rights organizations. They explained what we were about to launch, hoping for their support. They learned instead that the nine most prominent LGBT organizations that had previously subscribed to a "no lawsuits" statement in 2008 were now more determined than ever to pursue a nonlitigation strategy.

Drafted with the assumption that the California Supreme Court would uphold Proposition 8 as constitutional, they had prepared and then released a joint statement entitled "Why the Ballot Box and Not the Courts Should be the Next Step on Marriage in California," which called for a new ballot campaign to overturn it. Their reasoning was that the 2008 election had been so close, with the pro-equality forces gaining ground near the end, that a well-organized repeal effort would be likely to succeed. The statement dismissed the idea of a federal suit as "premature" and "a temptation we should resist." It urged instead a massive dialogue to persuade people that the cause of equality was just and worthy of a major referendum campaign. As for a federal judicial remedy, they concluded, "History says that the odds at the Supreme Court now are not so good."

When we considered these arguments against the case we planned to file, we had to ask ourselves, if not now, when? When *would* it be propitious to bring a federal constitutional challenge to the Supreme Court? Who would be the next justice to retire, and who would replace him or her? No one could predict when the composition of the Supreme Court might change—Supreme Court justices average twenty-five years on the bench—and whether the next change would be for the better. *No one* could predict when the timing would be better for a Supreme Court challenge.

After extended analysis, we had concluded and then reconcluded that we had a good chance of prevailing at the district court in San Francisco, in the Ninth Circuit Court of Appeals, and at the Supreme Court. We also considered the fact that $40 million had been spent to defeat Proposition 8, and yet it had passed by a margin of almost 600,000 votes. No one could predict that it would be possible to raise a comparable sum to put that same issue immediately back on the ballot and expect a different outcome. Moreover, another ballot-box defeat would surely be devastating and demoralizing. It was time to affirm that fundamental rights are not a matter to be determined by a popular vote. Gays and lesbians had lost election after election in various states. This was not a winning strategy. We have a Constitution, a Bill of Rights, and an independent judiciary so that minority rights cannot be abused. It was time to turn to the courts.

———

While the nine advocacy groups were preparing their concerted opposition, we completed our federal complaint. Theane's initial draft was revised by the entire California team. It was finally polished by Ted and his Washington colleagues Matt McGill and Amir Tayrani, and by David and his partners Bob Silver and Jeremy Goldman. In ten pages it introduced the plaintiffs, described how they were affected by Proposition 8, and asked the court to intervene on their behalf. Brief as the complaint was—every page of it was vital—the emotional heart of the document was the section that described the damage done by the official discrimination that was enshrined in Prop 8. After declaring that the California constitutional policy of exclusion resulted in "severe humiliation, emotional distress, pain, suffering, psychological harm, and stigma" for the plaintiffs, the complaint addressed the fundamental importance of the right to marriage, quoting from the *Loving* decision:

Marriage is a supremely important social institution, and the "freedom to marry has long been recognized as one of the vital personal rights essential to the orderly pursuit of happiness by free men." *Loving v. Virginia*, 388 U.S. 1, 12 (1967). Each day that Plaintiffs are denied the freedom to marry, they suffer an irreparable harm as the direct result of Defendants' violation of their constitutional rights.

In terms that anyone could understand, these two sentences stated the essence of our argument: *Loving*, along with many other cases, had established marriage as a constitutionally protected right. To deny that right was to make plaintiffs outcasts and create immense personal damage.

The complaint went on to explain that Prop 8 had been advanced not to achieve some worthy state purpose but on the basis of an "animus against a politically unpopular group." As a remedy the complaint asked for the court to declare that Proposition 8 violated the plaintiffs' Fourteenth Amendment rights to due process and equal protection and to enjoin the state from enforcing it.

The complaint listed Ted, members of the Gibson Dunn team, and David and his partner Ted Uno as attorneys for Jeff, Paul, Sandy, and Kris. The defendants included the various officials who were charged with implementing Prop 8, including the governor, the attorney general, and the county clerks who had rejected the plaintiffs' marriage license applications. After Ted signed it, it was shipped to Enrique Monagas in San Francisco.

———

At about 3 P.M. on Friday, May 22, after the California Supreme Court notified the public that its Proposition 8 opinion would be issued the following Tuesday, Enrique walked up to the entrance of the federal building in San Francisco on Golden Gate Avenue. A massive example of fifties-style bureaucratic architecture, the hulking twenty-one-story building fills an entire block between Polk Street and Larkin Street, where a cluster of Vietnamese restaurants reminds you why the neighborhood is called

Little Saigon. Named after longtime congressman Phillip Burton, the sky-scraper houses many different federal agencies, including the FBI, the U.S. Marshals Service, and the Bureau of Alcohol, Tobacco and Firearms. Parked all around the building, the marked and unmarked vehicles used by these agencies add an extra element of seriousness to the setting.

After a security screening that included a walk through a metal detector, Enrique went up to the sixteenth floor, where the clerk's office stood at the end of a long hallway. No one outside our legal team and the plaintiffs knew he was coming—or that we were at that moment about to file a complaint challenging Proposition 8. The clerk who accepted the complaint stamped it with the date and time—3:25 P.M.—and said something about how it "must be an important filing" because it had been hand-delivered by an attorney near the close of business on a Friday before a holiday. (Attorneys who want to limit or control the publicity related to a filing sometimes prefer to time deliveries this way because the press and public may be less attentive at the start of a long weekend.) Enrique surreptitiously crossed his fingers and said, "I haven't even read it," and sneaked a peek at the screen of the computer where the clerk recorded the complaint. He noticed that the initials VRW popped up on the form that the clerk was completing.

To avoid complaints about the assignment of cases, many courts use a system like the one at the U.S. district court in San Francisco, which allows a computer to pick a judge at random for each complaint filed. VRW stood for Chief Judge Vaughn R. Walker. As chief judge, Walker oversaw the administration of the court even as he handled his own caseload. Well liked by his colleagues, he was known for being both tough-minded and fair. Blessed with a deep and authoritative voice, the white-haired judge had, during twenty years on the bench, become such a fixture in the courthouse that only the veterans remembered that he almost hadn't made it there in the first place.

When President Reagan nominated Walker in 1987, City Attorney Louise Renne and dozens of congressional Democrats, including Senator Alan Cranston and San Francisco's representative, Nancy Pelosi, mounted a ferocious effort to block his confirmation by the Senate. Their opposition was based on Walker's membership in an all-male golf and athletic club and his role as the attorney who had represented the U.S. Olympic Committee in a suit that stopped the organizers of the so-called Gay Olympics from using the word "Olympics" to promote their games. The lawsuit had led his critics to complain that Walker was antigay; the club membership made him, in their eyes, antiwoman. Cranston, Pelosi, and the others did manage to block his appointment in 1987, but when President George H. W. Bush quietly renominated him in 1989, Walker won unanimous confirmation. In the time since, he had presided over many complex cases involving technology giants such as Microsoft and Oracle. It was also understood, by many lawyers and court officials, that Judge Walker was himself gay. Enrique was aware of these rumors, but he didn't think it would influence the judge's handling of the case. His reputation was as a smart, fair, and even-handed judge. We could not ask for more than that.

Our team of lawyers and advocates spent the Memorial Day weekend of 2009 waiting to announce our filing. On Tuesday, at 9 A.M. Pacific standard time, the California Supreme Court issued the decision we had expected all along: Proposition 8 was upheld, but the eighteen thousand couples who had been legally married in 2008 in the six months between the *In re Marriage Cases* and the passage of Proposition 8 would retain that status. The opinion was written by Chief Justice Ronald George and joined by four of the other six members of the panel. A sixth justice, Kathryn Werdegar, wrote her own concurring opinion. The only member of the court to dissent was Carlos Moreno, who wrote that he thought Prop 8 violated the California constitution.

Because it had been so widely anticipated, the court's decision was generally met with acceptance. Governor Arnold Schwarzenegger said that he believed that "one day California will recognize gay marriage," but in the meantime he would uphold the law as directed by the court. While small numbers of people took to the streets to protest, much more attention was focused on the repeal campaign, which was announced by the nine legal/activist groups less than ninety minutes after the news of the decision broke. "It's time to go on offense," said Rick Jacobs of the pro-equality Courage Campaign as he asked for donations to fund repeal campaign advertising. He was answered by the organizers of the original Prop 8 campaign, who asked their donors for "several million dollars to get our message out." One evangelical pastor from Huntington Beach declared, "I don't have any desire to get in a violent war with anyone over this, but we won't back down."

With the opposing sides resuming the same fight they had waged for the past year, we prepared for a press conference in a large ballroom at a prominent, historic hotel in downtown Los Angeles. As two reasonably well-known lawyers, thanks in part to our opposing roles in the *Bush v. Gore* case, we were able to draw a crowd of reporters and camera crews to what was publicized as a news-making announcement. To emphasize the point that this case was all about Americans and the principles of our Constitution, we set up sixteen flags on the stage behind the podium, which held a placard that read AMERICAN FOUNDATION FOR EQUAL RIGHTS. Underscoring the theme, AFER's logo was a set of three red-and-white stripes that looked as if they were waving as proudly as the Star-Spangled Banner.

We took the stage flanked by Chad Griffin and our clients, Sandy, Kris, Paul, and Jeff. Amid camera flashes, we announced that we had filed a federal lawsuit against Proposition 8, that a new rights organization—AFER—was backing us, and that the couples who stood to our left and our right were the plaintiffs. We explained that our complaint alleged violations of our clients' civil rights, but in layman's terms we were seeking to end discriminatory practices carried out under the authority of the government. Ted stated, "Creating a second class of citizens is discrimination, plain and simple. The Constitution of Thomas Jefferson, James Madison, and Abraham Lincoln does not permit it."

Somewhat astonished to see this cause led by two older, straight men who were last seen together in a courtroom battling against each other over the 2000 presidential election, the reporters responded with a barrage of questions. Why had we taken up this issue? How was it that we had come to be working together? Why did we think we could accomplish what other lawyers, with long-term commitments to equal rights, hadn't been able to? Ted was even pressed to reconcile his conservatism, including his role as someone who had been present at the founding of the conservative Federalist Society, with the marriage equality cause.

Ted explained that this case was about freedom, liberty, nondiscrimination, and the rights of all. The Federalist Society had never staked out a position regarding marriage rights for gay men and lesbian women, he explained. In fact, the Federalist Society does not take "positions"; it hosts debate and discussion. We acknowledged the "odd couple" quality of our collaboration. As Ted explained, "We are two lawyers from opposite ends of the political spectrum who have come together to support one of the most important issues of our time. The plaintiffs are Americans. They work hard. They pay their taxes. And they want to get married just like many of the rest of us. . . . Our nation was founded on the principle that all Americans are created equal. This case is about ensuring that every American is treated equally under the law. California has created a separate relationship for same-sex couples called domestic partnerships. That is separate, and that is not equal. . . . It is unconstitutional."

David then joked, "I must say, being up here on a platform with Ted Olson and all these lights makes me want to urge everybody to count every vote."

After the laughter died down, Ted continued, "David and I have both studied constitutional law and have studied the Supreme Court, and we think we know what we're doing." When asked about the course we would follow, we said that we had asked the district court for an injunction. If we lost there, we would appeal to the Ninth Circuit and all the way up to the Supreme Court, if necessary.

When he was questioned about our motivation in taking on the case, David's voice filled with emotion as he said:

> If you look into the eyes and hearts of people who are gay and talk to them about this issue, it reinforces in the most powerful way possible the fact that these individuals deserve to be treated equally. . . . No right is more fundamental than the right to marry the person that you love and to raise a family. The courts exist to reverse injustices. The purpose of our Constitution and

the purpose of our court system is to make sure that the promise of our Constitution is extended to every American. That's what this lawsuit is about. The concept of equality—equal rights and equal justice under the law—is not just in our Constitution. I believe it is in the hearts and souls of every American. And we have tolerated discrimination and injustice in the past because we have been blinded to the fact that the person being discriminated against is simply another human being, another American. That blindness has enabled us historically not to recognize the equality of people based on sex; based on race; based on religion; and now based on sexual orientation. This lawsuit is about the courts saying that no matter how blind people may be, the Constitution guarantees that everyone deserves the equal rights that every human being is entitled to. And we go to court because that is the place that those equal rights have been established time and again over the last hundred years.

To balance their reporting, most of the journalists at the press conference contacted leaders of the gay and lesbian rights establishment who, true to the statement they had just issued, explained that they had considered a federal suit but rejected the idea in favor of state-by-state efforts. "We think it's risky and premature," said Jennifer Pizer of Lambda Legal in an interview with the *New York Times*. The more gradual approach she favored had been developed "from working on these issues for decades," she added, "and our strategy grows from that work."

As of May 27, 2009, the strategy Pizer and her allies favored had yielded state court decisions that made same-sex marriage legal in just three states, Massachusetts, Connecticut, and Iowa. Meanwhile, in every state where legislators or voters had been asked to consider marriage equality, they had lost—even as public opinion polls showed gradually rising support for the issue in some places. From this record it seemed clear that the opponents of equality had the advantage in elections and statehouses. Perhaps the number of highly motivated opponents was simply greater than the number of highly motivated supporters, or maybe the church networks that they used gave them an organizational benefit. Whatever the reason, the state-by-state strategy that had been tried had enjoyed only limited success.

From the beginning our strategy called for a solid, carefully reasoned, and rigorously prepared case in court, with the result being a favorable court ruling bringing an end to Proposition 8. A concomitant goal was to influence public opinion—to help convince a large segment of the American public that discrimination on the basis of sexual orientation was wrong, damaging, and incompatible with American principles and ideals. It was important for gays and lesbians not only that they win the right to be married—and all that it meant to them and their families—but also that the American people accept that right, and welcome them as married individuals into American society as full equals.

In 1967 the Supreme Court in *Loving* had overturned the laws of the sixteen states that then prohibited interracial marriage. (As many as thirty states had had such prohibitions on the books during the years leading up to that decision.) Today very few Americans would question the constitutional right of persons of different races to be married. Indeed, in 2008 the American people elected as president the offspring of such a marriage. A Supreme Court decision that gave gays and lesbians the right to marry would be only a partial victory if it was not accompanied by a comparable level of acceptance by the American people.

The campaign to influence public opinion was at least as important as the campaign to secure a victory in court. And the best way to accomplish that goal was to persuade America that gays and lesbians were our brothers and sisters, family members, neighbors, and coworkers with the same dreams, aspirations, needs, strengths, and weaknesses as other Americans. The lawsuit was a perfect opportunity to launch that frontal attack. The litigation would complement our communications effort; our public engagement would complement the litigation. Our goal was the advancement of equal rights and the end of discrimination in court and in the arena of public opinion.

FIVE

Preliminary Skirmishes

In June 2009 Governor Arnold Schwarzenegger made it clear that he did not want to have anything to do with defending Proposition 8 in the case that we had filed. Although he had once vetoed a bill that would have authorized same-sex marriage in the state, he had come to support marriage equality wholeheartedly. Days after Prop 8 was adopted, he said he hoped the courts would overturn it. When notified of our suit, he announced that no state official would appear in Judge Walker's court to defend the measure. Then–attorney general Jerry Brown (now California governor) stated that he would file a brief arguing that the amendment be overturned.

To someone who hadn't followed the issue closely, such reactions might have seemed quite strange (although as we go to publication, several state attorneys general have made similar decisions in marriage equality suits in their respective states). Four citizens file a lawsuit challenging the constitutionality of a provision of a state constitution approved by a vote of the electorate, naming the governor, the attorney general, and various other state officials as defendants, but none of those officials would mount a defense. One might expect that the result would be that Proposition 8, in this context, would be left defenseless in the courtroom. That would seldom be the outcome, however, because the parties that sponsored the measure in the first place would want to come to its defense. In this case, the forces that wanted to restrict marriage to heterosexual couples had their own ample resources and infrastructure upon which to draw. Days after the governor and attorney general declared they would not defend Proposition 8, the groups and individuals who had initially brought the amendment to the voters came forward to say that they would defend it as "intervenors" in federal court.

California law accorded these "proponents" of Proposition 8, as they asserted in a motion and brief filed in the case, "a preferred status as [the] official advocate for Proposition 8," since, as they put it, they had "indefatigably labored in support of [it]." They each had been principals in the early stages of the battle, having been responsible for drafting the measure and raising the money—$37 million or more—that funded a campaign that eventually involved thousands of volunteers. They had also prepared the arguments in favor of the proposition that appeared in the official voter guide submitted statewide to the electorate. And they had defended the measure successfully before the California Supreme Court in *Strauss v. Horton*. They had anticipated that Jerry Brown, who had opposed Proposition 8, and had urged that it be invalidated, would be an inadequate representative for its defense. They asserted that they were therefore uniquely suited, both legally and by disposition, to defend it.

The intervenor group included Dennis Hollingsworth, Gail Knight, Martin Gutierrez, Hak-Shing William Tam, and Mark Jansson. ProtectMarriage.com–Yes on 8 was also named in a notice of intervention. On June 30, Judge Walker issued an order granting the proponents' request to intervene to defend the initiative. Our legal team did not oppose intervention and participation by the proponents at this stage. We were sure that the judge would grant their request in any event, and we felt that a vigorous, competent defense of Proposition 8 in the district court would make our ultimate victory, if we could achieve it, that much more credible. Judge Walker then called for a "case management conference." In the course of his order scheduling the conference, he identified several issues for the parties to consider and address, including the potential factors that would guide the level of scrutiny that he would be obliged to apply in considering the constitutionality of Proposition 8.

The Supreme Court has applied ascending levels of scrutiny to laws challenged as violating constitutional rights or infringing on the right to equal protection under the laws. The most lenient, or permissive, review, called "rational basis," is applied to laws that regulate economic activity, commerce, the environment, and so forth. In those areas, while the legislature may be perceived as acting unwisely, there is little reason generally to suspect improper motivations and, at the same time, a substantial basis for deferring to the political process. Broad authority is given by the Constitution to the legislative branch to regulate the nation's activities, including the economy, and courts are ill-equipped to second-guess legislative judgments in these arenas. Courts will thus defer to the legislative decisions if they can perceive any reasonable or rational objective for the measure under consideration.

On the other hand, where fundamental human rights or freedoms are at stake, the courts are considerably less deferential. If a law deprives citizens of a fundamental right, such as freedom of speech or the right to vote, or if a law discriminates between citizens based on characteristics such as race, the courts treat such measures as highly suspect and apply a standard of review referred to as "strict scrutiny." Here, courts feel much more responsible to protect against majoritarian encroachments on the rights of minorities or on basic freedoms, and much better equipped to act as a check on legislative impulses. Discriminatory measures that treat races differently, for example, are almost never justifiable, so courts are properly vigilant in the presence of—and highly suspicious regarding—such measures. They will be upheld only if government can show a "compelling" interest in enacting the measure, and that the law enacted is "narrowly tailored" to achieve the government's goal.

The courts have on occasion applied "intermediate scrutiny" to some measures, such as laws that apply different rules according to gender, requiring the showing of an important governmental interest substantially related to a legislative provision.

Needless to say, a law is much more likely to withstand judicial review under rational basis review than if subject to strict scrutiny. Thus the standard the judiciary applies to an enactment like Proposition 8 may have a substantial impact on whether it is upheld or overturned.

Judge Walker's order made it clear that in the process of deciding whether Proposition 8 was constitutional, he planned first to determine which test he would apply in conducting that analysis. In that respect he expressed interest in evidence that would demonstrate the degree to which gays and lesbians had historically been the victims of discrimination, whether they had the political power to defend themselves, whether their sexual orientation affected their ability to contribute to society, and whether sexual orientation was an immutable characteristic (that is, whether their sexuality was a matter of biology at birth or a decision, conduct, or characteristic that they had the power to change). He also asked the parties to address and present evidence on fundamental questions about marriage, discrimination, and child rearing.

———

Our opponents in the case were represented by a team that included California-based attorney Andrew Pugno, who had helped run the Prop 8 campaign, and Brian Raum of New York and Arizona. A graduate of Lee University, whose motto is "A Christ-Centered Liberal Arts Campus," Raum had earned his law degree in 1994 from Regent University School of Law, which televangelist Pat Robertson created to train leaders who would promote his religious convictions in the secular world. Although much of Raum's legal work had been in the area of employment law, he had attracted notice in the spring of 2008 by criticizing New York State officials for adopting polices that recognized the marriages of same-sex couples who were married in other states. In that instance Raum spoke for a group called the Alliance Defense Fund (which was renamed the Alliance Defending Freedom in 2012).

Created in 1994 by leaders of other major conservative Christian organizations, the original Alliance group was founded to spread religious values while fighting against marriage between individuals of the same sex and what organizers called the "homosexual agenda." This term reframed the efforts of gay men and lesbians to gain equality as an attack on conservative Christians, and it incited church-based election campaigns while aiding fund-raising efforts, which brought in more than $20 million per year. The Alliance promoted Proposition 8 and lent its support to its defense before the California Supreme Court, and then helped to finance the proponents in the *Perry* case.

Raum and Pugno recruited a prominent trial and appellate lawyer named Charles "Chuck" Cooper, who would be high on anyone's list of candidates to lead a long, hard, challenging legal fight. Washington-based, Cooper was an Alabama-born son of the South who wore French-cuff shirts, elegant suits, and spoke with a formality that one political writer called "Victorian copy book prose." He had been a clerk for Supreme Court associate justice William H. Rehnquist (later chief justice) before taking a job in the civil rights division of the Reagan Justice Department. Cooper described himself as an "unrepentant and avowed originalist," which meant he thought judges should determine and follow the intent of the framers of the Constitution. The flag over his law office bore the slogan VICTORY OR DEATH. He was a fine lawyer, unfailingly gracious and polite, and he had won some impressive victories in important cases. He was a formidable adversary.

When it came to issues involving the rights of gays and lesbians, Cooper had considerable experience in high-profile cases. He had filed a brief in favor of the Colorado constitutional amendment in the case of *Romer v. Evans* and had supported Hawaii's laws against same-sex marriage when its supreme court concluded that they discriminated against gays and lesbians and were constitutionally suspect. In both cases Cooper cited originalist principles, insisting that the laws that were under legal attack had been properly adopted and reflected the will of the people. In each of these cases, he was on the losing side, but he had consistently presented his arguments with skill and integrity.

With prominent attorneys and activist organizations on both sides, the Prop 8 battle was shaping up to be a classic contest of relatively equal teams. Our side, however, had to do some scrambling to catch up with our opponents when it came to public advocacy. While the Alliance Defense Fund was well established, AFER was a start-up operating on a modest budget, and we had to struggle to attain something close to an equal voice with the massive national fund-raising machines on the other side. Their side was motivated by a conservative Christian view of society that reserved marriage and parenthood for heterosexual couples. Many who contributed to the "traditional marriage" position were honorable, principled people who just could not accept the concept of marriage between persons of the same sex. Many were motivated by religious convictions and the belief that same-sex intimacy was a sin, immoral and indecent. Our supporters did not want to take away anything from those who enjoyed the right to marriage and all it brought; we just wanted equal access for gays and lesbians to the same happiness, respect, acceptance, benefits, and responsibilities.

———

Our first procedural step was to ask Judge Walker for an injunction that would suspend Proposition 8 during the course of the case. We argued that it caused immediate, continuous, immeasurable, and irreparable harm by singling out one group of Americans for separate, discriminatory treatment when it came to marriage. Domestic partnerships—or civil unions in some states—were just not the same as marriage. It was akin, we argued, to declaring that citizens of Chinese ancestry could have legal rights but could not call themselves U.S. citizens. We also argued that as a clearly vulnerable class of persons, subject to mistreatment based on immutable characteristics, gays and lesbians could not be shunted aside and denied rights enjoyed by other Californians. The immutability of sexual identity is something that science has gradually confirmed in the last few decades, and the tragic failure of various programs designed to "help" people change their sexual orientation underscored that fact.

Our opponents disagreed with us not only on immutability but on almost every other point we made. Prop 8, in their view, was merely an affirmation of the nation's centuries-old definition of marriage as a relationship between a man and a woman. They cited a case called *Baker v. Nelson,* which involved an early challenge by a gay couple to restrictions on their right to marry. Richard Baker wanted to wed fellow university student and gay rights activist James McConnell, but Gerald Nelson, district court clerk of Hennepin County, Minnesota, denied them a marriage license. The attorneys who represented Baker lost, decisively, as both a trial court and the Minnesota Supreme Court found that because the state had a compelling interest in procreation and child rearing, it could bar same-sex marriages. The U.S. Supreme Court declined to hear an appeal, a decision that had some precedential value, because it meant that at the time—1972—the Supreme Court did not see that it presented any substantial federal constitutional question.

Besides *Baker,* our opponents armed themselves with their own take on the *Loving v. Virginia* decision, arguing that the Supreme Court had determined in that case that the purpose of marriage was to produce children; only heterosexual couples, they argued, were able to fulfill this purpose. They denied that Prop 8 was based on discriminatory animus toward same-sex couples, since it applied equally to everyone: All men could marry only women, and all women could marry only men; our clients could marry anyone they wanted as long as it was someone of the opposite sex—overlooking the devastating consequences of forcing gays and lesbians to marry only the persons they could not, by their nature, love. Finally, they disputed the idea that gays and lesbians should receive special protection as a distinct minority because, as they noted, the Ninth Circuit Court of Appeals had previously found that sexual orientation "is behavioral" and thus changeable.

As a work of legal heft, our opponents' response to our request for an immediate injunction was about as good as it could be. It repeatedly invoked the mantra "traditional marriage," suggesting that it was sacrosanct. It addressed the major points we had made and offered the essential arguments against same-sex marriage that had historically been made.

———

Judge Walker may have been moved by our appeal based upon the ongoing harm to gays and lesbians that our briefs described. But he approached our motion for an immediate injunction, as he did everything else throughout the case, with a careful, balanced, and dispassionate objectivity. Most lawyers who had appeared before Judge Walker had praised him as temperamentally suited to managing a controversial case with fairness and equanimity, two traits that may have been influenced by his midwestern upbringing, born and raised in the tiny farm town of Watseka, Illinois. His own father had once studied the law but ended his education short of a degree when the United States entered the Second World War. A worn copy of *Black's Law Dictionary* remained in the house, and Walker has said that as a boy he leafed through it with care approaching reverence. His parents never pushed him toward one profession or another, though, and in high school he was good at everything from math and science to theater and debate. When radio station WGFA ("World's Greatest Farming Area") began to broadcast in 1961, Walker scored a job announcing the morning agricultural report. Farmers who tuned in at 6 A.M. heard a deep, authoritative voice deliver bushel prices for corn and wheat. When the show was over, radio personality Walker hopped on his bicycle and metamorphosed back into high school student Walker. He left Watseka for undergraduate studies at the University of Michigan and eventually completed law school at Stanford. After a clerkship at federal district court in Los Angeles he entered private practice with one of the most prominent firms in California.

In his twenty years on the bench, Judge Walker had developed a personal philosophy regarding the role of the courts in society. He placed a high value on the contribution trials could make to the public understanding of difficult issues. More than any other forum—debates, speeches, legislative hearings—a trial allowed for facts to be uncovered, balanced, weighed, and contested. The famous Scopes Trial of 1925, the battle over evolution and creationism in public schools, led the country to a better comprehension of science and education. More recently, proceedings involving executives of fraudulently run companies had opened a window on the workings of duplicitous businesses that went from boom to bust, taking investors with them. Although few trials ever rise to the historic significance of the Scopes case, every one presented an opportunity to establish a public record. When cases were subsequently considered by appellate courts, the value of that record, and the performance of the trial judge involved, would be meticulously weighed and evaluated. If upheld, a trial court's factual findings could have an immense and permanent impact on history, culture, and law.

A definitive record can only be established, of course, if a judge enables the litigants to present a full case. This doesn't always happen in constitutional cases. Many judges confronted with our complaint on Prop 8 would have opted to request briefs and declarations and then issued a ruling based on written arguments and authorities. This procedure, called summary judgment, would have been much more expeditious and spared the judge the difficult task of sorting out the controversies that would present themselves regarding this case's key issues of sex, family, discrimination, stigma, history, marriage, rights, responsibilities, and equality. It would have been far less work for Judge Walker to take the easier path.

Judge Walker's history on the bench, however, demonstrated that he did not shrink from cases with complicated issues laden with conflict, having presided over Apple's 1994 copyright infringement case against Microsoft and the U.S. government's 2004 challenge to software giant Oracle's ultimate takeover of a firm called PeopleSoft.

In his first substantive order in our case, Judge Walker indicated he would deny our request for an immediate preliminary injunction. Instead the order stated that "the court is inclined to proceed directly and expeditiously to the merits." He was going to put Proposition 8 on trial, and to accomplish this task he asked us to submit evidence to address nineteen factual questions:

- The history of discrimination gays and lesbians have faced
- Whether the characteristics defining gays and lesbians as a class might in any way affect their ability to contribute to society
- Whether sexual orientation can be changed, and if so, whether gays and lesbians should be encouraged to change it
- The relative political power of gays and lesbians, including successes of both pro-gay and antigay legislation
- The long-standing definition of marriage in California
- Whether the exclusion of same-sex couples from marriage leads to increased stability in opposite-sex marriage
- Whether permitting same-sex couples to marry destabilizes opposite-sex marriage
- Whether a married mother and father provide the optimal child-rearing environment
- Whether excluding same-sex couples from marriage promotes this environment
- Whether and how California has acted to promote these interests in other family law contexts
- Whether or not Prop 8 discriminates based on sexual orientation or gender or both
- Whether the availability of opposite-sex marriage is a meaningful option for gays and lesbians
- Whether the ban on same-sex marriage meaningfully restricts options available to heterosexuals
- Whether requiring one man and one woman in marriage promotes stereotypical gender roles
- Whether Prop 8 was passed with a discriminatory intent

- The voters' motivation or motivations for supporting Prop 8, including advertisements and ballot literature considered by California voters
- The differences in actual practice of registered domestic partnerships, civil unions, and marriage
- Whether married couples are treated differently from domestic partners in governmental and nongovernmental contexts
- Whether the right [to marriage] asserted by plaintiffs is "deeply rooted in this Nation's history and tradition" and thus subject to strict scrutiny under the due process clause

These nineteen questions in Judge Walker's order issued June 30, 2009, less than five weeks after Enrique Monagas filed our complaint, addressed all the issues that would establish predicates for the arguments for and against marriage equality. Taken together they suggested extremely careful and deep thinking about what it means to be a lesbian woman or gay man in twenty-first-century America.

The nation, too, seemed on the threshold of willingness to take the issues presented by Proposition 8 seriously. A couple of weeks before the judge sent us his order, President Obama and the First Lady entertained a group of gay and lesbian activists in the East Room of the White House in celebration of the fortieth anniversary of the Stonewall uprising.

Earlier in his career, President Obama had opposed what virtually everyone was calling same-sex marriage. But he would later say that he was "evolving." As a candidate President Obama had endorsed the cause of gays and lesbians, promising to roll back the Defense of Marriage Act and the military's "Don't Ask, Don't Tell" policy, which allowed gays and lesbians to serve only if they kept in the closet— remained silent about their sexual orientation. At the time we started our case he had not yet acted to fulfill his promises, and still resisted endorsing marriage equality, but no previous president had been as receptive on this issue of equality, and the East Room event was an encouraging sign of change. The attendees included former ambassador James Hormel; Gene Robinson, an openly gay bishop in the Episcopal Church; and Chad Griffin.

Having worked on political campaigns and then in the Clinton White House, Chad knew many of the guests at the Stonewall anniversary celebration. The event gave him a chance to talk politics and policy with people who understood both very well. Although he was fast becoming a prominent leader in the movement to advance equality, he was still a young, aggressive, outspoken activist more willing than most to take assertive stands. In part this was because he never stopped thinking about gays and lesbians, especially younger ones, living in places like his home state of Arkansas. They were still waiting for new laws against discrimination and the social change that was sweeping more rapidly on the nation's coasts.

———

In the weeks after our complaint was filed, San Francisco's city attorney and three of the gay rights groups that had initially opposed even the idea of a court battle over Prop 8 sought to intervene on our side. Although we would have been happy to have assistance in a less formal way, we were not enthusiastic about adding additional litigants. We were, first and foremost, lawyers representing specific clients—Sandy, Kris, Paul, and Jeff—and we needed to control the case to get the best result for them. We did not want to fight with other lawyers about the direction, timing, and strategy of the case, the identity of witnesses, and the way to express legal arguments. We did not want balkanized arguments, time-consuming debates about who would argue what. We wanted a controlled, coherent, and consistent message. Accordingly we rejected would-be intervenors' offers and opposed their motions to intervene. With perhaps a little too much zeal, Chad took up the task of responding to them in a letter that noted their effort to "undermine" our effort and expressed concern whether they "would zealously and effectively litigate this case if you were successful in intervening."

When the recipients didn't respond to Chad's letter, and then mischaracterized our position to the press, Chad shared with journalists what he had written. The aspiring intervenors had been very public and pointedly critical in their "Make Change, Not Lawsuits" policy statement. Nevertheless they continued to insist that Judge Walker let them participate in the trial.

———

On July 2, 2009, days after Judge Walker gave us his nineteen questions, the parties assembled in a courtroom high in the Phillip Burton Federal Building. A modernist design with wood paneling on three sides and a slab of beige-colored stone behind the bench, the chamber was softly lit and modestly outfitted with straight-backed wooden benches and a judge's bench elevated just a few feet above the main floor.

About a dozen reporters and twenty-one attorneys gathered in the court. Among them were several representing those groups that had formerly opposed the suit but now wanted to be part of the case, including the ACLU, Lambda Legal, and the National Center for Lesbian Rights. Judge Walker, dignified in his black robe, white hair, and Vandyke beard, appeared precisely at ten o'clock, taking his seat beneath the seal of the U.S. District Court, Northern District of California, which features the eagle, olive branch, and arrows of the Great Seal of the United States. When he noticed how many lawyers were present he quipped, "Well, you know, simply because you appear doesn't mean you to have to talk." Throughout this case Judge Walker often introduced just the right light touch that, while retaining firm control on the courtroom, put everyone at ease.

Judge Walker approved the proponents' request to defend Prop 8. After having heard arguments from all of the potential intervenors on our side, he decided that only the City of San Francisco could show it had an interest in the case that would not be well represented by our team. The city attorney would be permitted to intervene on our side, but only to address its governmental and economic interests, which had been established over decades of municipal activism and social programming that had made San Francisco into a notably diverse and thriving community and a mecca for gays and lesbians.

With respect to our request for an injunction, Judge Walker stated his reluctance to grant one but allowed us to make our argument in support of it. Ted told the court, "Every day that Proposition 8 is enforced perpetuates a tragic injustice on tens of thousands of Californians," and emphasized that "the United States Supreme Court has held again and again that the right to marry is the most important relation in life and a right of fundamental importance to all citizens."

Chuck Cooper rose to respond, arguing that what we were in effect seeking was "to sweep away not only Proposition 8 and the sovereign will of the people in the state, but the common definition of marriage and the laws of forty-three other states and the federal government in the Defense of Marriage Act. . . . The plaintiff's claim also condemns as irrational, as bigoted, the universal definition of marriage that has hitherto prevailed by law in America and in virtually every known society for as long as the subject of marriage has been governed by law."

Judge Walker listened attentively, giving everyone the full opportunity to be heard. He noted the likelihood that this case would eventually wind up in the Ninth Circuit Court of Appeals and then perhaps the U.S. Supreme Court:

> I'm reasonably sure, given the issues involved and the personnel that are in the courtroom, that this case is only touching down in this court, that it will have a life after this court, and what happens here, in many ways, is only a prelude to what is going to happen later.
>
> So I am inclined to think that *how* we do things here is more important than *what* we do. That our job in this case, at this point, is to make a record. And I want to give the plaintiffs, the defendants, and the intervenors [proponents] the opportunity to make the record that they think is appropriate for the decision. And so I think we've got our work cut out for us.

Judge Walker's stated goal was a speedy trial, as complete as justice could provide. More than once he used the phrase "roll up our sleeves" to remind us that he wanted us to work hard and expeditiously. "I used to practice law myself," he reminded us, "and I know the value of a deadline." He asked the parties to negotiate over the matter of pretrial discovery, which is the process that litigants use to uncover the facts in a dispute, and suggested a thirty-day deadline to get things rolling.

Discovery includes document demands (which require each side and selected third parties to turn over relevant documents), interrogatories (written questions that each side can direct to the other), and depositions (in which each side can require people with relevant knowledge to answer orally questions under oath with a stenographer, and often a videographer, keeping the record of each question and answer). In every case certain documents may be withheld because they relate to the attorney-client relationship or are otherwise privileged, as, for example, a doctor's communication with a patient. Although certain privileges are generally easy to recognize, the discovery process is often marked by intense conflicts over evidence that one side seeks, and another withholds, based on a claim of privilege. Judges or referees working for judges settle these disputes on an individual basis. (Judge Walker appointed a magistrate judge named Joseph Spero to rule on many of these disputes.) Of course, as evidence is released and read, litigants typically submit further requests for documents referenced in the papers they receive. This process is something like a treasure hunt, with each find bringing the requesting side closer to victory. For the side holding the evidence, the best offense is often a good defense, which is why Chuck Cooper announced, "I'm not going to look for any e-mails in this case."

Upon hearing this Judge Walker interrupted to say, "Those are sometimes very handy, as you know, Mr. Cooper."

The audience in the courtroom reacted with laughter. Most everyone was well aware that in our search for evidence that Proposition 8 was the product of malice, animosity, ill will, or discriminatory intent, e-mails exchanged by the proponents could be very revealing. Knowing this, Cooper responded, "I don't want his clients' e-mails, and I'm sure he doesn't want mine."

We didn't have to refute Cooper's claim, because the judge wasn't going to decide any discovery questions that day. He wanted instead for us to spend the coming month negotiating over the process and settling as many issues as we could. Cooper briefly resisted this idea, insisting that his side was playing catch-up and could need more time. Judge Walker clearly disagreed, and even offered us the immediate use of his jury room so we could "sit down and roll up your sleeves and talk about some issues." He noted that the longer two parties have to talk, the more likely they are to find points of agreement.

The well-mannered and invariably respectful Cooper yielded. "Yes, indeed," he said. "And, Your Honor, thirty days it is."

Our opponents plainly and viscerally did not want a trial in the *Perry* case. They did not want the pro–Proposition 8 campaign planning and rhetoric exposed, and they did not want to respond with actual evidence to the complex and controversial questions that Judge Walker had raised. How could they prove that permitting same-sex marriage destabilizes opposite-sex marriage? How could they disprove the long and tragic history of discrimination that gays and lesbians had experienced in America? How could they prove that sexual orientation could be changed?

So they made one last try to avoid the awkwardness and potentially devastating consequences, to them, of a trial. On September 9, Cooper filed a motion for summary judgment, asking Judge Walker to uphold Proposition 8 as a matter of law, without a trial. Their motion was accompanied by a long supporting brief with citations to 130 or so judicial decisions, the constitutions of nearly every state, and references to learned writings from such living and dead luminaries as Edmund Burke, William Jefferson Clinton, William Blackstone, Alfred Kinsey, Barack Obama, Aldous Huxley, Samuel Johnson, James Q. Wilson, and Plato, to name just a fraction. (Nothing from Zorba the Greek.) The brief argued that marriage between a man and woman was the way it had always been and there were no facts to adjudicate in a trial— that was the way it should remain.

We responded in our brief that Cooper's invocation in his brief of the phrase "traditional definition of marriage" thirty-nine times in precisely those words, and in countless additional verbal variations, amounted to no more than a "the way things have always been" argument and was no more valid in this case than it was in the school segregation and interracial marriage cases.

The case came on for argument on October 14 before Judge Walker and produced one of the most memorable and decisive moments in the case.

Did he just say what I thought he said? These words silently coursed through many of our minds during an exchange between Cooper and Judge Walker. Our opponent had just uttered words that we sent rocketing back to him again and again in briefs and arguments throughout the case.

One of our central themes in this case was that depriving gays and lesbians of the right to marry causes grave harm to them and their children but according them that right would not harm the "traditional" institution of marriage between opposite-sex persons.

Proving that proposition was not a simple matter because it is easy to assert that any change in marriage could change the institution and make it less desirable to opposite-sex couples. We knew that this wasn't true, but how to prove it? In the trial, we planned to put on numerous experts who could help us establish that marriage between persons of the same sex did not discourage heterosexual couples from getting married, cause them to divorce, or discourage them from having children. The notion was laughable, but it is always difficult to prove a negative.

And to our surprise and great relief, Cooper handed us a telling concession on this very point that he would immediately and continuously regret.

Cooper was arguing in court that day that the judge should rule in his favor without a trial because limiting marriage to a man and a woman furthered the state's interest in procreation and the conception of children. Judge Walker first punctured this balloon by interjecting, "Well, the last marriage that I performed, Mr. Cooper, involved a groom who was ninety-five and the bride was eighty-three. I did not demand that they prove that they intended to engage in a procreative activity. Now, was I missing something?"

Over the laughter that ensued Cooper, undeterred, persisted, insisting that the "central purpose . . . for the [man/woman] institution of marriage [is the] simple biological reality that same-sex couples do not naturally procreate."

Judge Walker remained skeptical, observing that, on the one hand, "procreation doesn't require marriage" and, on the other, it is "certainly not a precondition of marriage to be able to prove that you can have children."

Cooper soldiered on. He insisted that the issue was not "the individual's motivation to get married. . . . It's the state's purpose that's important here. And if the state has any conceivable rational purpose, I have to win."

At this point, Judge Walker drove to the core of Cooper's case—and ours—and called for a direct, unequivocal answer. "Assume that I agree [that the state's interest in marriage is essentially procreative]. How does permitting same-sex marriage impair or adversely affect that interest?"

After telling the judge that "that's not the legally relevant question," seldom a productive response to a question that a judge obviously perceives as relevant or he wouldn't have asked it, Cooper bobbed and weaved. But Walker had been a judge too long to let a lawyer slip the hook that easily. "What," he repeated, "is the harm to the procreative purpose or function of marriage that you outline of permitting same-sex marriage?"

Cooper is a smart man, and he had practiced law for forty years. He knew a dangerous question when he heard one. He tried yet another pirouette, this time involving a digression into "channeling procreative activity into enduring relationships." But Judge Walker wasn't buying that one either and bored in:

"I'm asking you to tell me how it would harm opposite-sex marriages. . . . Let's play on the same playing field for once."

Mr. Cooper: "Your Honor, my answer is: *I don't know. I don't know.*"

At this point, the clocks in the courtroom figuratively stopped and there was a perceptible collective intake of breath. If marriage was a valuable relationship (which Cooper was conceding), if withholding it from gays and lesbians was harmful to them (which we could certainly prove), and if granting that right to same-sex couples would not impose any knowable harm to opposite-sex marriages, what was left of Cooper's case?

To be fair, Cooper's point, once he was able to collect his thoughts—and his whole case seemed to boil down to this—was that since the consequences to opposite-sex marriages by allowing same-sex marriages were unknown, and apparently unknowable, California had the right to prevent it from happening. He tried to rephrase his "I don't know." Unleashing a barrage of double negatives, he pleaded, "I . . . submit that it is not self-evident that there is no chance of any harm. And unless it is, the people of California are entitled not to run the risk . . . unless Mr. Olson and his colleagues can prove that there is no harm that can possibly come from this, then the people of California are entitled to make the decision they did."

Of course, this would mean that virtually any law could be constitutionally justified by the "I don't know" standard. The courts are not that willing to defer totally to legislative actions simply because the consequences may be unknowable.

At the end of the trial, in his closing argument, Cooper tried to walk back his concession. He stated that he had often "wished I could have those three words ['I don't know'] back." The problem was that he had committed truth. In the end, neither he nor his trial witnesses nor his colleagues knew of any harm that would result from allowing same-sex couples to have the same right to marry that opposite-sex couples enjoyed. Neither the words nor the facts that motivated them could be retracted. Marriage was being denied and grave harm was being done for no known reason.

SIX

Assembling the Evidence

Well before the end of summer, Judge Walker announced that he intended to start the trial in the second week of January 2010. It was an ambitious goal, giving us just a few months, including the holidays in November and December, to do all the work needed to move from our first appearance in his courtroom to a history-making trial. However, we were pleased with the tight schedule, which we believed would give us just enough time, if we all worked overtime. In addition to discovery, we had to interview and prepare fact witnesses, select experts from around the world and assist in the preparation of their reports, and continue to refine our legal and factual arguments.

When Ted was asked by one of the Gibson Dunn lawyers on the case to seek additional time, he replied that whatever would be hard on us would be as hard or harder on the other side. We were confident that we had as much—or more—horsepower. We intended to do nothing to slow this case down.

For as long as there have been courts of law, attorneys have appealed to the court of public opinion on their clients' behalf. The idea isn't to influence a judge or a jury directly, but rather, especially in today's media-driven world, to influence the social and intellectual discourse and the atmosphere in which decision making occurs, and to prepare the public to accept the results you seek. In addition to the interest the two of us could be expected to generate, we relied on Chad Griffin and a talented AFER team, together with David's equally talented director of communications, Dawn Schneider, to make our case to the public. While no one article or broadcast will make people generally more open-minded and empathetic toward a particular issue, repeated coverage that presents a legal point of view regarding that issue or the plaintiffs as fuller human beings can have an effect. We thought it was important for us to use the publicity we could command, thanks to the case, to call attention to the fact that people who may hold different political views can still seek and find common ground. We believe that productive cross-party alliances can not only solve problems but make the public square a happier place.

The opening gambit in this effort was, of course, the press conference when we filed the complaint, and media appearances we made on that day and in the days thereafter. Next was an op-ed piece David wrote for the *Wall Street Journal*. As the most respected and influential conservative opinion forum, the *Journal* was not the place where most people would have expected to find David Boies, Al Gore's champion, making the case for marriage equality. The *New York Times, Washington Post,* or *Los Angeles Times* might have been a more predictable fit for his views. But we wanted to begin connecting with a constituency that hadn't fully considered our side of the issue, and demonstrate that we had the courage of our convictions. David began:

> Recently, Ted Olson and I brought a lawsuit asking the courts to now declare unconstitutional California's Proposition 8 limitation of marriage to people of the opposite sex. We acted together because of our mutual commitment to the importance of this cause, and to emphasize that this is not a Republican or Democratic issue, not a liberal or conservative issue, but an issue of enforcing our Constitution's guarantee of equal protection and due process to all citizens.

David described the history of Supreme Court rulings that have held that the right to marry is so fundamental that it may not be abridged even where it might appear sensible to do so. (One case struck down a Missouri law that prevented imprisoned felons from marrying;

another case invalidated a Wisconsin law that barred child-support scofflaws from getting another marriage license.) He argued that laws on same-sex marriage served no legitimate purpose, finding it "difficult to the point of impossibility to imagine love-struck heterosexuals contemplating marriage to decide against it because gays and lesbians also have the right to marry," and asserted that

> there is no longer any credible contention that depriving gays and lesbians of basic rights will cause them to change their sexual orientation. Even if there was, the attempt would be constitutionally defective. But, in fact, the sexual orientation of gays and lesbians is as much a God-given characteristic as the color of their skin or the sexual orientation of their straight brothers and sisters. It is also a condition that, like race, has historically been subject to abusive and often violent discrimination. It is precisely where a minority's basic human rights are abridged that our Constitution's promise of due process and equal protection is most vital.

If the eight published letters responding to his piece were any indication, David had not completely succeeded in overcoming the opposition, certainly, at least not the readers of the *Wall Street Journal*. One respondent allowed that he (seven of eight who commented were men) was not "entirely unpersuaded" but then insisted that polygamy would naturally follow equal marriage rights for same-sex couples. Another confessed that marriage equality might well be inevitable but maintained that it should be accomplished by ballot initiatives and not in court. Mostly, though, those who did respond opposed equality on the basis that the framers of the Constitution would never have approved of such a measure. But we did not expect to change public opinion with one opinion piece. That was going to require a sustained, prolonged effort in every forum available. This was just the start.

Days after David's op-ed appeared, other papers began publishing articles about the former courtroom adversaries turned allies, and each piece gave us an opportunity to explain why our clients were being harmed by illegal discrimination. Patt Morrison of the *Los Angeles Times* plumbed her colorful imagination to describe us as "a version of Hepburn and Tracy in *Adam's Rib*," the 1949 George Cukor comedy about a married couple who are lawyers battling on opposite sides of a case. Jo Becker of the *New York Times* wrote a lengthy story about the case that was featured on her paper's front page, where a million or so readers could learn our rationale for filing the case together, and the outlines of our argument. She also gave roughly equal time to Cooper and fellow conservatives, who admitted they were somewhat aghast at Ted's choice of clients. She quoted the now deceased Judge Robert Bork, a close friend of Ted's and someone for whom he had enormous respect and admiration. Bork said he chose not to discuss the issue with Ted but expressed polite antipathy to his new case.

Our effort to educate and influence public opinion continued throughout the case, on television, radio, and in print. One example came as the trial began in January 2010 in the form of a lengthy cover piece for *Newsweek* by Ted entitled "The Conservative Case for Gay Marriage: The Republican Lawyer Who Won *Bush v. Gore* Is Fighting a New Battle for Equal Rights for All." In it he explained "why same-sex marriage is an American value" and should, especially, be embraced by conservatives. The introduction to the piece, by *Newsweek* writer Eve Conant, quoted one conservative scholar expressing his "surprise, followed by disgust," but grudgingly acknowledging, "There's a definite chance he'll win. That's what makes it all the more outrageous that he's pushing this."

Any discomfort Ted felt about the animosity directed toward him was balanced by support from many other quarters. He was moved by the friendship that he had developed with Rob and Michele Reiner, Chad Griffin, and others on the team. He also received overwhelming encouragement within Gibson Dunn, where his colleagues often made a point of expressing support for the case. One of these moments came just weeks after the suit was filed and the press attention began. Ted walked into the law library at the firm's Washington office one evening. The only other lawyer in the room, a woman, stopped her work and told him, "You and I haven't worked together, but I'm a lesbian. My partner and I have two children." She expressed a tearful thanks for his bringing the firm's resources to bear on behalf of the Prop 8 challenge and putting his reputation and status on the line for equality.

———

While our legal work drew nationwide attention, opponents of marriage equality kept the pressure on at the state level. In Maine, where the state legislature had passed a law permitting same-sex marriage, which the governor had signed, a campaign had been started to repeal it with a voter referendum. This effort was led by some of the same consultants who had guided Proposition 8 in California, including a strategist named Frank Schubert, who worked on behalf of conservative Christian causes, individual candidates, and the tobacco, timber, and drug industries. Meanwhile, in Iowa, the National Organization for Marriage (NOM) began a campaign to overturn a state supreme court decision that had legalized same-sex marriage. Their focus was on electing state lawmakers who would craft, propose, and vote for a constitutional amendment banning it. This was to be a long-term project, requiring precinct-level work to elect legislators who would have to vote in favor of the amendment in successive legislative terms. At the very earliest the measure would appear on a ballot in 2014.

The NOM activists and Frank Schubert were both politically and religiously inspired. Schubert made prayer a part of his business meetings, and NOM's executive director, Brian Brown, had previously worked for a Connecticut organization devoted to promoting Judeo-Christian values in society and state government. While religious values can, and often do, influence policy debates, the same provision of the Constitution that protects the free exercise of religion prohibits "an establishment of religion." This means that government cannot enforce or impose one's religious beliefs or tenets on others. For this reason the people who campaigned against marriage equality were ordinarily careful to present their arguments in terms of "traditional" values instead of conservative Christian dogma, and they rarely if ever discussed the church-connected donors who provided almost all of their funding. While NOM and Schubert were effective in conveying their message, they also aided our cause: Their opposition, in a sense, helped clarify the debate.

It almost goes without saying that the best contests—and lawsuits *are* intense contests, often with immense stakes—involve combatants well matched in skill, motivation, and strength. Throughout this contest, Chuck Cooper and Brian Raum and their team fought us, ably and aggressively, at every step. Early on, they resisted our requests for documents related to the Proposition 8 campaign. We wanted to obtain information that would reveal the motivations of those who conceived of Prop 8 and devised and conducted the campaign to pass it. We also asked for all the materials—including but not limited to print, video, audio, and electronic communications—that had been distributed by the campaign.

Cooper and Raum tried to limit our access to their clients' records, which would make it more difficult for us to make our case and would also keep those records out of the hands of the press and public. Withholding what they admitted were thousands of pages of material, they insisted to Judge Walker that the documents "are not fit and appropriate for judicial inquiry, and that in fact, would raise the gravest possible First Amendment issues."

The First Amendment to the U.S. Constitution states in full, "Congress shall make no law respecting an establishment of religion, or prohibiting the free exercise thereof; or abridging the freedom of speech, or of the press; or the right of the people peaceably to assemble, and to petition the Government for a redress of grievances." Over time it has been applied by the courts to protect citizens from government actions, including court orders, that would make them vulnerable to harassment or reprisals or have a significant restrictive effect on their political or expressive activities. For example, in a famous case, the NAACP was allowed to protect its membership rolls from disclosure to protect against harassment. However, courts have tested claims of certain privileges against strict standards, requiring those who claim them to show they would genuinely be harmed by disclosures. Sometimes judges even review material page by page, identifying which portions can be admitted into court proceedings or otherwise publicly disclosed. They also have the option to order disclosure subject to redactions of sensitive material. In the case of printed material, the result can be pages with blacked-out names, sentences, and entire paragraphs.

At an August hearing conducted to deal with the discovery disagreement, Cooper said he could find no previous case where the proponents of a ballot measure were required to make public the records of their campaign. "We think it's [a] gravely serious issue," he told Judge Walker. "We would urge the court to give us an opportunity to fight this out."

Pressed by the judge, Cooper backtracked and acknowledged that discovery had been allowed in *Romer v. Evans,* which was relevant because both that case and ours dealt with a referendum withdrawing the rights of gays and lesbians. "But there was no discovery taken into—that we've been able to find, in that case or any other—into the subjective motivations of the voters," he quickly added. "Or into the subjective motivation presumably of their proxies, those that organized the referendum effort, and those who organized and provided the strategy for the campaign for the referendum itself." Although he said he would be willing to hand over the public campaign materials that had been approved by state officials, he wanted to deny us anything that had been distributed less publicly. He and his colleagues also raised privacy claims, arguing that even when they had gathered at Memorial Park in Cupertino and on street corners in San Francisco's Chinatown, records of what was said and done were private and could be withheld.

The motivations of political organizers and voters had been material to the issues in *Romer* and were likewise relevant to our claim, since we contended in *Perry* that animus toward gays and lesbians and their relationships was at least one factor in establishing the law that discriminated against our clients. Our ability to explore this issue would be inhibited if we could not review the full record of the appeals to voters. We felt entitled to learn the actual extent to which the proponents had used bigoted and/or deceptive claims about same-sex couples to foster hatred and fear.

In response to Cooper's position on discovery, David stressed, first, that opposing lawyers could find many areas of agreement on public documents and officially sanctioned materials. Other items occupied what he called a "gray area" that would require more effort to illuminate. Then he turned to Judge Walker's proposed schedule and the reason we were all in the room that day: how to achieve the prompt and fair resolution of our claim. "If we are going to get this process going, and really achieve what I know the court's objective is and what all of our objective is," David stated, "which is a prompt resolution of this, I think we need to get started. And I think that we can get started on fact discovery, we can get started in preparing expert reports now."

David thus aligned our interests with those of Judge Walker, who had come to the hearing already armed with a timetable. The judge suggested that by October 2 we identify all the expert witnesses we might call, only six weeks away. Two more months would be allotted to depositions and other discovery. A pretrial conference would be held on December 17, with the trial commencing with opening statements on January 11.

"Your Honor, I think that is easily doable," answered David with casualness that masked our enthusiasm for the judge's tight schedule. With some small adjustments made to accommodate variable schedules, the timetable was set and we retired from the courtroom to commence our work.

In the end, after additional disputes and with the assistance of Judge Walker and his judicial magistrate assistant, most of the issues were resolved in our favor. We were to find quite a trove of documents and other materials revealing rather poisonous pro–Prop 8 campaign rhetoric.

As we sought documents held by the defendants, we prepared our clients to be deposed by the other side and, ultimately, to testify at trial.

We also worked to line up the very best experts in history, politics, psychology, and many other fields. In any trial the pursuit of expert witnesses is a little like diving into graduate study of a compelling new subject: You read deeply to understand the field, find the most respected authorities, and then consult them about your case. For our suit we discovered that most of the experts we contacted were eager to participate, even though it would require them to write substantial reports, submit to questioning in depositions, and probably appear at the trial.

Our expert witness list included Nancy Cott of Harvard and George Chauncey of Yale, who were experts on the history of marriage and discrimination, respectively. Our other expert witnesses were Lee Badgett, Gregory Herek, Michael Lamb, Ilan Meyer, Letitia Peplau, and Gary Segura. They were highly qualified and widely respected authorities who could discuss, among other things, the psychological and economic benefits that accrue to married people, the effects of being stigmatized, the raising of children, and the political power, or rather powerlessness, of gays and lesbians as individuals and in organized groups.

The defendants eventually designated six expert witnesses, including David Blankenhorn, who held a master's degree in history but had spent much of his working life as a public advocate on behalf of the kind of families—two heterosexual parents raising their children— one might associate with a 1950s *Ozzie and Harriet* version of America. The defense also named Paul Nathanson to discuss the definition and purpose of marriage and Katherine Young to discuss religious attitudes toward Proposition 8, two Canadian-based religious studies professors who had collaborated on several books, and who had testified in prior state cases concerning same-sex marriage. Professor Loren Marks of Louisiana State University was named as an expert who would testify that children do best when raised by two heterosexual parents. Kenneth Miller of Claremont McKenna College was chosen by the defendants as an expert in political science, and they listed Oxford philosophy professor Daniel Robinson, whose most recent book, *Consciousness and Mental Life*, examined advances in neuroscience in light of what great thinkers have proposed on the nature of human awareness.

Consciousness and Mental Life is dense and arcane, but the lawyers on our team made their way through it, as well as everything else we could find that had been said or written by the defense's expert witnesses. The court's procedures and practices allowed us to conduct this vetting of the experts and then depose them under oath in order to establish their expertise or discredit them. Expert witnesses must meet standards established in the Supreme Court case *Daubert v. Merrell Dow Pharmaceuticals,* which held that an expert must be qualified and must offer relevant, reliable opinion testimony. In the run-up to trials, attorneys often investigate and depose one another's expert witnesses and then ask the judge to rule on whether they will be allowed to testify.

As the member of our team most experienced in examining, probing, and testing witnesses in the crucible of litigation, David led our effort to examine the defendants' experts. Although David may employ a deposition to probe a witness's qualifications, his approach invariably goes beyond the *Daubert* protocol. For him a deposition also presents an opportunity to find new evidence, or avenues of examination that moderate a witness's testimony or even turn a witness from an enemy into an ally. To do this he absorbs and digests everything about a witness and his or her record and then uses that information to engage the witness in a conversation. As most psychologists agree, most people can't help but reveal themselves in the course of conversation. The trick is in letting them do it, and recognizing and exploiting it when it happens.

———

Both Paul Nathanson and Katherine Young were experienced advocates and each had produced a detailed expert report in support of the defendants' position that marriage always had been, and should be, limited to heterosexual relationships. Because of the importance of the opinions they expressed, and their experience in prior marriage equality litigation, David decided to depose these two experts personally. A team of lawyers, including Rosanne Baxter, Beko Reblitz-Richardson, and Rick Bettan from Boies Schiller and others from Gibson Dunn, laboriously read, analyzed, and indexed everything the two professors had written or said. Armed with this ammunition, in November, with two months remaining before the trial, David flew to Montreal to depose Nathanson and Young. Dr. Nathanson, who was deposed first, arrived at the conference room dressed all in black, with his silvery hair combed back from his high forehead. Depositions are conducted in a formal manner, with the witness seated opposite the questioners and a court reporter recording the proceedings. Lawyers have the option of also having a video recording made, an option (wisely, it turned out) we exercised. Deponents often feel ill at ease in such a setting, and it is usually productive to get right to the heart of the matter before a witness has a chance to get comfortable. David did just that.

He attacked Nathanson's expertise and credibility early on, both to neutralize him as an effective witness for the defendants and to soften him up to possibly extract helpful admissions that would support us. David led the witness to agree that he lacked any real expertise in sociology, anthropology, or several other related fields. He also got him to acknowledge that he had written his report without any serious study of California's history with marriage equality or of the experience of countries where same-sex couples were permitted to marry, including his home country of Canada. The psychological effect of having to concede that he wasn't truly an expert in so many related fields and that his knowledge was so limited showed in Nathanson's body language, as he began to slump in his seat and stiffen defensively.

David asked, "Now, with respect to the fear of gay people, do you believe that everyone who fears gay people does so for malicious or neurotic reasons?"

Peter Patterson, a young attorney sent by the defendants to shepherd the professor through the proceeding, objected on the grounds that the questions called for speculation. Nathanson, picking up the hint, replied, "I have no idea. I can't get into anyone's head."

David could have argued that the question asked not for an analysis of subjective motivation but for whether there was any objective reason to fear gay people other than malice or neurosis. Instead he used Nathanson's statement to undercut the witness's report.

"Well, in fact, you *do* try to get into people's head in your report, do you not, sir?"

"Do I?" said an increasingly nervous Nathanson.

"Do you try to discuss people's motivation in your report?" David asked.

"To the extent that I try to allow for various possible motivations."

In fact, as Nathanson went on to admit, his report for the defense was made up almost in its entirety of assessments of the religious motivations of people who favored or opposed marriage equality.

David forced Nathanson to answer "I don't know" to the question of what proportion of people in the United States or California were prejudiced against gay citizens. David then switched directions, asking, "Do you have an opinion as to whether gay people, gay couples today, in some instances, are raising children?"

"Yes," answered Nathanson.

"And what is that opinion?"

Again, Patterson interrupted with an objection. When the questioning resumed, David asked if Nathanson still remembered the original question. Nathanson responded, "What do I think of gay people who have children . . . gay couples . . ."

"No," replied David, "actually, that wasn't quite the question, but it's interesting that you would interpret it that way."

David's question hadn't yet been about Nathanson's opinions on gay parenthood but rather a simple inquiry into whether the professor was aware that "gay couples . . . are raising children." Without direct prompting Nathanson had revealed clues as to what was going through his mind in the way he recalled the question.

David walked Nathanson through a series of questions about how virtually all major academic, scientific, and medical organizations representing everyone from anthropologists to psychoanalysts had issued statements in favor of marriage equality. Nathanson also agreed that no one had ever published a study that used scientific evidence to show that being raised by same-sex parents posed any special problems for children and conceded that no study had established that the existence of families headed by couples of the same sex had any effect whatsoever on heterosexual families.

Nathanson wanted to be seen as a fair and reasonable person, which is what most of us want to do when we answer questions; it is human nature to want to be seen in the best light, and to get along with others. This can be especially true when we feel uncomfortable, or feel our integrity or competence is under attack. As the day wore on, Nathanson's attempts to recover his credibility led him to become a better witness for us than for our opponents. Before the day was over he would tell us that he thought that for many centuries society and religions have been hostile to gay men and lesbians; that roughly half the people who supported Proposition 8 were motivated by religion, and that their faiths regarded sexual relationships between two men or two women to be sinful; that advocates of racial segregation once claimed that their racist practices protected the "family"; and that there were valid religious reasons for supporting marriage equality. Perhaps most important, Nathanson agreed that gay and lesbian couples were raising children in California and other places and that their families would be strengthened if they were permitted to marry. By the end of the day a visibly wrung-out Nathanson had given us so much testimony favorable to our cause that David suspected—correctly, as it would turn out—that the defendants would withdraw him from their list of witnesses.

When David began his deposition of Nathanson's colleague Katherine Young, she appeared to have been instructed not to fall into the Nathanson trap of being so agreeable. At one point early in the questioning, she tried to take control of the deposition, interrupting David to say, "I would like to make an intervention here."

"I'm sure you would," David said firmly, with just a hint of amusement in his voice, "but as your counsel explained to you, depositions do not involve interventions. Depositions involve me asking the questions, you giving the answers. [Opposing counsel] will get a chance to examine you about anything you want to say or speeches you want to make or what you refer to as interventions that you want to make, but I think he will instruct you that I can ask the questions now and you need to answer them."

As the deposition went on, Young repeatedly had to admit that she was not aware of key research and findings, or the reports of professional organizations, concerning the subject matter of her testimony—and that the research and reports she was aware of contradicted her opinions. She also ultimately agreed with our principal arguments. Yes, she said, gay men and lesbians suffered discrimination based on bigotry. Yes, their families would be strengthened if they were permitted to marry. Young also testified that:

- "Gay men and lesbians possess the same potential and desire for sustained loving and lasting relationships as heterosexuals."
- If there is a single parent, "it doesn't make any difference whether that single parent is gay or straight."
- "Same-sex couples are raising children and have the same potential and desire as heterosexual couples to love and parent children."

Young also contradicted the defendants' assertion that same-sex marriage was a novelty of the last two or three decades. Under David's questioning, she described same-sex marriages that existed in pre-Christian cultures of Europe, Asia, Africa, and North America.

Near the end of Young's examination, David turned to the religious basis underlying discrimination against gays and lesbians, and the parallels that existed between prejudices against homosexuals and prejudices against women and African Americans and other minorities. The point was not that religions should not be able to define their own creeds; the First Amendment guarantees the free exercise of religion. The point was that the First Amendment also prohibits the establishment of religion, and laws should not impose one religion's beliefs even on its own adherents, let alone other citizens.

Her testimony continued:

> Q: We talked earlier about the fact that gay people have histori-
> cally been subject to prejudice and discrimination, you re-
> call that?
>
> A: Yes.
>
> Q: Now, it's the case that women have also historically been sub-
> ject to prejudice and discrimination, correct?
>
> A: Correct.
>
> Q: And the prejudice and discrimination against women, like
> the prejudice and discrimination against gay people, was of-
> ten justified by religio[us] assertions and beliefs, correct?
>
> A: Sometimes it was, yes.
>
> Q: Often it was, correct?
>
> A: Often it was.
>
> Q: And the discrimination and prejudice against women was
> also often justified by the argument that it promoted or pro-
> tected the traditional family, correct?
>
> A: Yes.
>
> Q: And various racial groups, including blacks, have histori-
> cally been subject to prejudice and discrimination, correct?
>
> A: Correct.
>
> Q: And that prejudice and discrimination, again, like the preju-
> dice and discrimination against gay[s] and lesbians, was of-
> ten justified by religion, correct?
>
> A: Yes.

Lawyers will sometimes say that you never want to ask a question
of a hostile witness unless you know the answer. That is particularly
true during a trial when an unexpected or unfavorable answer, once
given, is largely irretrievable. But a deposition allows a lot more latitude. That is the time when it is helpful to find out what a witness will
say on various subjects. David had been convinced, based on his earlier questioning and Young's writings, that he could get her to admit
the role of religion in rationalizing discrimination against gays,

women, and African Americans—and that it was useful to show the parallels. However, we also wanted to prove that legislating based on religious beliefs was inconsistent with American values and the U.S. Constitution. Could he get Young to agree to that? He couldn't be certain, but near the end of his examination he asked:

> Q: And do you have a view as to whether, in the United States today, law continues to be based on religion?
> A: No, because you have the doctrine of the separation of church and state.

In the end, Young's name, like Nathanson's, would be withdrawn from the defendants' witness list. She had ultimately been too reasonable and far too vulnerable to a skilled cross-examination to serve as a reliable advocate for the other side. In fact, at trial we would introduce into evidence in our case, over the defendants' objections, the videos of both her deposition and the deposition of Professor Nathanson. The irony of the defendants trying to keep the court from hearing testimony from their own experts was not lost on Judge Walker or the courtroom audience.

———

One by one defense witnesses were dropped by Cooper and his team after their depositions. The power of the deposition experience is such that witnesses often withdraw (or are withdrawn) from a case after their views are tested by opposing counsel. But rarely does someone who inserted himself into a case as a party attempt to back out of a case entirely. In the *Perry* case, however, one did just that.

Hak-Shing William Tam was a Chinese American evangelical Christian leader who had served as an official citizen sponsor of Proposition 8. He held a doctorate in chemical engineering, and in many Prop 8 campaign documents he was called "Dr. Bill Tam." He had been invited to take on this role by the organizers of ProtectMarriage.com, who assembled a host of conservative religious activists to back the amendment. In the months leading up to the election, Tam had abandoned his cosmetics business to crisscross the state to deliver speeches and rally volunteers. He had spent considerable time in churches that serve various Asian American communities, and he had written letters, granted interviews, and appeared in televised debates on behalf of the cause. When our case was filed, Tam joined the other proposition proponents as an intervenor/defendant.

With Tam's lawyers opposing most of our requests for campaign documents that would reveal the motivations of the Prop 8 sponsors, we had to start with materials already in the public domain. Gathering them was more difficult than one might imagine because a great deal of the effort in support of the amendment took place in the subculture of California's conservative Christian community, which, while sizable, exists largely outside the media mainstream. Activities hosted by the churches that serve this community might draw hundreds or even thousands of people and never be noticed by political reporters. But traces of this activity could be found on publicly available Web sites, and with effort it was possible to reconstruct at least some of the Prop 8 campaign's messages.

As we dug for evidence we unearthed materials that supported our contention that antipathy toward or fear of gays and lesbians had been at least part of the Prop 8 advocacy. One stark example was a letter that began with the greeting "A Message from Bill Tam (Sharon Chinese Baptist Church of San Francisco)." Apparently posted by a member of the church, another letter, also attributed to Tam, urged readers to support Proposition 8 to prevent the eventual legalization of both prostitution and pedophilia. "After legalizing same-sex marriage, they want to legalize prostitution," the letter warned. "What will be next? On their agenda list is: legalizing having sex with children." The "Message from Bill Tam" letter, which spoke ominously of a "gay agenda," continued:

> I'd like to ask you to talk to your church pastor about educating your church youths on the issue of SSM [same-sex marriage]. I suggest the church to teach youths about the issues of

sex, marriage and family, as a package. SSM can be part of the curriculum. We must give them the proper Biblical values so that they are immune to the teachings from the public schools. This is our biggest battlefield—our next generation. It is a battle of the mind. Satan is working on our youths. If we and our churches don't do our part, we'll certainly lose our kids. They'll one day surrender to Satan. Everything we do in building Prop 8 would be given up by the next generation. If you would like me to speak to your pastor about this, let me know.

Although in some evangelical Christian circles, discussions about Satan and a "battle of the mind" over future generations may be commonplace, this particular letter was full of derogatory slurs and would be seen as steeped in prejudice in virtually any context. Some people have long tried to associate gays and lesbians with pedophilia, though every serious study of this crime has shown no such correlation. The same is true for prostitution. And as far as we could tell, the term "gay agenda" was coined by conservative Christian activists who have long sought to suggest that gay men in America were united in a monolithic pursuit not only of equality but of a radical sexual program that would destroy the country's moral fiber. It seemed to be effective in some quarters at least in creating an enemy for some people to fear, but the notion of a gay agenda that embraced priorities like the sexual abuse of children would have been ridiculous if it weren't so pernicious.

In our judgment Tam's letter was proof of antigay animus in portions of the Yes on 8 campaign, and attorneys Ethan Dettmer of Gibson Dunn and Terry Stewart of the City and County of San Francisco, who deposed him for our side, asked him to discuss it under oath. When they read aloud the statements in one of his hateful letters, Tam's attorneys, Nicole Moss and Andrew Pugno, seemed implicitly to agree with our assessment. They began to advise Tam against answering our questions and insisted that the letter was not a public document and was instead his private property.

"There is no establishment that this is a public document," said Pugno.

"If you can get it off the Internet, it is pretty damn public," protested Terry Stewart.

"Absolutely not," replied Pugno. "You haven't asked any questions that establish his intent or consent to have this published. You know, if I steal your personal information and post it on the Internet, it is not public."

Tam persisted in refusing to answer questions about the letter, but our team was able to get him to confirm his long record of speaking on issues pertaining to homosexuality and society, including his contention that the movie *Brokeback Mountain* "breaks families" and his belief that "70 percent of male homosexuals have been sexually abused." He also confirmed the translations of Chinese-language documents obtained from a Web site of a group he served as executive director that argued, "If homosexuality was a normal act, then diseases such as AIDS, hepatitis, pneumonia and other deadly diseases would not appear. Homosexuality also existed in ancient times. And if it was the natural behavior of humans, modern male homosexuals would have uteruses/ovaries so as to be able to produce the next generation. Female homosexuals would have male reproductive organs. Therefore, homosexuality is against common sense and is not normal behavior."

Sometime after his deposition Tam apparently realized that what he had said to members of evangelical churches might not reflect well on him with the general populace. He decided that he didn't want his statements about gays and lesbians made public and sought to avoid the possibility that he might be called by plaintiffs as a witness at trial. He asked to remove himself from the Prop 8 defense team and had his lawyer send a motion to that effect to the judge. He asserted that he had endured online threats and neighborhood confrontations and feared for his safety and the safety of his family.

The tone of the lawyer's motion was that of someone who had eagerly entered a fight only to discover that his adversary was every bit as determined and equally eager for the confrontation. Faced with the extreme public statements he had made, Tam now wanted to avoid any chance that he might be held accountable. His lawyer begged for Judge Walker's indulgence, explaining that his client was "tired and wants peace."

Judge Walker received Tam's request and set it aside. Tam would ultimately testify at trial, and his animosity toward gays would become part of the trial record.

As the prospect of cross-examination sent William Tam scurrying for cover, and academics like Professors Young and Nathanson retreated under a barrage of deposition questions, the defendants found themselves approaching the trial date with few real assets. One who remained was David Blankenhorn, a self-described expert, and frequent lecturer, on the institution of marriage. At his deposition, conducted by Chris Dusseault of Gibson Dunn, he discussed leaving his work as a young, street-level community organizer to found an organization he called the Institute for American Values, which was described as fostering scholarly collaboration on subjects related to marriage and family life. He has served as its president since its founding in 1988.

Blankenhorn decried the rise of divorce, out-of-wedlock births, and the declining number of two-parent families, and advocated the return of conventional family units led by a mother and father and against the trend toward motherhood for single women. These positions resonated with Christian conservatives and other advocates of "traditional family values," and much of the funding for his institute had come from conservative-leaning foundations. However, Blankenhorn was not reflexively conservative on all social issues, and his style was thoughtful and reflective, not aggressive and dogmatic.

Educated at Harvard and the University of Warwick in Coventry, England, Blankenhorn identified himself as a liberal Democrat and positioned himself as someone who had developed his brief on behalf of traditional marriage during community service work that brought him face-to-face with the ways that children are affected by being raised in single-parent households. He testified that he became alarmed by the absence of fathers in the lives of many such children. Turning that alarm into action, he wrote *Fatherless America* (1995), which fueled a policy conversation about the role of men in family life.

In response to Chris Dusseault's questions, Blankenhorn managed to speak extemporaneously in entire paragraphs that filled 342 pages of transcript. Read carefully, the record showed a thoughtful man anxious to be considered fair and reasonable. He was a potentially important witness for the defendants, both because he was an experienced and articulate advocate for his (and their) views and because his thoughtful, reflective manner could make the case for Prop 8 seem less about bigotry and more about preserving something valuable in heterosexual marriage. However, his very thoughtfulness combined with a fervent desire to be seen as fair and reasonable could make him a dangerous witness for the defendants. It was with mixed emotions that we saw that Blankenhorn remained on the defendants' witness list after his deposition.

———

Defendants were, of course, permitted to depose the plaintiffs' witnesses as well. All of our experts were dutifully interrogated, but our adversaries' attorneys didn't manage to move any of them off their respective positions. Having endured peer reviews and the rigors of teaching and academic conferences, they knew what they believed and how to defend their work. In the end each one remained on our list, ready to testify if called. Our clients were equally unshakable in their depositions, even though they were unaccustomed to the kind of scrutiny and the degree of interrogation that occurs in a deposition.

We had helped them with mock depositions beforehand in which we stressed the importance of direct, careful answers that addressed the questions asked, and no more. David prepared Jeff and Paul in Los Angeles, while Ted Boutrous traveled to San Francisco to work with Kris and Sandy. Sandy, who would undergo the toughest questioning in her real deposition, would later recall that during her eight-hour prep sessions with Ted she came to feel as if Ted was out to get her, pressing her as he did with questions about her marriage earlier in her life to Matthew Stier.

"How could you have been married to a man and now want to be married to a woman?" he asked.

"Did you do your best to keep your commitment to your husband?"

"When did you know you were attracted to women?"

"Are you a lesbian, a heterosexual, or a bisexual?"

"When did you know you were a lesbian?"

"How did your parents react?"

"You had children when you were married. Do you think divorce is good for children?

"Do you love your children?

As Sandy answered these and a hundred other questions, she initially felt shocked and hurt by Ted's assertive, even aggressive behavior. *What happened to that nice, smart man who was supposed to be on my side?* she wondered. She knew, and appreciated as the process unfolded, however, to quell her feelings of betrayal—*This is an exercise,* she reminded herself—and formulated answers that were both truthful and true to her ideals.

In their real depositions, Kris, Sandy, Paul, and Jeff responded with calm self-assurance to a barrage of probing questions about sexual orientation, relationships, and marriage. With every answer, especially those that related to understanding their sexuality and the challenge of living in a world that discriminated against them, our clients demonstrated an unmistakable strength of character and conviction. They had been required by a sometimes hostile society to reflect deeply on their identities, values, and actions. They knew who they were.

As we anticipated, Brian Raum pressed Sandy on the subject of her eleven-year marriage to Matthew Stier, which ended in 1999 as she fell in love with Kris. He focused a great deal on the fact that she had committed herself to a heterosexual relationship, which produced two children, but had then fallen in love with a woman. As Raum explained, "To the extent that Ms. Stier's sexual orientation is at issue in the case, I'd like to establish when she identified that sexual orientation."

Unstated, but certainly understood by all, was that Raum was trying to address the issue of the "immutability" of sexual identity. In court, our side would demonstrate that being gay or lesbian is not a choice but an immutable trait. Our opponents planned to argue that people choose their sexual orientation and could therefore choose to be heterosexual in order to qualify for and enjoy marriage to an opposite-sex person—a silly proposition at best, but a theory some people profess.

Very few people would feel comfortable answering the kinds of questions Raum put to Sandy, but our mock depositions, not to mention her own life, had prepared her well. Gay and lesbian individuals often find themselves in discussions that heterosexual people rarely, if ever, have to confront. Even the most supportive family, friends, and acquaintances want to know about the nature of their personal experience with their sexual orientation, and this is doubly true whenever a controversy like Prop 8 arises. Just as an African American may be asked by whites to explain "the African American point of view" or "the African American experience," a lesbian will often find herself in the uncomfortable position of being asked to speak for lesbians in general. For some individuals such discussions can become awkward when they veer into subjects like "When did you know you were attracted to someone of the same sex?" or "Does your family accept you?" Particularly when posed by someone who seeks to deny you equal rights, such questions are infuriating. Nevertheless, Sandy answered every one in a calm and direct way.

Sandy explained that she had felt attracted to women when she was quite young—at college age—but that she had fallen in love with Matthew and was attracted to him when they were married. "It was my goal," she said, "to have a meaningful marriage."

After years of turmoil, Sandy met Kris and felt a profound connection. Sandy and Matthew divorced, and she then began an exclusive long-term relationship with Kris. They moved in together and created a family that included Kris's two sons and Sandy's two sons. In 2004 Sandy and Kris were married during the period when Mayor Gavin Newsom had ordered the county clerk to grant licenses to same-sex couples. Though the courts eventually voided their union, their desire to be married remained strong.

Through a series of questions Raum drew out the information that Sandy's mother had not attended the wedding ceremony when she married Kris, although her brother and sister had traveled from Iowa to be there. Raum asked her, in several ways, to explain her mother's absence. Sandy replied that her mother was a loving parent who was also a devout Catholic who valued the sacramental aspect of marriage. To her, Sandy explained, "My marriage doesn't fit within maybe the parameters of what one would call a sacrament."

"And do you respect her position in that regard?" Raum continued.

"I respect my mother's dedication to the religion that she is dedicated to, very much so."

"But do you disagree with her view in regard to marriage?"

"I don't disagree with her viewing marriage as a sacrament for the religion that she is dedicated to," Sandy said. "That is very much her choice, and I respect it. But I don't personally have the same belief system or conviction. So, in that sense, I do disagree."

With her answer, Sandy refused to permit Raum to box her into a limited view of marriage. She did so again when he tried to get her to say that she and Kris wanted to be married so they could receive benefits under state law. She countered that the reason she sought to be married was that "it's important to me to be a contributing member of society. It's important to me to be a good parent. It's important to me to be a good community member." Marriage, which represents a declaration of commitment and reinforces both a relationship and family life, would help her accomplish all of these goals.

Realizing that the track he was on was unproductive, Raum turned to testing Sandy's claim that she had been harmed by antilesbian bigotry in society. When she recounted specific instances of harassment—taunts shouted from cars, snide remarks at clubs—Raum asked, "Have you received any counseling or medical treatment as a result of your emotional distress, pain, suffering, or psychological harm?" Sandy candidly confessed that she had indeed sought therapy for this reason. "I have gone to therapy over the years very specifically to talk about the issues of being an out lesbian in our society and the impact in family and friend relationships, yes."

Raum returned to the subject of Sandy's parents, asking if her father had brought anything unique to her upbringing and family—the inference, of course, being that men as fathers are irreplaceable in children's lives. "My parents were both good parents," Sandy replied. "They both brought something important, but that something important that they brought was love and dedication and total acceptance and support of their children."

Disarmingly honest, Sandy seemed to confound Raum with her answers. Pressed on whether she would ever be attracted to a man, she answered in a way that left it in the realm of possibility. She refused, however, to be categorized as bisexual, insisting, "I consider myself to be gay."

No question Raum posed, however personal, unbalanced Sandy, even when he asked if her children had trouble "grappling with the concept of their mom identifying as a lesbian." They didn't, she assured him, and with every reply she displayed a generous view of humanity, one that included herself. Raised to respect honesty, kindness, and compassion, Sandy projected those qualities effortlessly.

———

Thirty-four depositions were conducted in the ninety days before the trial. During this same period we continued to skirmish over the production of documents, with the defendants appealing rulings that we won in our pursuit of materials that were distributed to donors and potential donors to the Prop 8 campaign. Judge Walker had reviewed dozens of documents and approved about a third of them for release to us, but this still left thousands in dispute.

In the six months between our first pretrial hearing and opening statements on January 11, 2010, Judge Walker ultimately rendered more than thirty rulings to resolve pretrial disputes. Taking into account the magistrate judge's decisions and rulings from the appellate court, the number of pretrial orders exceeded fifty. None, however, provoked more discussion and debate than Judge Walker's decision to telecast the trial live to a few selected federal courthouses around the country and on a delayed basis on the Internet site YouTube.

We enthusiastically supported the broadcast because public interest in the trial was so great, not only in the United States but around the world. Anything that helps people understand how the justice system works is good in and of itself. What happens in a public courthouse, with limited exceptions, we believed, should be open and accessible to the public—in real time—and not restricted to the small number of people who could get into the courtroom. The proponents of Proposition 8 vigorously opposed the decision. "Given the highly contentious and politicized nature of Proposition 8 and the issue of same-sex marriage in general," Cooper told Judge Walker, "the possibility of compromised safety, witness intimidation, and/or harassment of trial participants is very real." As evidence he cited the criticisms and calls for boycotts that arose when the major donors to the Prop 8 campaign were revealed. Internet-based activists had organized boycotts of three California hotels and a storage facility—hardly an adequate basis for depriving the public of an opportunity to see the trial, we argued.

Additional impetus for broadcasting the trial came from a dozen or so media companies that banded together, calling themselves the Media Coalition, and hired attorneys to make the case for what they called "gavel-to-gavel" video coverage. Public video access to courtroom proceedings can be traced back to the 1961 war crimes trial in Israel of the infamous Nazi Adolf Eichmann, which was among the first in history to be televised in its entirety. More recently the 1995 trial of O. J. Simpson on murder charges marked the modern fascination with high-profile cases. From that point onward, trials became a TV staple, providing inexpensive, high-drama programming. However, such proceedings generally took place in state courts. On the federal level the Second and Ninth Circuit Courts of Appeals had allowed a number of broadcasts on appellate proceedings, and some district courts had experimented with a few broadcasts in the early 1990s.

Three days before Christmas 2009, we joined Chuck Cooper and Brian Raum in Judge Walker's courtroom to debate the question of a live or delayed broadcast of the trial. Higher-court officials had approved a pilot program for the broadcasting of civil trials not involving juries. While our case qualified as such, district court judges were still awaiting approval to start the experiment. Judge Walker said that a broadcast could not go forward until he had gotten a "green light" from the chief judge of the Ninth Circuit Court of Appeals, Alex Kozinski.

Less than a week before opening statements, Judge Kozinski approved broadcasting the trial, saying, "We hope that being able to see and hear what transpires in the courtroom will lead to a better public understanding of our judicial processes and enhanced confidence in the rule of law. The experiment is designed to help us find the right balance between the public's right to access to the courts and the parties' right to a fair and dignified proceeding." The judge noted that "the public has demanded greater access to our courtrooms, we have provided it and it has not caused problems."

It was the right decision. This was a nonjury trial of a major constitutional question affecting all the citizens of California. There was no danger of publicity that might affect the right of a criminal defendant to a fair trial. If there ever was a case in which the public had a powerful interest, this was it.

The defendants immediately appealed to the Ninth Circuit, where they lost again, and then rushed to file with the Supreme Court of the United States. Chief Justice John Roberts had previously made it clear that he didn't want cameras in the Supreme Court, and similar sentiments had been expressed by several other justices. In general, they believed that cameras would negatively affect the way the justices worked, and that any benefit that might accrue to the public didn't outweigh this potential harm. On the Monday our trial began, Chief Justice Roberts and Justices Scalia, Kennedy, Thomas, and Alito joined in issuing a decision to stop the broadcast. They accepted the applicants' argument that "irreparable harm would likely result from the District Court's actions" and found that Judge Walker had not followed proper procedures when he approved the broadcast. In their view the judge had not provided ample time for the parties to contest the issue and had acted in haste.

In a dissent written by Justice Steven Breyer, the four other members of the Court noted that the parties in our case had been dealing with the specific question of a broadcast for months, and that the issue of television cameras in court in general had been discussed in legal circles since the 1990s. "The parties, the intervenors, other judges, the public—all had an opportunity to comment," he wrote. As for the harm a broadcast might cause, Justice Breyer noted that forty-two states and two federal district courts allowed courtroom broadcasts of trials, and that all of the witnesses who might testify in ours were publicly known. They had each published or spoken publicly about their opposition to marriage equality. Given these factors, Justice Breyer concluded, "the scales tip heavily against, not in favor" of interfering with the broadcast.

We believed the real reason our opponents wanted to bar cameras was because they didn't want the public to have an opportunity to see our evidence and compare it to theirs (or their lack of it). One thing that we and our opponents seemed to agree on was that the more people heard and knew about this issue, the better it was for us and the worse it was for them. Except for the relatively small group admitted to the courtroom every day, the public would be denied the opportunity to see and hear the proceedings. The trial would still be permitted to be videotaped, but the video would be available only to counsel and the court.

Although the issue of broadcasting the trial was now behind us, we continued to struggle over documents being withheld by the defense. Our discovery battles would continue right up to and beyond the start of the trial on January 11, 2010.

A trial, even a nonjury trial, is a complex theatrical production. The players (witnesses, lawyers) have to be prepared for their roles. Props (exhibits, documents, videotaped depositions) have to be in place; timing and sequences have to be anticipated and planned. In a case as highly publicized as this, it is also necessary to prepare for press briefings during lunch breaks and at the end of the day. Any failure to attend to details or lapses in timing, any failure properly to produce or challenge evidence could prove to be fatal later in the case, perhaps on appeal. A trial is preparation, preparation, preparation, and meticulous execution. It also involves skill and artistry—but skill and artistry are rarely effective without planning and disciplined execution.

Ted spent the days preceding the trial preparing his opening statement. He knew that his words, the first words the world would hear once the trial began, not only would set the stage for the ensuing trial and focus the courtroom on the prism through which we hoped the case would be viewed, but would be widely reported and analyzed, sending the message to the world of what this case was all about.

Judge Walker was likely to interrupt Ted's opening statement, as he had done during lawyers' presentations earlier in the case. This is generally what happens during legal arguments—lawyers are frequently interrupted with observations, questions, even arguments from judges. Ted prepared for that contingency while carefully rehearsing his general outline and thematic remarks with his colleagues, who listened and offered suggestions over the weekend preceding the trial.

David, meanwhile, worked to prepare his examinations of our witnesses and his cross-examination of the defendants' witnesses. Ted Boutrous, Chris Dusseault, Matt McGill, and others prepared their respective expert witnesses for their direct testimony regarding the history of marriage, discrimination in America against gays and lesbians, the upbringing of children in gay households, marriage and divorce in states and nations that allowed gay marriage, the political vulnerability of gays and lesbians, the damage done by discrimination and stigma, the immutability of sexual orientation, and other important issues pertinent to Proposition 8, many of which had been raised by Judge Walker as potential subjects for fact finding at the trial.

Jeremy Goldman, Steve Holtzman, and Josh Schiller worked preparing outlines of potential cross-examination points based on the analysis they and many, many other lawyers and paralegals were doing of all the publications and statements of the defendants' witnesses.

Other members of the legal team were assembling documents and exhibits to be used during the trial and preparing summaries of the anticipated testimony of opposing witnesses, including testimony and materials from the proponents of Proposition 8. The key issues involved included the arguments made to convince the voters to vote for the measure, the tactics employed to enact it, and the source of its funding. Still other team members were preparing legal briefs with respect to issues expected to arise during the course of the trial, the admissibility of certain evidence, and other legal questions.

On the Sunday before opening arguments, we met with Ted Boutrous over lunch at Tadich Grill, billed as San Francisco's oldest restaurant, established in 1849. We shared our satisfaction over the state of our preparation and our pride in the legal team from our two law firms over California chardonnay (a screwdriver for David), sand dabs, and San Francisco sourdough French bread. The three of us raised a toast to our clients and our soon-to-begin case. The plaintiffs, lawyers, witnesses, and supporting actors in the challenge to Proposition 8 were as ready as they possibly could be. Everyone knew his or her role. We were infused with energy, enthusiasm, and anticipation. The curtain was about to rise.

SEVEN

The Trial I

O n Monday, January 11, 2010, America awakened to coast-to-coast media coverage about the case that would be making history that would begin that morning in San Francisco in Judge Vaughn R. Walker's court. The federal constitutional challenge to California's Proposition 8, which had dashed the dreams of so many citizens, and which had consumed our time, energy, and passion for over a year, was finally reaching a crescendo.

For Reagan-era attorney general Edwin Meese, Ted's longtime friend, the prospect of our trial was, as he described it in an op-ed in the *New York Times,* "disquieting." As he explained, he believed that Judge Walker would be deviating from the practice of other judges who had considered marriage equality, who had taken into account the opinions of experts, reviewed records, and heard arguments without requiring a trial where experts, and other witnesses, would have to testify under oath subject to cross examination. Walker, Meese worried, was attempting to discover the intent of the proponents while effectively "putting the sponsors of Proposition 8, and the people who voted for it, on trial." As a result, wrote Meese, "the plaintiffs will aggressively exploit this opportunity to assert that the sponsors exhibited bigotry toward homosexuals, or that religious views motivated the adoption of Proposition 8. They'll argue that prohibiting gay marriage is akin to racial discrimination."

Although we respected Attorney General Meese's defense of what he called "traditional marriage, and the rights of the voters," we believed our case was about basic human and constitutional rights, which could not be trumped by a majority vote or the way things had always been. No American minority group subject to official discrimination had ever won equal rights without making appeals to the justice system somewhere along the way. The judiciary is the place where discriminatory policies, no matter how thickly encrusted with tradition, or accepted as unchangeable by a majority, may be overcome by reason, fairness, and the rule of law.

We disagreed with Meese about the way Judge Walker was managing the case and on the constitutionality of Proposition 8. And with the offense he seemed to take at the actual idea of a trial. Our forefathers had fought for that right—the opportunity to be heard, to testify, to confront witnesses. The concept of a trial was at the core of American justice. But Meese seemed right about one thing: "No matter how the judge rules," he wrote, "the *Perry* case is destined for appeals and a final decision in the United States Supreme Court." The stakes in what we were about to begin were very much in the thoughts of our large group—four clients, a dozen lawyers, and even more supporters—as we arrived at the federal courthouse in a small caravan of vans and automobiles. Sandy, Kris, Paul, and Jeff looked as if they had barely slept, as indeed they hadn't, but the scene on the street seemed to revive them.

Having gathered hours before the 9:06 A.M. start of the trial, hundreds of marriage equality supporters had jammed the sidewalk in front of the courthouse carrying signs with statements like WE ALL DESERVE THE FREEDOM TO MARRY and waving cardboard hearts colored fluorescent pink. One demonstrator held a sign that said, TYPICAL STRAIGHT WOMAN IN FAVOR OF EQUAL RIGHTS. At dawn singer-songwriter Melanie DeMore had performed "Over the Rainbow." After she sang, Lance Black reminded the crowd that despite progress in places like San Francisco, bigotry still contributed to suicides and murders of gay and lesbian Americans. "Now is the time," he said, for those who had experienced discrimination to hear they have "brothers and sisters, gay and straight."

Gay rights activists Del Martin (LEFT) and Phyllis Lyon (RIGHT) are married by San Francisco mayor Gavin Newsom in 2008. Martin and Lyon were the first couple to be married in San Francisco when same-sex marriage was briefly allowed in California before voters passed Proposition 8.

The "Yes on 8" and "No on 8" campaigns polarized Californians during the run-up to election day.

AFP/Getty Images

David, who was the lead attorney for the Gore campaign, talks with the media in Tallahassee, Florida, during the recount proceedings in November 2000.

Courtesy of the authors

Ted, lead lawyer for the Bush campaign, addresses reporters outside the U.S. Supreme Court.

A friendship develops between former adversaries: together with our wives, Lady Booth Olson and Mary Boies, on a bike trip in Umbria in 2008.

Sandy Stier and Kris Perry, along with Paul Katami and Jeff Zarrillo, were ideal couples to lead the charge for marriage equality.

The American Foundation for Equal Rights (AFER) team in May 2009 at the Biltmore Hotel in Los Angeles, just before the press conference announcing our challenge to Proposition 8. From left to right: Jeff Zarrillo, Paul Katami, Chad Griffin, Kris Perry, Ted Olson, David Boies, Sandy Stier, Bruce Cohen, Yusef Robb, Kristina Schake.

We held a press conference on May 27, 2009, announcing our challenge to Proposition 8. Jeff and Paul stand next to us.

Vaughn Walker, chief judge for the U.S. District Court for the Northern District of California, who would preside over *Perry v. Schwarzenegger*, the federal constitutional challenge to Proposition 8.

The AFER team in the Gibson Dunn offices following our opening statements in federal district court in January 2010. From left to right: Adam Umhoefer, Kristina Schake, Kris Perry, Sandy Stier, Ted Olson, David Boies, Paul Katami, Jeff Zarrillo, Chad Griffin.

Anthony Pugno, general counsel for Protect Marriage, a group of conservative and religious activist groups united in opposition to same-sex marriage.

Charles Cooper, the lead attorney for supporters of Proposition 8.

Chad Griffin, founder of AFER, in the Gibson Dunn offices in June 2010 preparing for closing arguments before federal district court judge Vaughn Walker.

We share a moment in San Francisco just before our press conference following Judge Walker's decision to invalidate Proposition 8.

Gibson Dunn partner and renowned constitutional law expert Ted Boutrous, left, breaking down Judge Walker's decision in the Gibson Dunn offices in San Francisco.

David in December 2010, just before entering the Ninth Circuit Court of Appeals, where a three-judge panel would decide on the appeal of Judge Walker's decision.

The AFER team outside the Ninth Circuit Court of Appeals. From left to right: Jason Lipton, a paralegal from David's firm; Gibson Dunn attorney Russell Gold; Gibson Dunn attorney Enrique Monagas; and documentarians Ryan White and Rebekah Fergusson.

David, Mary, and the AFER team in the Gibson Dunn offices preparing for arguments before the appeals court.

U.S. Ninth Circuit Court of Appeals judges Stephen Reinhardt and Randy N. Smith listen to arguments during the appeal.

Same-sex couples embrace during a rally outside the Phillip Burton Federal Building in San Francisco during the appeal hearing.

Ted speaks to reporters outside the California Supreme Court following arguments as to whether Proposition 8 supporters have standing to defend the ballot measure in court.

In 2011 Dustin Lance Black created the play *8*, which portrays the closing arguments of *Perry v. Schwarzenegger*, featuring an all-star cast in the leading roles at its premieres in New York City and Los Angeles. George Clooney played David in the Los Angeles premiere, with Martin Sheen taking the role of Ted.

David appears with moderator David Gregory on *Meet the Press* two days before opening arguments begin.

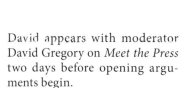

Ted taking part in a moot session in preparation for his opening argument before the Supreme Court in March 2013.

Rob and Michele Reiner, Adam Umhoefer of AFER, Dustin Lance Black, and Ken Mehlman watching the Proposition 8 oral arguments before the Supreme Court on March 26, 2013.

An artist's rendering of Solicitor General Donald Verrilli addressing the Supreme Court. We are seated behind him.

Opponents and supporters of same-sex marriage outside the Supreme Court during opening arguments.

Our press conference in front of the Supreme Court after oral arguments.

On the Supreme Court steps minutes after the Court's ruling to invalidate Proposition 8: Adam Umhoefer, Jeff Zarrillo and Paul Katami, David, Sandy Stier and Kris Perry, Chad Griffin.

David at a press conference after the Supreme Court's ruling. Ted was arguing a case in Virginia that day and unfortunately had to miss the decision.

Immediately after the decision we all flew to Los Angeles to celebrate.

Paul and Jeff are married by Los Angeles mayor Antonio Villaraigosa at City Hall on June 28, 2013, two days after the Supreme Court's verdict.

California attorney general Kamala Harris officiates at Kris and Sandy's wedding the same day.

While we waited for the trial to start, we were acutely aware that our clients, who would testify this day to open the trial, were feeling the pressure born of decades of experience in a society that often greeted them with hostility. They knew how much was riding on their shoulders. For our part, decades of courtroom experience had helped us to remain (at least outwardly) calm as we prepared for Ted's opening statement.

In the courtroom, seats were reserved for supporters and guests of the plaintiffs and defendants on opposite sides of the courtroom. We were on the right, as you faced the front of the court, and among the audience were Chad Griffin, other members of the AFER family, Lady Booth Olson, Mary Boies, our colleagues on the legal team, Rob and Michele Reiner, Bruce Cohen, and Lance Black. Across the aisle were members of the National Organization for Marriage leadership and proponents and supporters of Proposition 8. Members of the public had lined up early to get the few remaining seats. Judge Walker had also arranged for an overflow courtroom one flight above us where additional members of the public could watch the proceedings via a closed-circuit television feed.

Members of the audience supporting marriage equality shared an almost joyful anticipation that this was an historic civil rights case with the potential of changing the way gays and lesbians were viewed and treated. The people seated on the defendants' side of the courtroom, in contrast, seemed solemn and apprehensive.

As the legal team entered the courtroom each day, and throughout the trial, the citizens patiently standing in line would reach out to us, shaking hands, offering gestures of encouragement and gratitude. The emotion was warm and very close to the surface. Over the course of the trial we would come to realize that the group who did manage to get a seat in Judge Walker's courtroom included many of the same individuals every day. Longtime gay residents of San Francisco, many of whom had been in long-term committed relationships, were present in force. One male couple told Ted partway through the trial that they had been together for over forty years. Although they had never expected to be able to marry, they said, with tears in their eyes, that if we were successful in our case they had decided they would do so.

The Opening Statements

Ted began his opening statement with a simple declaration: "This case is about marriage and equality. Plaintiffs are being denied the right to marry and to equality under the law." He stated that the U.S. Supreme Court had repeatedly described the right to marry as one of the "most vital personal rights essential to the orderly pursuit of happiness, a basic civil right, a component of the constitutional rights to liberty, privacy, association, an intimate choice, an expression of emotional support and public commitment, the exercise of spiritual unity and a fulfillment of one's self."

These words had been chosen carefully and had been the product of considerable deliberation. They were a distillation of language from Supreme Court opinions, including concepts articulated in Justice Kennedy's opinions in cases involving the rights of homosexuals, and were intended to set the theme for the case and the tone of the trial. Happiness, spirituality, equality, dignity, privacy, association, support, and identity—all these were bound up in marriage and all were being denied to gay and lesbian Californians.

Just thirty seconds after Ted began, Judge Walker asked, "Does the right to marry, as secured by the Constitution, mean the right to have a marriage license issued by the state?"

Ted answered, "Well, to the extent that the state asserts the right to regulate marriage, and it utilizes the form of a license to do so, I would think that would follow."

"Why?" Judge Walker persisted.

"I'm not sure I understand the import of the question," replied Ted, "because, as I said, it seems to me that if there is a right to marry in the Constitution, and the court upholds the right to the individuals that we are representing to marry—"

"Well, what you're saying is that that right presumes that the state has a duty to issue marriage licenses."

"Well, it would have a duty to issue a marriage license where it would constitutionally require it under the Constitution, and that would be coextensive with the constitutional right itself. It is certainly appropriate—"

"Could the state get out of the marriage license business?" asked Judge Walker.

"Yes, I believe it could," said Ted.

With this line of questioning Judge Walker revealed his somewhat libertarian cast of mind and demonstrated that he would guide the proceedings in order to examine fully the issues that he believed were relevant.

Ted continued. He began with the fact that marriage is a fundamental right that has been repeatedly affirmed by no lesser authority than the U.S. Supreme Court as many as fourteen times. The signal case in this regard was, of course, *Loving v. Virginia,* which ended bans on interracial marriage in 1967. Had President Obama's black father and white mother tried to marry in Virginia before their son was born, "it would have been against the law," Ted reminded the court.

He went on to argue that:

- Proposition 8 discriminated against our clients and other gay men and lesbians by consigning them to a status that is "separate, unequal, and less advantageous."
- The amendment violated the Constitution by creating a second-class status for citizens based on an aspect of their identity—sexuality—that, like race, is immutable.
- No overarching social good was achieved by this discrimination, which in fact harmed many individuals and families.
- Proponents of Prop 8 acted irrationally and were motivated by animus. Both factors disqualified state efforts to limit the rights of any group of citizens.

Our clients would supply the emotional power behind our legal arguments with their own testimony, although Ted did focus the court on the reality that "this government-sponsored societal stigmatization causes grave—the experts will tell us—grave psychological and physical harms to gay men and lesbians and their families. And it increases [that] likelihood, because we are branding them as different, as inferior and as less worthy, and their relationships as less worthy of recognition; it increases the likelihood they will experience discrimination and harassment. It causes immeasurable harm.

"Proposition 8 ended the dream of marriage, the most important relation in life [in the words of the Supreme Court] for the plaintiffs and hundreds of thousands of Californians," he continued. "[It] slammed the door to marriage to gay and lesbian citizens." He reminded Judge Walker that months before Proposition 8 was enacted in response to the California Supreme Court decision, that court had found that denial of the right to marry to gays and lesbians relegated them to "second-class citizenship." Proposition 8 returned them to that status and officially notified them and their families that their relationships were inferior and not worthy of recognition. Proposition 8 thus restored discrimination against a class of individuals that the California Supreme Court had expressly rejected, adding to a long history of discrimination against gays and lesbians in California.

Speaking from the bench, the judge noted that Americans are often surprised by the rights that judges manage to find in the Constitution, giving Ted an opening that he quickly took. This trial, he asserted, "will be an education. Attitudes change when people are educated. . . . If the American people could see what you're going to see, from the plaintiffs themselves, what that discrimination does to them every day, and what it does to their families and to their relationships when they go somewhere and they can't introduce the person that they love as their spouse, they have to explain what in the world a domestic partnership is, what that does. What that does may surprise some people. Surprise in the sense that it opens people's minds to the damage that we are doing when we discriminate on this basis."

Ted went on to explain that the evidence from experts would show that this discriminatory classification served no legitimate purpose. In California convicted murderers and child molesters enjoyed the freedom to marry. The ability to procreate could not be a legitimate justification for denying marriage, because the ability or intention to procreate had never been a condition to marriage, and Proposition 8 allowed gays and lesbians to have and to raise children.

Judge Walker asked why the courts should intervene in a political process that had seen the voters of California enact Proposition 8. "Because that is why we have courts," Ted answered. "And that is why we have a Constitution. That is why we have the Fourteenth Amendment." When individuals were excluded from schools and not allowed to marry the person of their choice because of the color of their skin, they sought relief in the courts. "We wouldn't need a Constitution if we left everything to the political process," Ted pointed out, because if we did, "the majority would always prevail, which is a great thing about democracy, but it's not so good if you are a . . . disfavored minority or you're new or you're different. . . . What Prop 8 does is label gay and lesbian persons as different, inferior, unequal, and disfavored. It says to them, 'Your relationship is not the same.' . . . It stigmatizes gays and lesbians. It classifies them as outcasts. It causes needless and unrelenting pain and isolation and humiliation. We have courts to declare enactments like Proposition 8 that take our citizens, our worthy, loving, upstanding citizens who are being treated differently and being hurt every single day, we have courts to declare those measures unconstitutional. And that is why we are here today."

The opening statement on behalf of the defendants was made by Chuck Cooper, who stressed the core American value of democracy as represented by the direct vote of California's citizens. Fifty-two percent of them had voted for Proposition 8, and as they did, he argued, California joined sister states that had in recent years enshrined the traditional definition of marriage in their constitutions, while many more states and the federal government had enacted clarifying statutes to the same effect. Only five states had opened the institution of marriage to same-sex couples, and three of them had had it imposed upon them by judges. Cooper also played his own Obama card, quoting the president, who had said, "I do not support gay marriage. Marriage has religious and social connotations, and I consider marriage to be between a man and a woman."

While the president's position remained, according to many sources, "evolving" under the influence of Mrs. Obama and others, it was true that President Obama was still opposed to same-sex marriage, much to the frustration of untold numbers of his supporters, including Chad Griffin.

Cooper maintained that *Loving v. Virginia* was not relevant to our case because it did not deal with what he considered society's real vested interest in marriage: procreation. (In fact, bans on interracial marriage were explicitly in part motivated by racist concerns over the children these marriages might produce.) "The purpose of the institution of marriage," declared Cooper, "the central purpose, is to promote procreation and to channel naturally procreative sexual activity between men and women into stable enduring unions for the purpose."

"Is that the only purpose of marriage?" asked Judge Walker.

"Your Honor," Cooper replied, "it is the central and, we would submit, defining purpose of marriage. It is the—it is the basis on which and the reason on which marriage as an institution has been universal across societies and cultures throughout history; two, because it is a pro-child societal institution. The evidence will show—"

"Where do the other values associated with marriage come in; companionship, support?" Judge Walker interrupted. "All of those things that attend a marriage that have nothing to do with procreation. What's the evidence going to show, that those are secondary, unimportant values associated with marriage?" Cooper responded with his theme that "this debate goes to the definition of marriage and . . . whether it's going to be deinstitutionalized."

After a bit more questioning, Cooper focused again on his key point, explaining that his star witness, David Blankenhorn, "will testify that a broad consensus of leading scholars suggests that across history and cultures marriage is fundamentally a pro-child social institution anchored in socially approved sexual intercourse between a man and a woman. And the core need that marriage, he will testify, aims to meet is the child's need to be emotionally, morally, practically, and legally affiliated with the woman and the man whose sexual union brought the child into the world."

And there it was. At the heart of Cooper's defense was the "historic definition of marriage" presented now by a single expert witness whose qualifications, it would soon become clear, were limited at best.

Cooper's argument that marriage was, at its core, simply an institution to foster responsible procreation and child rearing was inconsistent with numerous Supreme Court cases holding that the constitutional right to marry was grounded in individual rights—a phrase Cooper had rejected as a purpose for marriage—to "personal fulfillment and expression of love," including, for example, a holding that imprisoned felons, with no opportunity for procreation or child rearing, had a constitutional right to marry. As in so many other spheres of life, people today are freer than ever to follow their hearts, which seemed to us, and most Americans, a good idea.

Moreover, Cooper still did not have an answer, other than "I don't know," to the question of—even assuming that heterosexual marriage was simply an institution for child rearing—how in the world heterosexual marriage would be weakened or harmed by permitting gay and lesbian citizens to marry the person they loved.

With the opening statements completed, it became time to turn to the presentation of the evidence upon which the case would be decided. We had said from the beginning that we intended to prove three things: first, that marriage was a fundamental right; second, that denying gay and lesbian citizens the right to marry seriously harmed them and the children they were raising; third, that banning same-sex marriage did not harm heterosexual marriage. It was now time to prove each of these points. The opening ceremonies were over. The trial was now to begin.

Based on the opening statements, each of those three might seem obvious. Sometimes, however, a trial is important to prove what every-one at some level already knows.

The Plaintiffs

A plaintiff has certain disadvantages at trial, including the burden of proof. One of the offsetting advantages is the right to be the first to present evidence. By selecting the witnesses the court will hear first, the plaintiff has the opportunity to set the stage, build a framework, and determine what facts will begin to shape the record. The plaintiffs' first witnesses provide an opportunity to breathe life into the key points for their side of the case, to stamp an impression that succeed-ing witnesses and other evidence can reinforce.

Sometimes the best first witnesses are the plaintiffs themselves. But such a strategy carries risks. If the plaintiffs come across poorly or make damaging admissions during cross-examination, their case may never recover. Despite the risks involved, everyone agreed that our case should begin with Jeff, Paul, Kris, and Sandy. They were what this trial was all about. The lawyers were simply the instruments through which their story would be told.

Change seldom comes easy, and for those who have been scarred by prejudice or discrimination, living as openly gay required some measure of courage. Even more courage was required when confronting those who have actively and aggressively campaigned to relegate gays to second-class status. This was precisely what our clients were going to have to encounter on the opening day of the trial. Jeff Zarrillo was called to testify first and was examined by David. After a few background questions, David asked, "Are you gay?" Jeff answered, "Yes, I am."

In decades past David's question and Jeff's answer might have pro-duced a moment of high drama. In Judge Walker's courtroom no one reacted with even mild surprise. Jeff explained what it was like to grow up gay in Brick, New Jersey, during the 1980s and 1990s. Schoolmates used homophobic slurs and made antigay remarks so casually that they didn't even notice how they affected Jeff. "Ultimately you get to the point where you are comfortable with yourself," he added, but this process required him to accept and somehow internalize the fact that some people might dislike him, discriminate against him, or even hate him, simply because he was gay. Jeff testified that although he had always been gay, the hostility gay Americans faced caused him to conceal his sexual orientation for years, and that he had not come out to his friends and family in New Jersey until he was thirty.

As Jeff spoke in a firm and steady voice, his seriousness was unmistakable. Unmistakable too was the happiness that crossed his face when David asked him about his partner of nine years, Paul. As we did in every case, we had prepared our plaintiffs for their testimony by going over with them in advance the questions we were planning to ask, as well as the questions they might be asked on cross-examination. However, in preparing Jeff for his testimony, David had intentionally not raised the subject of his feelings for Paul. David wanted to be sure that Jeff's answer in court would come across as naturally and unrehearsed as possible.

After identifying Paul, David asked, "Tell me a little bit about that man."

Jeff replied:

> He's the love of my life. I love him probably more than I love myself. I would do anything for him. I would put his needs ahead of my own.
>
> I would be with him in sickness and in health, for richer, for poorer, till death do us part, just like the vows. I would do anything for him. And I want nothing more than to marry him.

It was a powerful start to the trial. Jeff's love for Paul was unmistakable, genuine, and powerful. Everyone in the courtroom, Judge Walker and defense counsel included, were affected; many blinked back tears.

In response to David's questions, Jeff discussed the importance of marriage to him and Paul. "The word 'marriage' has a special meaning. It's why we're here today. If it wasn't so important, we wouldn't be here today." Jeff explained that California's domestic partnership alternative relegated gay couples to "second-class citizenship, maybe even third-class citizenship." He described the awkwardness of checking into a hotel, opening a joint bank account, and trying to explain the ring he wore. He testified that marriage would validate his relationship with Paul, and validate him and Paul themselves. He explained that he and Paul were reluctant to have children until they could marry because of the protections and acceptance that their marriage would provide their children.

In less than an hour Jeff had succeeded in putting a human face on what the fight for marriage equality was all about, far better than any lawyer's brief or argument could. David completed his examination by asking:

> Q: Now, assume that the State of California continues to tell you that you can't get married to someone of the same sex. Might that lead you to desire to get married and marry somebody of the opposite sex?
>
> A: No.
>
> (LAUGHTER)
>
> Q: Why not?
>
> A: I have no attraction, desire, to be with a member of the opposite sex.
>
> Q: Do you think if somehow you were able to be forced into a marriage with somebody of the opposite sex, that would lead to a stable, loving relationship?
>
> A: Again, no.
>
> MR. BOIES: Your Honor, I have no more questions.

What followed surprised the courtroom:

> THE COURT: Cross-examination?
>
> MR. RAUM: No.

THE COURT: No cross-examination. Very well, then. Mr. Zarrillo, sir, you may step down.

Judge Walker generally kept a poker face during the trial, but when
he repeated, "No cross-examination," his tone reflected that he had not
expected the defendants' decision not to confront Jeff at all. Given the
power, confidence, and emotion with which Jeff spoke, the defendants'
decision was not necessarily a bad one. But it underscored how little
they had to say about the principal points of our case.

Paul followed his partner to the witness chair. A fitness expert and
actor, Paul is comfortable speaking in public and was a more assertive
witness. David planned to use him not only to reinforce the points Jeff
had made, but to introduce and put in context Proposition 8 itself. Paul
described the pain caused by being told by his state that he was a second-
class citizen who could not marry the person he loved. "I'm a proud
man. I'm proud to be gay. I'm a natural-born gay. I love Jeff more than
myself. And being excluded in that way is so incredibly harmful to me.
I can't speak as an expert. I can speak as a human being that's lived it."

Paul testified how he too had delayed coming out because of his
community's hostility to gays and lesbians—and how after he had
come out he had been subjected to slurs and insults, and on occasion
rocks and eggs. He also echoed Jeff's testimony on the importance to
children of having their parents married.

When David turned to the subject of Proposition 8, Paul recalled
how he felt insulted by the campaign to ban same-sex marriage on the
basis of somehow protecting children from people like him. "'Protect
the children' is a big part of the campaign," he said. "And when I think
of protecting your children, you protect them from people who will
perpetrate crimes against them, people who might get them hooked on
a drug, a pedophile, or some person that you need protecting from.
You don't protect yourself from an amicable person or a good person.
You protect yourself from things that can harm you physically, emotionally. And [it is] so insulting, even the insinuation that I would be
part of that category. . . . But to lump this issue into 'protect your family, protect your children,' that invokes to me that we are some sort of

perpetrator; that my getting married to Jeff is going to harm some child somewhere. And it's so damning, and it's so angering, because I love kids."

David went on to use Paul to introduce a series of videos that had been used as TV ads, Internet appeals, or at campaign events by proponents of Proposition 8. The first one, "It's Already Happened," opens with a little girl exclaiming to her mother that in school she learned "how a prince married a prince, and I can marry a princess." The scene freezes as a man in jacket and tie appears onscreen to ask, "Think it can't happen?" and then warns, "It's already happened." The spot ends with the message, "Protect our children. Restore marriage." Another video, "Stand Up for Proposition 8," showed a freight train speeding down some tracks with a voice-over that warned, "The devil wants to blur the lines between right and wrong when it comes to family structure." The video implored people to support "biblical marriage" and ended with a call for Prop 8 supporters to "stand up for righteousness."

Brian Raum, the defendants' counsel responsible for dealing with Jeff and Paul, objected to the use of the "Stand Up for Proposition 8" video on the ground that there was no proof it had been produced by Protect-Marriage.com, an official proponent of Proposition 8. This was part of an attempt by the defendants to distance themselves from some of the more blatant appeals to prejudice that had fueled the Prop 8 campaign.

There were plenty of egregious appeals to prejudice from the defendants themselves, as David's examination of Mr. Tam would later reveal. However, as David argued more generally later, there was no basis for the defendants to "try to draw a distinction between what they call the official campaign and the unofficial campaign. In fact, it's all one campaign. And the attempt to sort of step back for purposes of this litigation and pretend there was only really an official campaign, and they didn't know anything about or have any knowledge of what was going on with everybody else, I think, is not credible."

Raum's objection was particularly weak with respect to the "Stand Up" video, since, as David pointed out, the video prominently featured Ron Prentice, the chairman of ProtectMarriage.com. The video was admitted into evidence.

Our purpose in getting the videos into evidence was to display to the court what the messaging of the Prop 8 campaign was intended to accomplish—namely, depicting gays and lesbians as sinful, evil, dangerous, threatening. The videos showed that for many of its supporters, the purpose of Prop 8 was to ban same-sex marriage based on a religious and moral view that homosexuality was sinful, wrong, threatening, and "unnatural."

We also used the videos to rebut the defendants' sanitized litigation posture that Prop 8 was simply an effort to preserve heterosexual marriage, and to emphasize the personal damage inflicted by government-sanctioned discrimination against a class of citizens.

Paul described the effect of being told that his relationship with Jeff was somehow wrong and that "marriage is not for you people." He testified that "regardless of how proud you are, you still feel a bit ashamed. And I shouldn't have to feel ashamed. Being gay doesn't make me any less American. It doesn't change my patriotism. It doesn't change the fact that I pay my taxes, and I own a home, and I want to start a family. But in that moment, being gay means I'm unequal. I'm less than. I am undesirable. I have been relegated to a corner."

Paul emphasized that "when your state sanctions something that segregates you, it fortifies people's biases. . . . It gives them an excuse." And he explained that permitting gay citizens to marry the person they loved could not hurt anyone. "All I want is to be married. And that affects no one except for my husband, my family, my friends, our concentric circles."

Paul, like Jeff before him and Kris and Sandy after him, was a sensational witness whose testimony made our case more effectively than anything we could say. There is a tendency with such an effective witness to keep asking questions because it is going so well. But a lawyer also needs to know when to stop. Paul had only been on the stand for a little more than an hour when he completed an answer as to why it was harmful and wrong for a state to discriminate between those who can marry and those who can't based on sexual orientation. "We're not a country about us and them. We're supposed to be a country about us, all of us, working in concert, doing things together. That's why we have these protections. My state is supposed to protect me. It's not supposed to discriminate against me."

There was only one sensible thing for David to say:

> MR. BOIES: Your Honor, I have no more questions.

This time Raum did cross-examine. But the result was simply to reinforce the impact of Paul's testimony. He would have been better off with the decision he had made with Jeff—not to cross-examine. He did not even attempt to challenge our basic points that banning same-sex marriage seriously harmed gay and lesbian citizens and the children they were raising without benefiting anyone.

Raum's primary point was that the intent of Prop 8 was not to protect children from gays but to protect children from learning about gays and sex in school, in first and second grade as opposed to later grades. In response to repeated questions, Paul responded that that was not what the campaign videos and literature said. David's redirect questioning was brief:

> BY MR. BOIES:
> Q: As you understood it, was there anything in Proposition 8 about what was going to be taught in schools?
> A: No.
> Q: Was there anything in Proposition 8 that talked about whether kids would be taught about sex in second grade as opposed to sixth or eighth grade?
> A: To my understanding, not at all.
> MR. BOIES: No more questions, Your Honor.

The lightest moment of the day came when Kris Perry was examined by Ted. After they covered her background and discussed how she met Sandy, Kris recalled realizing that she had fallen in love with Sandy. Ted asked her, "How did she feel about you?"

"She told me she loved me too," answered Kris.

"We will be asking her to verify that," said Ted.

Kris visibly relaxed. Moments later she offered a poignant bit of commentary on marriage, as she hoped it might be:

> I have never really let myself want it until now. Growing up as a lesbian, you don't let yourself want it, because everyone tells you [you] are never going to have it. So in some ways it's hard for me to grasp what it would even mean, but I do see other people who are married and I—and I think what it looks like is that you are honored and respected by your family. Your children know what your relationship is. And when you leave your home and you go to work or you go out in the world, people know what your relationship means. And so then everyone can, in a sense, join in supporting your relationship, which at this point I can only observe it as an outsider. I don't have any first-hand experience with what that must be like.

Kris described in moving testimony how she felt when informed that her earlier marriage to Sandy during the Mayor Newsom episode was not valid:

> The part of me that was disbelieving and unsure of it in the first place was confirmed. . . . When you're gay, you think you don't really deserve things . . . I'm not good enough to be married.

And, in words no lawyer could have written for her, she answered Ted's question about the meaning of this case to her, and to others:

> Q: If the courts of the United States . . . ultimately decided that you and other . . . persons seeking to marry someone of the same sex could indeed, did indeed have the constitutional right to get married, do you think that would have an effect on other acts of discrimination against you?
> A: I believe for me personally, as a lesbian, that if I had grown up in a world where the most important decision I was going to make as an adult was treated the same way as everybody

else's decision, that I would not have been treated the way I was growing up or as an adult.

There's something so humiliating about everybody knowing that you want to make that decision and you don't get to do that, you know, it's hard to face the people at work and the people even here right now. And many of you have this, but I don't.

So I have to still find a way to feel okay and not take every bit of discriminatory behavior toward me too personally because in the end that will only hurt me and my family.

So if Prop 8 were undone and kids like me growing up in Bakersfield right now could never know what this felt like, then I assume that their entire lives would be on a higher arc. They would live with a higher sense of themselves that would improve the quality of their entire life.

Sandy's testimony was equally poignant, compelling, and memorable. Like her fellow plaintiffs she painted an indelible picture of discrimination, its pain, and its effects on simple daily life. Because Sandy had been married, she had the personal experience to compare marriage to domestic partnership. "It's not the same," she said firmly. Referring to encounters with others, she said, "I don't want to have to explain myself . . . in a way that would indicate there must be something wrong with me."

The claims of the Prop 8 campaigners seemed all the more preposterous when examined in the real-world context of the love that Sandy and Kris expressed for each other. It was hard to imagine two people who were more devoted, who more movingly embodied the very ideal of marriage. Kris had proposed to Sandy and the two had wed when San Francisco briefly granted marriage licenses to same-sex couples, but their happiness soon turned to disappointment, as Sandy recalled:

We received a document from the city . . . that [our marriage] was invalidated. And I felt so outraged and hurt by that and humiliated.

And I felt like everybody who had come to our wedding and gone out of their way and bought us lovely gifts and celebrated with us must feel a level of humiliation themselves.

Sandy and Kris had entered into a California domestic partnership—called a civil union in some states—but to Sandy, "There is certainly nothing about domestic partnership . . . that indicates love and commitment that are inherent in marriage. . . . It's just a legal document. . . . It has nothing to do with marriage. Nothing." Marriage has a fundamentally different connotation in our society, Sandy explained. "We have a loving, committed relationship. We are not business partners. We are not social partners. We are not glorified roommates. . . . We want to be married. It's a different relationship."

Being married "would provide me with a sense of inclusion in the social fabric. . . . I think I would feel more respected by other people and I feel like our relationship is more respected and that I could hold my head up high . . . in our family and . . . our family could feel proud."

Sandy finished her testimony by describing, in a way no lawyer could convey, what it would mean to her to be married:

> Well, I think it would change my life dramatically. The first time somebody said to me, "Are you married," and I said, "Yes," I would think, "Ah, that feels good. It feels good and honest and true."
>
> I would feel more secure. I would feel more accepted. I would feel more pride. . . . I would feel less like I had to protect my kids or worry about them or worry that they feel any . . . sense of not belonging.
>
> So I think there are immediate, very real and very desirable personal gains that I would experience. And, of course, [our] family.
>
> But on a different level, you know, as a parent you are always thinking about that other generation, that next generation, because you are—they are in your house. So you are constantly

thinking about the world that you're—the society you are in, what are you doing for them? And are we building a good world for them? And I really want that.

I want our kids to have a better life than we have right now. When they grow up. I want it to be better for them. And their kids, I want their lives to be better, too.

So I really do think about that generation and the possibility of having grandchildren someday and having them live in a world where they grow up and whoever they fall in love with, it's okay, because they can be honored and they can be true to themselves and they can be accepted by society and protected by their government. And that's what I hope can be the outcome of this case in the long run.

And as somebody who is from one of those conservative little pockets of the country where there isn't necessarily a lot of difference in the types of people that are there, having those legal protections is everything. It's important for these kids that don't have ready access to all types of people to at least feel like the option to be true to yourself is an option that they can have too.

And that's what I hope for. I hope for something for Kris and I, but we are big, strong women. You know, we are in a good place in our lives right now. So we would benefit from it greatly, but other people over time, I think, would benefit in such a more profound life-changing way.

These unrehearsed words seemed at the time, and to this day, to express it all. We felt that if everyone in America could hear that testimony, and the words and feelings of Kris, Jeff, and Paul, opposition to marriage equality would melt away. In the courtroom there were very few dry eyes.

At such an emotionally powerful moment in a trial, the danger of amplifying the devastating impact of testimony like Sandy's by allowing her to repeat and reinforce it on cross-examination was great. Our opponents offered probably the only response that made any sense: "We have no questions, Your Honor."

The Experts

Our trial witnesses included top experts from around the world in subjects relevant to marriage equality:

- M. V. Lee Badgett, University of Massachusetts professor of economics, who would testify about the economic harm and inequalities resulting from bans on same-sex marriage.
- George Chauncey, Yale professor of history, who would testify about the history of homosexual discrimination, love, and intimacy.
- Nancy Cott, Harvard professor of history, who would testify about the history of marriage.
- Edmund Egan, chief economist for the City of San Francisco, who would testify about the economic burdens imposed by Prop 8.
- Michael Lamb, Cambridge University professor and head of the Department of Social and Developmental Psychology, who would testify about child and adolescent development in same-sex households and the benefits to children of marriage equality.
- Ilan Meyer, Columbia University associate professor of public health, who would testify about the social stigma resulting from discrimination against gay and lesbian citizens, and the mental health consequences of such discrimination.
- Letitia Anne Peplau, UCLA professor of psychology, who would testify about the benefits of marriage and their effects on health and well-being; the similarities between

same-sex and opposite-sex couples; and the benefits of permitting same-sex couples to marry.

- Gary Segura, Stanford University professor of American politics, who would testify about the relative political power, and political vulnerability, of gay and lesbian citizens.

Our first expert witness, Harvard historian Nancy Cott, had authored one of the definitive texts on the history of marriage and testified that throughout history, many conceptions of marriage have existed, and the institution of marriage has repeatedly adapted to societal changes. The Bible's accounts of marriage include references to polygamy practiced in certain Jewish communities, and at the time the United States was founded, many of the world's people lived in societies where one-man-one-woman was not the established norm. Cott also offered some compelling testimony about the significance of marriage as a civil right. In antebellum America, the denial of slaves' right to marry was a reaffirmation of their second-class status. They were property, not free people. Their owner could not let them form matrimonial bonds. This issue even arose in the infamous Dred Scott case before the Supreme Court, which denied a slave's petition for freedom when he was living in a free state. The justices' decision noted that state prohibitions on Scott's freedom to marry evinced his inferior status as property and supported the Court's decision to reject his claim. When the slaves were freed, they flocked to get married, Cott testified. This was a major, tangible sign of their newly found liberty.

In testimony that ran into the following day, Professor Cott dismantled much of the argument in favor of Prop 8. Heterosexual intercourse and the children who might result were not the main purpose of the state's interest in marriage, she explained. "The larger purpose [places the] emphasis on the household formation that marriage founds, and the stability of that household formation, its contribution to social order, to economic benefit, to governance." Similarly, she testified, the government's interest in this relationship has been as much about "supporting adults" as it has been about supporting children.

One of the most salient aspects of Cott's testimony addressed the social implications of our case, linking it to the revolution in women's rights that began with the suffrage movement of the nineteenth century and accelerated in the late 1950s. Widely associated with the liberation made possible by the birth control pill, this movement brought about new laws and norms that allowed individuals and couples to transcend traditional gender roles. Women no longer stood as "dependents" in relationships where men were considered "providers." Resisted at every turn by social conservatives, these steps toward equality enabled people to choose their roles, and led in turn to the possibility of same-sex marriage: If men and women were no longer required to fulfill gender-based marriage roles, gender no longer needed to be the exclusive definition of the relationship. Understood in this context, the argument over marriage equality was just the latest development in a social transformation that began in earnest over fifty years earlier, and has raged at dinner tables, in the media, in election campaigns and legislatures ever since.

The cross-examination of Cott by Cooper partner David H. Thompson quickly turned prickly as he began to quiz her on the laws governing marriage in the thirteen original states at the time of the nation's founding. "So you have no idea whether the majority of states at the founding of the country did not have a prohibition on interracial marriage," asked Thompson.

"That is an irrelevant question, really, because—"

"On redirect you can give a speech," said Thompson, interrupting Cott. "It's yes or no now."

"Okay. Fine."

"So you don't know?"

"I don't know precisely how many of the original thirteen colonies had such laws."

Thompson succeeded in irritating Cott, but not shaking her, even as he referred to arguments that equality might lead toward "a slippery slope to licensing polygamy." She simply explained patiently why polygamy was quite different, and prohibited for sound reasons that had nothing to do with marriage between an individual and another of the same sex.

He didn't score any better against Yale historian George Chauncey, who described the sweeping legal oppression of gays and lesbians in the twentieth century and the rise in the mass media of false claims that gay men were inclined to drug abuse and pedophilia. Chauncey explained how this demonization continued through Anita Bryant's virulently antigay Save Our Children campaign of the late 1970s. Chauncey pointed out that the arguments made on behalf of Prop 8 had resonated "with a similar intent and uses some of the same imagery."

Dr. Lee Badgett, a professor and director of the Center for Public Policy and Administration at the University of Massachusetts and research director of the Williams Institute at UCLA Law School, was one of the world's leading experts on same-sex marriage and had authored books and peer-reviewed articles on the subject. Professor Badgett gave detailed testimony outlining the economic harm that Proposition 8 inflicted on same-sex couples and their children. She also testified that marriage gave "greater validation and social acceptance" of relationships, leading to greater family stability.

Gary Segura, a Stanford political scientist, explained that despite the election of the occasional legislator and mayor, the community of gay and lesbian Americans was relatively powerless politically and at the same time frequently under attack by social conservatives who used ballot measures to both stigmatize them and deny them protections. "There is no group in American society," he reported, "who has been targeted by ballot initiatives more than gays and lesbians." The response of the community's allies, meanwhile, has often been half-hearted. He cited President Obama, with his yet-to-have-evolved opposition to gay marriage, as an "ally who can't be counted on." Of course, President Obama was to become a very powerful ally before the end of this case.

The defense poked away at Segura's assertions, hoping to undermine our claim that our clients were part of a minority that deserved protection. But despite hours of laborious cross-examination, Cooper's team was repeatedly unable to shake the testimony or conviction of our witnesses. Much of the cross was boring, repetitious, and, frankly, deadening. At one point, one of the defense lawyers even managed to get under Judge Walker's skin as he tediously questioned one of our witnesses about dozens of different studies. Is it true, he asked, that some lesbian mothers might not set limits as firmly as they should? At this the judge remarked drily, "Perhaps this is not the only area in which setting limits would be helpful."

However, Judge Walker gave defendants' counsel very wide latitude to ask questions and introduce evidence, permitting the defendants to ask literally hundreds of questions (sometimes repeatedly) and agreeing to take judicial notice of documents that didn't seem even remotely germane. This process consumed hours of court time, and while standing-room-only crowds packed every session, the tedium began to weigh upon everyone.

In addition to our experts we offered testimony from witnesses about their personal experiences. Jerry Sanders, the Republican mayor of San Diego, testified to the discrimination against gays and lesbians he had observed in his twenty-six years in the San Diego Police Department, the last six years as chief of police. He also testified about how he had come to sign a resolution passed by the San Diego City Council in 2007 supporting San Francisco's efforts to achieve marriage equality. Even though he has a lesbian daughter with whom he was very close, he had been a supporter of civil unions as an alternative to same-sex marriage until 2007. When he was considering whether to sign or veto the resolution, he had a meeting with a group of gay friends and neighbors in order to hear their views.

"Well, you know, I suppose what I expected was that they'd say civil unions are fine. I guess I was absolutely shocked at the depth of the hurt, the depth of the feeling, the depth of the comments that came from them.

"I remember one of our neighbors, who I have known for quite some time, said, basically, 'I walk by here—my partner and I walk by here all the time, with our children. And you always stop, when you are doing yard work, and say hello to them and talk to them. You know, we're a family just like you're a family.'

"One of our other neighbors said that she had children just like I did; they loved the children just as much; and that they felt their children deserved parents, also, and they deserved to have parents who were married.

"The depth of feeling was unbelievable. The depth of the hurt. And also I could see the harm I had done by considering the veto."

Especially poignant testimony was provided by Ryan Kendall, who spoke of the pain he suffered as his parents, who were conservative evangelical Christians, sent him to "reversal therapy" when he was fourteen, and how extraordinarily damaging to him that "therapy" was. Now thoroughly discredited, these so-called treatments were supposed to transform gay people into heterosexuals. After a year and a half in the program, he said, "I was just as gay as when I started."

Each day we spent long hours at court, and each evening we met with a large contingent of associates and partners who were carefully reading the thousands of pages of documents that had been produced as the trial proceeded. We kept receiving boxes and boxes filled with files. In the hope of finding new and important evidence, our team worked while we attended the trial and through the night on a formerly vacant floor of the downtown skyscraper where Gibson Dunn had its offices. With their assistance we were able to refine our strategy and arguments and develop new lines of questioning for the witnesses who might be presented by the other side.

The scene in the offices where lawyers combed through the documents resembled a cross between an all-nighter in a college dormitory and the search for the golden ticket in *Willie Wonka and the Chocolate Factory* (a comparison aptly made by Enrique Monagas). Chris Dusseault oversaw much of this effort and imposed a few rules, including a ban on junk food to prevent what he called "carb comas." On the fourth night of the trial, one of the young associates saw him in a hallway and confessed, "We ordered some pizza. It's going to be here any minute." Chris reassured him that it was all right to break the carb rule, especially since the research group had discovered many documents that refuted the defendants' assertion that the Prop 8 campaign was run by disparate groups that were not centrally organized. They had used this claim to justify withholding letters and other documents that they maintained were private and irrelevant. What this material actually

revealed was the coordination of efforts by the leaders of ProtectMar-
riage.com, who managed the timing and content of communications
and funneled money to those who paid for events and advertising.

We also found a great deal of communication that established the
pervasive involvement of Mormon and Catholic groups. One letter,
sent to California's Catholic bishops by the director of Prop 8's central
organization, noted:

> The Catholic Conference has played a substantial role in
> inviting Catholic faithful to put their faith in action by volun-
> teering and donating. Led by the Knights of Columbus na-
> tional donation of $1.15 million, other million-dollar donors,
> and countless major donors, and with a significant percentage
> of the 90,000 online donors, the Catholic community has
> stepped up. Of course, this campaign owes an enormous debt
> to the LDS Church. I will comment specifically at a later time,
> under separate cover, about their financial, organizational and
> management contribution to the success of the effort. The
> ProtectMarriage.com campaign has surpassed $37 million in
> donations.

Any doubt that the churches and other religious organizations had
worked together on a single election campaign was dispelled when we
found a "Statement of Unity" that bound them under centralized authority. It placed control over media interviews, campaign messages,
and fund-raising in the hands of ProtectMarriage.com and its consultants, Frank Schubert and Jeff Flint. The copy we received had been
signed by Bill Tam, and when it turned up, it made it more imperative
that this reluctant defendant testify. Judge Walker agreed that we could
call him.

The night before we called Tam to the stand, David, as he often does
before a critical cross-examination, talked with Mary about how to
approach the witness. Getting the most from a hostile witness is one
of the most difficult tasks a trial lawyer faces, and it is important to
understand the witness's character, the relevant evidence that can be

used with the witness, and the best way to combine the two to extract helpful, and minimize harmful, testimony. Mary's advice was valuable both because of her own skills as a lawyer and because she, like Lady, rivaled David and Ted in knowledge about and commitment to the case. They agreed that just as we had used our plaintiffs to put a human face on the harm and unfairness of discrimination, the goal with Tam would be to reveal the dark side of the Prop 8 campaign, using, where possible, Tam's own words and documents.

From the very start of his questioning by David, Tam tried to play down his knowledge of and role in the Prop 8 campaign. For example:

> Q: The next organization is Family Research Council. Was that one of the organizations that was part of the ProtectMarriage.com coalition supporting Proposition 8?
>
> A: Now, I—I really don't know why they put these names on there. You have to ask them, not me, because I have no position of knowing which organization or person on this list is their coalition. I really don't know.
>
> Q: Dr. Tam, my question to you was whether the Family Research Council was one of the organizations that was part of the ProtectMarriage.com coalition supporting Proposition 8. Yes, no, or I don't know?
>
> A: I don't know.
>
> Q: Do you know what the Family Research Council is?
>
> A: I know what it is.
>
> Q: Let me try to be clear. The Family Research Council was one of the organizations that you got e-mails from and that were listed as joint addressees with you and your organization in connection with Proposition 8, correct?
>
> A: Could be.

Throughout his testimony, Tam did his best to evade any responsibility for having a role as a leader of the Prop 8 campaign, despite the documents we produced that indicated he was. At various points he insisted that the organizers were only "being nice" to him by referring to him as a leader and that he was ignorant of other parties who were plainly his active allies in the cause. When David showed Tam an e-mail he wrote declaring that his organization "is playing a major role to put 1-man-1-woman marriage into California's constitution," Tam, confronted with his own words, finally had to admit, "I was playing a major role." He also admitted that he had invested "substantial time, effort, and personal resources in campaigning for Proposition 8."

Even more troubling than Tam's evasions were the ideas that he had put forward to support Proposition 8. As an example David presented him with a Web page published by his group that stated that homosexuals were twelve times more likely to molest children. With a tone that expressed his incredulity, David queried him:

Q: Now, do you believe that homosexuals are twelve times more
   likely to molest children? Do you believe that?
A: Yeah, based on the different literature that I've read.
Q: Oh. And what literature have you read, sir, that says that?
A: Um, I've read what is posted here.
Q: And what is it? Tell me what it is that you read.
A: I don't remember.
Q: Who—who authored it?
A: Some from, apparently, academic papers.
Q: What academic papers, sir?
A: I don't remember.
Q: Well, do you remember any of them?
A: No.
Q: Was it in a—a journal, or was it in a book that you read?
A: Some could be news. Some could be from journals.
Q: It could be. I'm not asking you what it could be. You told me
   you'd read something that said that homosexuals were twelve
   times more likely to molest children. You told me that, right?
A: Yes.
Q: Okay. Now, I'm asking you what you read. Was it a book?
A: I don't remember.

Q: Was it an article?

A: I don't remember.

Q: Who wrote it?

A: I don't know.

In the next document David presented, Tam had warned that San Francisco was under "the rule of homosexuals." When David asked, "The mayor was a homosexual, was he, according to you?" Tam answered, "I don't think so."

"You don't think so?" replied David. "No, I don't think so either, actually. So if you knew the mayor wasn't homosexual, why are you telling people in part of the Proposition 8 campaign that San Francisco is under the rule of homosexuals?"

Stammering a bit, Tam then said, "Well, you see, Mayor Newsom passed out the same-sex marriage licenses in 2004. And if he is not a friend of them, why would he do that?"

"When you say that San Francisco was under the rule of homosexuals, did you mean San Francisco was under the rule of heterosexuals that were friends of homosexuals? Is that what you meant?"

"Could be."

"Could be?"

"Yeah, you know, I'm not a lawyer. I don't write things so specifically. You know, that well defined."

The truth, obvious to everyone in the courtroom, was that Tam had been a leader in a richly financed, extensive campaign for a carefully crafted amendment to California's constitution using deceptive, bigoted, and erroneous claims intended to inflame his constituency. His Web site reported that after same-sex marriage was approved in the Netherlands, it also legalized incest and polygamy. None of these accusations were true, and it eventually became clear that Tam had no basis for his reckless claims.

Q: And you say, "Netherlands legalized same-sex marriage in 2001, and to date incest and polygamy became legal." Do you see that?

A: Yes.

Q: Now, did you agree with that, sir?

A: Yes.

Q: Who told you that, sir? Where did you get that idea?

A: It's in the Internet.

Q: In the Internet?

A: Yeah.

Q: Somewhere out in the Internet it says that the Netherlands legalized incest and polygamy in 2005?

A: Frankly, I did not write this, all right? Polygamy was legalized in 2005. Another person in the organization found it and he showed me that.

Q: And you just put it out there to convince voters to vote for Proposition 8?

A: Well, I—I look at the document and I think that was true.

We would have been happy to end the proceedings with Tam's testimony hanging in the air and move on to closing arguments. However, the other side insisted on continuing, presumably deciding that they needed to present at least some evidence. This proved to be, for them, an unfortunate decision.

EIGHT

The Trial II

I n the end the defense would call only two witnesses. The first, Professor Kenneth Miller of Claremont McKenna College, was offered as
an expert on the political power of the gay and lesbian communities.
He was supposed to make the case that they did not merit protection
as a minority because, contrary to what our expert, Gary Segura, had
testified, they did in fact possess significant political power.

This was relevant because one of the factors courts consider in determining whether a group is a suspect class entitled to greater judicial
scrutiny of laws adversely affecting it is whether the class has political
power sufficient to protect itself. While public opinion was certainly
moving away from hard-core prejudice, anyone who could claim that
gays and lesbians didn't deserve protected status would have to take
into account the fact that bias attacks, hate crimes, and discrimination
were still commonplace, and that political advocates like William Tam
felt they could score points and win votes with base appeals to bigotry.
Then there was the matter of the dozens of recently enacted state and
national bans on marriage equality. If the gay community was a politically powerful group, why had it lost all of these battles?

Kenneth Miller was not the best man to answer all such questions.
A political scientist who had authored a book on politics and helped
edit another, he had done little work on the power of gays and lesbians
or Prop 8. Before an expert witness is permitted to testify, the other
side is given an opportunity, called voir dire—literally, "to speak the

truth"—to determine whether the witness is qualified to give expert testimony. Given Miller's background, David planned to confront him aggressively on his qualifications during voir dire. If he could demonstrate that the witness's qualifications were weak or nonexistent, Miller might not be allowed to testify at all. And if he did testify, Judge Walker would be aware of the witness's weaknesses as he listened, while the witness himself might well be disciplined by the experience.

Voir dire can be a tough business, and it certainly was in this case. Beginning with questions about the work Miller had published in the United States on gay and lesbian issues, David quickly established that the professor had never authored anything on the history of discrimination against these groups. Miller confessed that until recently he hadn't known that the Mattachine Society was one of the first major gay rights organizations in America, and on the stand he failed to recognize the name of the first openly gay legislator in the country, Allan Spear.

Judge Walker ultimately decided that Miller's knowledge was not so limited as to disqualify him entirely, and the witness was allowed to testify. But David had noticed something odd in Miller's expert report to the court: It included an index of articles that seemed to include a great many items that were noted in other defense witness reports. David suspected that Miller hadn't done all that reading and had instead been handed citations to pad his index by our opposing counsel. But the judge would not ordinarily permit inquiry into communications with counsel, so David waited until Miller brought the subject up first.

Early in David's cross-examination, in an attempt to bolster his qualifications. Miller volunteered, "I investigated everything that was in my report."

"I beg your pardon, sir?"

"I investigated everything that was in my report."

"Personally?"

"Personally."

For emphasis David repeated, "Personally investigated it," and then paused and asked, "For example, every statement in there is something that you personally investigated; is that true?"

"I believe that's true, yes."

David moved quickly, directing the witness to look at the index to his own report. Miller was asked whether the many items he cited were the product of his own research or whether defense counsel had provided them. (The judge dismissed an objection to this line of questioning—Professor Miller had "opened the door" to the subject.) "Some of them were provided for me by counsel," Miller replied. "I found most of them myself."

David then asked Miller to read down the list and circle the articles, books, or chapters he had found himself. If he was unsure about the provenance of any of them he could annotate them with a question mark. Miller looked a little tentative as he undertook this task. When he finished, his marked-up index showed that only about a hundred sources were ones that he had personally investigated, he was uncertain as to about 250 entries, and he was certain that 83 had been provided by defendants' counsel. The point had been made to the judge. The witness and opposing counsel had been engaged in a rather clumsy effort to bulk up the witness's credibility.

Under David's questioning Miller revealed that he was uncertain about the legal protections offered to gays and lesbians in various states and that he couldn't speak authoritatively about the level of violence directed at these populations. When asked to define the commonly used term "gay bashing," he struggled. He acknowledged that he hadn't read the writings of many of the important scholars in the area of social science in which he claimed expertise, and he confessed to having little or no understanding of discrimination against gays and lesbians in the private sector. He did, however, agree that members of these groups constituted a recognizable minority, that they continued to suffer from discrimination, and that Proposition 8 was itself discriminatory.

In his direct examination, Miller had asserted that gay and lesbian citizens had political power because even though they were a small minority they had many powerful allies. David asked:

Q: Now, despite all these allies, Proposition 8 did pass, correct?
A: Yes, it passed.
(LAUGHTER)

David also noted that the same organizations that Miller said were allies of gay and lesbian citizens were also allies of women and African American citizens—two groups that the courts already identified as suspect classes. Miller claimed not to know whether African Americans had more political power today than the LGBT community.

Miller also claimed that he didn't know whether gays and lesbians were underrepresented in elected office because he couldn't determine the denominator representing the total number of gay and lesbian citizens. David responded:

> Q: Well, sir, take California. You know that no openly gay or lesbian person has ever, in the history of the state, been elected to statewide office, correct, sir?
>
> A: No openly gay person, that's correct.
>
> Q: Not governor, not lieutenant governor, not attorney general, not senator, correct, sir?
>
> A: That's correct.
>
> Q: So in that case, whatever the denominator would be, the numerator would be zero, correct?
>
> (LAUGHTER)

Perhaps the best part of David's cross-examination of Miller came from Miller's own writings that had been brought to David's attention the night before. Remarkably, Miller had published articles that concluded, based on a study of nine hundred initiatives, that in California "initiative constitutional amendments and initiative statutes undermine the authority and flexibility of representative government"; that "direct democracy can actually be less democratic than representative democracy . . . and violates . . . fairness"; and that the initiative process "violates procedural guarantees observed by almost every freely elected legislature in the world."

Miller agreed that the danger of initiatives was particularly great when a majority took away rights not of everyone but only of a minority, and that initiatives that "differentially affect minorities can easily tap into a vein of antiminority sentiment in the electorate." A clearer indictment of Proposition 8 was hard to imagine—and it came from one of the defendants' own witnesses.

Eleven days into the proceedings, with the end of the trial in sight, the defense of Proposition 8 was down to David Blankenhorn, an expert with modest credentials who soon became quite ambivalent about the starring role he had agreed to play. Trouper that he was, Blankenhorn began his testimony by describing his education—Harvard undergrad, University of Warwick master's degree—and his early career as a community organizer in poor neighborhoods of Boston. It was there, while still in his twenties, that he came to believe that many of the nation's social problems were linked to families without fathers. By age thirty-two he had founded the Institute for American Values to focus attention on marriage, families, and the well-being of children. Since then he had published nonacademic books on these topics, served on various committees and commissions, and gained a following as an advocate for the type of family—father, mother, children—into which he was born in 1955. When Cooper finished his questions designed to qualify Blankenhorn as an expert, he turned to Judge Walker and said, "Your Honor, I would like to tender Mr. Blankenhorn as an expert on the subject of marriage, fatherhood, and family structures."

Judge Walker replied, "Very well," and then, directing his attention to our side of the room, asked, "Voir dire?"

"Yes, Your Honor," answered David.

With Kenneth Miller's voir dire fresh in their collective memory, the audience in the courtroom seemed to draw themselves forward in anticipation of what was to happen next. David had made an exhaustive study of Blankenhorn's work and his many public statements and had reached some conclusions about his values and self-image. David sensed, from what he had read, that Blankenhorn (who frequently referenced his Harvard undergraduate degree and postgraduate work in Great Britain) was a man who craved admiration and affirmation as an intellectual. Blankenhorn also emphasized that although he was from the South, and a spokesperson for conservative causes, he personally harbored no racial, gender, or even sexual orientation prejudices. He wanted to be seen as open-minded, accepting, modern, and, above all, "reasonable."

Blankenhorn presented David with a number of possible vulnerabilities and opportunities to be explored in cross-examination. Before trying to do so, however, David wanted to soften Blankenhorn up by putting him on the defensive in voir dire.

David asked Blankenhorn to explain that his degree from Warwick was granted not for his study of marriage or families but of nineteenth-century cabinetmakers. Blankenhorn sparred with David over whether any of his studies had been peer-reviewed, but ultimately revealed that only two of his publications had been subject to that kind of scrutiny, and that neither had anything to do with same-sex marriage or the effects of same-sex marriage.

David got Blankenhorn to confirm that he had never taught at the college or university level; that he was not an expert in sociology, anthropology, or psychology; and that he had not undertaken any scientific study related to marriage equality. Blankenhorn then added, "I want to say what I did do, though, if I may be permitted."

"No," David said, provoking laughter as he added, "I'm sure you would like to answer questions that I'm not asking, sir. And you'll have a chance to do that with your counsel."

Judge Walker agreed that in a jury trial the decision to let Blankenhorn testify as an expert would be "a close one." However, since Walker was himself the sole arbiter of fact, he said he would agree to hear Blankenhorn's testimony and weigh it against his "qualifications, his background, training, and experience, and the reasons that he offers for his opinions." David had made the point he wanted—that this witness was a weak foundation upon which the defense was resting virtually its entire case.

In response to Cooper's direct examination, Blankenhorn then testified that the main purpose of marriage was the socially approved sexual intercourse and the protection of children within a family. "Marriage can look very different in different places and different times," he said. "But what's so astonishing about this is that it's always doing this thing. East, west, north, south, a thousand years ago, today, it's doing this thing. So this thing must be pretty important. It must be pretty fundamental."

Blankenhorn acknowledged that other "adult-centric" views of marriage did exist, and that there were many benefits people derived from being married, in addition to the creation of a family. He also recognized the existence of homophobia as something "I regret and deplore . . . and wish it would go away." However, he argued there was no evidence that antigay and antilesbian animus motivated those who would restrict marriage to heterosexuals. "I'm telling you that I have looked for it," he stated, "and I cannot find it."

Responding to questions about what he regarded as the best model for a family to raise children, he said that when it came to "delinquency, or educational achievement, or occupational success, or the likelihood of experiencing abuse and neglect . . . the two-biological-parent, married-couple home, in a stable marriage, is the best model from the child's point of view."

Finally, Blankenhorn attempted to justify efforts to restrict marriage to opposite-sex couples. They were effectively saving marriage from the process of "deinstitutionalization," he asserted, which he said was taking place as marriage was being redefined and in many cases simply ignored by single parents. The old rules, which barred same-sex couples from marrying, had made the institution stable, he argued. "The rules that govern the institution become less comprehensible and clear and . . . less authoritative. And when its structure becomes less stable, less able to give robust shape to the institution, it's like a—kind of a shrinking process. And as a result of deinstitutionalization—you don't have to think about marriage. You could think about, you know, a baseball team or a museum, or any—any institution. When you take away its rules and you weaken its structures, scholars say that you're seeing deinstitutionalization."

This view—that any change in the institution of marriage necessarily weakened it—was entirely tautological. Every change was labeled "deinstitutionalization" and by definition bad. However good it sounded on the surface, it proved nothing. It also failed to take into account, as Blankenhorn would soon concede on cross-examination, the many changes to marriage over the years (including greater rights for women and permitting interracial marriages).

Even before cross started, we believed Blankenhorn offered a very weak justification for excluding a new group of individuals—gays and lesbians—who wanted to marry and pour their hearts and souls into making their relationships work.

———

David's cross-examination continued the theme of his voir dire, emphasizing that Blankenhorn's direct testimony relied virtually exclusively on work done by other people, and that Blankenhorn was merely reporting on what selected scholars had said. The witness was initially reluctant to further admit his own lack of qualifications:

> Q: You're just a transmitter of the findings of these scholars, correct?
> A: Well, you're putting words in my mouth now.
> Q: No, sir.
> A: Yes, sir.

David then read Blankenhorn what the witness had admitted at his deposition:

> "I'm simply repeating things that they say. I can assure you, I'm not making any of this up on my own. These are not my own conclusions. I'm a transmitter here of findings for these eminent scholars."

The court, of course, did not need Blankenhorn to summarize what others had said. That such was the case was bad enough. That he initially resisted admitting it further reduced his credibility.

In addition, much of what Blankenhorn was repeating was now decades old and so could not take into account modern developments like the many same-sex couples who had become adoptive parents and the recent experiences of married gay and lesbian couples who had been raising children. In fact, as Blankenhorn admitted, virtually all of the research he quoted was based on comparisons of children in two-parent families headed by opposite-sex couples and single-parent families. Since two caring adults will usually be able to offer more to a child than one, any finding that argued that the best situation for children involved a mother and father in a stable home was mainly about arithmetic. It did not take into consideration the particular gender of the parents.

Moreover, Blankenhorn's conclusions were less nuanced than those reached by many of the experts he quoted and depended on his selective use of their findings. Scientists acknowledge complexity and the limitations of opinions and the importance of empirical testing. Advocates form opinions and often find support for those opinions in everything they see. But that kind of thinking is quite vulnerable to cross-examination.

David directed Blankenhorn to read aloud a paragraph he relied on from a book he had used as a source. The passage in question stated that children who grow up in single-parent homes are "worse off" than those raised in two-parent homes. "That is your understanding?" asked David. "Yes, sir," answered Blankenhorn.

"Now, did you read this entire chapter?" David continued.

"I read the entire book."

"Let me see if you remember reading the very next page, the first full paragraph," David said, and proceeded to read it aloud: "But are single motherhood and father absence, therefore, the root cause of child poverty, school failure, and juvenile delinquency? Our findings lead us to say no. While living with just one parent increases the risk of each of these negative outcomes, it is not the only or even the major cause of them."

As Blankenhorn became embarrassed, his desire to appear fair and reasonable caused him to try to give speeches rather than answer questions. This led Judge Walker, about ten minutes into David's cross, to admonish the witness:

THE COURT: Mr. Blankenhorn, counsel is entitled to an answer
   to his question.
THE WITNESS: May I ask a—
THE COURT: That's how this process works. There is a question
   and then there's an answer. The answer has to respond to the
   question.

The admonishment added to the witness's obvious discomfort and
desire to recover his standing. Soon thereafter Blankenhorn agreed:
"My answer to your question is that I believe that adopting same-sex
marriage would be likely to improve the well-being of gay and lesbian
households and their children." It was a powerful admission from the
defendants' chief witness. In fact, when David suggested that Blankenhorn believed that two biological parents made up the ideal family, the
witness had corrected him: "The studies show that adoptive parents,
because of the rigorous screening process that they undertake before
becoming adoptive parents, actually on some outcomes outstrip the
biological parents in terms of providing protective care for their
children."

That was also a very helpful answer to our case. "Yes, I was going to
come to that," David said, accepting an important and vital concession
for same-sex couples, "and I appreciate your getting there." Blankenhorn also agreed that there was no scientific evidence indicating that
children suffer from being raised by people of the same sex.

Blankenhorn's concessions were interspersed with evasiveness. For
example, when David asked him whether he knew of any social science
research that predicted that a law that opened marriage to same-sex
couples would cause any harm, Blankenhorn replied, "I know the answer. I cannot answer you accurately if the only words I'm allowed to
choose from is 'yes' or 'no.'" His evasiveness continued as he was
forced to retreat from his direct testimony and was confronted with
inconsistencies.

Blankenhorn believed that there were three "rules of the game" for
marriage: that marriage be between people of opposite genders, that it

be limited to just two people, and that the relationship involve sexual intercourse. One by one these "rules" fell by the wayside.

With respect to his "rule of opposites," Blankenhorn claimed not to be aware of the testimony his fellow expert witness for the defendants, Professor Young, had given in her deposition detailing societies where there were marriages between members of the same sex.

With respect to his "rule of two," Blankenhorn initially testified that over the last three hundred years "almost every single marriage has been between two people." He was then forced to admit that more than 80 percent of societies permit polygamy, and that he did not actually know, even approximately, what the percentage of polygamous marriages was. He only made things worse by trying to justify himself by asserting that polygamous marriages where a man had five wives at the same time were consistent with his "rule of two" if the man married his wives one at a time.

With respect to his "rule of sex," the witness first denied he was aware of any instances where prisoners or others who could not have sex were permitted to marry, calling such a situation "hypothetical":

> Q: Well, sir, you know perfectly well that these are not sort of just hypothetical cases. Correct, sir?
> A: No, sir.
> Q: You don't? You don't? Like this example of the incarcerated prisoner, you know perfectly well that that's a real example from a real court case, don't you, sir?
> A: No, sir. I do not.
> Q: You don't?
> A: Why would you try to put words in my mouth of that nature?

By now everyone in the courtroom knew what was coming next. David read from Blankenhorn's testimony at his deposition: "In recent years, there has been a growing permission on the part of courts to accept married couples who cannot have sexual intercourse. For example, when one spouse is in prison."

On occasion Blankenhorn's evasiveness provoked laughter from the audience. At one point, he complained, "It's actually not a laughing matter to me, Mr. Boies." "Mr. Boies is not laughing at you," Judge Walker interjected. "He's amused at the back-and-forth, as I think many of us who are observing this are."

Judge Walker generally listened to this testimony with forbearance, seemingly determined to give the defense every opportunity to make its case—even if that meant indulging a recalcitrant witness for hours on end. He did caution Blankenhorn early on that the court would weigh all the evidence presented, including "the demeanor of the witnesses. And the demeanor of the witnesses is sometimes gauged, importantly, by the responsiveness of the witness to the questions that he's asked." This caution undoubtedly increased the pressure on Blankenhorn.

Blankenhorn eventually admitted that none of the academics he cited—the genuine experts in the field—had predicted that same-sex marriage would damage heterosexual marriages. This was a key concession, because it supported our position that permitting same-sex marriage harmed no one.

But perhaps the most valuable testimony came at the end of a long and contentious cross-examination when Blankenhorn, after agreeing that equality and inclusiveness were core American values, agreed that "we would be more, emphasize more, American on the day we permitted same-sex marriage than we were on the day before."

By the end of his testimony, Blankenhorn had provided far more support for our case than he had for the defense. He had admitted that barring same-sex marriage harmed gays and lesbians and harmed children raised by gay and lesbian couples, that there was no evidence such a ban served any legitimate interest, and that the ban was inconsistent with core American values.

———

After two and a half weeks, the evidentiary phase of the trial ended in undramatic fashion as Judge Walker explained that he would grant both sides thirty days to submit more documents, and after that deadline he would study the entire record and then summon us back for closing arguments. His final, gracious words were "I would just like to take a moment to personally congratulate you and tell you what a good job you've all done."

After Judge Walker dismissed us, we shook hands with opposing counsel and left the courtroom. In the hallway a crowd of supporters waited, applauding and cheering as we emerged. There was considerable camaraderie and hugging. It is fair to say that all of us felt that we had put on a powerful, compelling case for an end to marriage discrimination against our clients and hundreds of thousands like them. Appeals were inevitable, no matter what Judge Walker decided, and we still had the challenge of the closing argument, but we felt that we had provided a sound foundation for what was to follow.

NINE

David's Cross-Examination

Theodore B. Olson

Trials can often be exercises in tedium. Lawyers are not genetically bred to be short of wind or concise. Determined to develop every scrap of evidence, with ample redundancy, they tend to grind away for hours and sometimes even days at a time, gnawing on a witness like a dog with a cherished bone.

Exciting, game-changing moments seldom occur in real trials the way they invariably do in movies starring Tom Cruise, Richard Gere, and the like. But when they do, they often take place during cross-examination, when a lawyer has the opportunity to convert harmful testimony into a game-changer.

That actually did happen during the *Perry* trial. That is not to say that we would have lost the case were it not for the points scored during David's cross-examinations. We had overwhelming evidence on our side, balanced against the scant support that had been offered by our opponents. But in my judgment the fireworks, when they did come, sealed the victory for us. And it was marvelous to observe.

Being a trial lawyer is hard work. It involves long hours, dealing with enormous pressure and constant stress, and the capacity to withstand surprise, criticism, public humiliation from judges, and the occasional crushing defeat. Very few lawyers can successfully deal with all that, and among the few who can, a genuinely outstanding trial lawyer is, if not exactly a myth, fairly close to one.

David is one of those blue diamonds, gifted with a unique

combination of charisma, intelligence, mental agility, spontaneity, focus, energy, and indefatigability, to mention just a few of his qualities.

The fact that he has also overcome dyslexia is by now well known, as his career and abilities have been written about often, most recently in Malcolm Gladwell's book about that other David, *David and Goliath,* and he himself has discussed publicly the nature of that challenge, what it has meant to him, and how he has adapted to it.

David's dyslexia does not prevent him from reading. He has clearly conquered that part of his condition, and when he prepares for trial he reads prodigiously and with intense concentration, absorbing the relevant material thoroughly and storing it seemingly verbatim in his memory.

Nor does David's dyslexia affect his ability to write. He crafts legal arguments that are seamless, precise, orderly, and compelling. His learning disability has, if anything, helped his mind remember, organize, sharpen, and produce cogent arguments distilled to their essence.

But David really excels when he speaks. His style is so focused that the listener is unconsciously drawn into the vortex. He presents his arguments in skillfully organized syllogisms that march from facially unassailable premise to seemingly incontrovertible conclusion. Having been drawn into that current, one has little choice but to become convinced. I have often been so captivated by what David is saying, somewhat mesmerized by his arguments, that I find myself mentally nodding in agreement—even when I am on the other side of a case. Needless to say, in those circumstances I manage to repress any subliminal tendency to manifest even the slightest hint that I might be persuaded by the logic or sensibility of his position.

David was a great colleague throughout the four-plus years of the Proposition 8 case. We faced considerable challenges and many difficult decisions, and, naturally, consulted and debated internally about them. Yet somehow we never disagreed about strategy, timing, or approach at the end of our deliberative process. We worked together almost as if we were brothers, or even twins. Often I seemed able to anticipate what he was going to say or do. By the same token he often seemed to read my mind. I found that remarkable, given that we were such robust opponents during the 2000 election recount saga.

Cross-examination is the toughest test of a trial lawyer's mettle, and often the best trial lawyers are only competent in this area. An incompetent lawyer will fail to weaken, discredit, or soften a witness or identify the weaknesses in adverse testimony. At the other extreme, some lawyers may attack a witness with such excessive aggression, sarcasm, or hostility that the judge or jury winds up identifying with the witness and angry at the lawyer. Sometimes cross-examination serves only to reinforce a witness's evidence, and the lawyer is left to back away in embarrassment.

David is better at cross-examination than any trial lawyer I have ever seen. He seems to have the perfect combination of instinct, experience, tenacity, and patience. His cross-examination of General William Westmoreland early in his career in the general's libel suit against CBS is still legendary, as is his cross-examination of Bill Gates when he was representing the United States in its antitrust case against Microsoft in 1998. There have been many other such cases, and aspiring trial lawyers could profit by taking a law school course consisting exclusively of David's classic cross-examinations. That may not guarantee them success, but it would be a step in the right direction.

Volumes have been written about the art of cross-examination. They typically offer conventional wisdom: questions never to ask, styles to avoid, safe lines of attack, and various shibboleths well known to practitioners. But as with many other crafts that involve instinct, art, and innate skills, each lawyer adept at cross-examination has his own style, much like a classical pianist or a matador.

The *Perry* case was a paradigmatic example of David's cross-examination skills. First, his questioning of several of our opponents' proposed expert witnesses in depositions prior to the trial so thoroughly weakened their testimony that most of them were withdrawn as witnesses on the eve of trial. Our opponents claimed that their suddenly shrinking witness list was a response to Judge Walker's plan to stream a video of the trial to a few other federal courthouses (and post it on YouTube), because the witnesses were afraid of harassment and intimidation if their testimony was to be widely disseminated. But that excuse strained credulity, to put it mildly, as these were paid expert witnesses who had written about and lectured on the subjects about which they were expected to testify. None of them had shunned publicity in the past, their views were widely known, and they were all aware from the outset that they would give their testimony in open court in a highly public trial. They had likewise consented to videotaped depositions that were also intended to be made publicly available. Finally, of course, the Supreme Court had halted Judge Walker's plan to stream the proceedings outside the courtroom during the trial, so they no longer had to fear that exposure when the trial officially began.

In fact, the only thing that had changed since these experts agreed to testify was that they had been subject to thorough, probing cross-examinations. Some were conducted by other members of our trial team, who had done superb work exploiting weaknesses in their testimony; some were conducted by David, who had succeeded in undermining their confidence and softening their spines. Were they now to walk into the courtroom, raise their hands for the oath, and take their seat in that witness box, they would face cross-examination by David. If he were to do to them what he had done to many others before them, it would be not only embarrassing but damaging to their reputations. Most decided that it wasn't worth the risk. Let someone else walk into that minefield.

David has said that cross-examination is the true test during a trial. A witness is alone up there on a witness stand. He or she does not know what to expect, has sworn to tell the truth, and must answer question after question after question. The right to confront adverse witnesses in a criminal case is guaranteed by the Sixth Amendment to the Constitution for a very good reason: It is the acid test of the adversary system, which is at the heart of our system of justice. It is one thing to make assertions; it is quite another to have to defend them on a witness stand.

David has many special approaches and techniques, including meticulous preparation, and will, I would hope, expound on them in a book dedicated to that subject someday. But among his most notable skills are patience and focus. He can't be brushed aside or worn down by an evasive witness. He will calmly persevere, certain of what he is going for, and he will remember exactly, literally verbatim, what a witness said in answer to a prior question an hour before, several hours earlier, or even the previous day. He has an avuncular style—gracious, polite, respectful—but intense and relentless nevertheless.

He can change the subject suddenly, catching a witness off balance, and yet return to that subject at a point when the witness has gone on to think about something else. He is adroit, quick, and hypnotic, and is so disarmingly easygoing, agreeable, and charming that it is easy to see, in retrospect, how a witness could slip or slide into a position from which there is no escape. But if you are that witness, even if you sense it is coming, it is like sinking into quicksand. The harder one struggles, the more powerful the undertow.

David knows that most witnesses want to be liked and to appear fair and reasonable. Otherwise, of course, they look defensive, stubborn, truculent, and unreliable, which undermines their credibility and effectively enables David to have made his point. But if they do try to present themselves as reasonable, flexible, and decent, David will gently take them to places they had no intention of going.

Of the two witnesses who remained willing to testify against the plaintiffs in the *Perry* case, David Blankenhorn was the most important, as he was the "expert" on marriage whom our opponents had relied on the most. Again and again in the pretrial proceedings and in their opening statement, Cooper and his team relied on and cited Blankenhorn. By the end of the trial, he was all they had left. And by the end of David's cross-examination, not only did they not have Blankenhorn, we did.

We have discussed the Blankenhorn testimony in great detail and described how he wound up being a witness who supported virtually everything we could have asked for in a witness *for* marriage equality. It was a remarkable transformation, and it was a special thrill for me to have a seat beside David as he made it happen. I won't repeat that process, but just summarize what he accomplished in his few hours with the witness.

David first undermined Blankenhorn's qualifications as a credible expert witness in this trial. Judge Walker ultimately determined that Blankenhorn was both unqualified and unreliable—and thus effectively of no affirmative use to the defense team. David challenged his credibility by patiently taking Blankenhorn through a recitation of his credentials, establishing that: (1) Blankenhorn's thesis for his master's degree was "a study of two cabinetmakers' unions in nineteenth-century Britain"—not exactly the stuff from which a marriage equality expert in the twenty-first century would be made; (2) he had never taught a course in any college or university on marriage, fatherhood, or family structure; (3) he had no degree in psychology, psychiatry, or anthropology; (4) he had never taught any course at any college or university; and (5) he had never conducted a scientific study on the effects of permitting same-sex marriage in any jurisdiction. Since this was a trial without a jury, Judge Walker allowed Blankenhorn to continue to testify, but his value as a witness—and his self-confidence—was already at this point severely undermined. Something like the Stockholm syndrome took over at this point, and Blankenhorn submitted to the cross-examiner's leadership.

At times Blankenhorn attempted resistance as David took him through his methodical, substantive cross-examination, but he was ultimately led to acknowledge that despite having testified that children were better off being raised by biological parents, in fact "two adoptive parents raising a child from birth . . . actually on some outcomes *outstrip* the biological parents in terms of providing protective care for their children." He likewise acknowledged that he was not aware of *any* studies showing that children raised from birth by a gay or lesbian couple have worse outcomes than children raised from birth by two biological parents. He then conceded that "adopting same-sex marriage would be likely to improve the well-being of gay and lesbian households and their children." This was followed by a concession that the "principle of equal human dignity must apply to gay and lesbian persons," and we as a nation "would be more, emphasize more, American on the day we permitted same-sex marriages than we were on the day before."

To cap it off, toward the end of his testimony on cross-examination,

Blankenhorn reiterated aloud his agreement with a statement he had written:

> Gay marriage would be a victory for the worthy ideas of tolerance and inclusion. It would likely decrease the number of those in society who tend to be viewed warily as "other" and increase the number who are accepted as part of "us." In that respect, gay marriage would be a victory for, and another key expansion of, the American idea.

And:

> Gay marriage might contribute over time to a decline in anti-gay prejudice as well as, more specifically, a reduction in anti-gay hate crimes.

We could hardly have written statements more central to the themes of equality, decency, and respect that we had set out to prove during this trial. If Blankenhorn had been our witness, his statements would not have had nearly the impact that they did coming from the lead witness for the opponents of same-sex marriage. David's cross-examination skillfully painted a picture with our opponent's brush that would live permanently as an endorsement of marriage equality.

TEN

Ted's Closing

David Boies

I n every contest of persuasion there comes the moment of truth. For a political candidate it is election day. For a salesman, it is when it is time to ask for the order. For a trial lawyer, it is the closing argument.

A closing argument seeks to persuade a judge to adopt the legal standards that the lawyer has argued for, to find facts that the lawyer believes he has proved, and to hold, based on those facts and legal standards, that his side prevails. Everything that a lawyer does at trial, and everything that he does to prepare for trial, is, or at least should be, directed toward this moment.

The *Perry* closing argument was heard on June 16, 2010, almost five months after the last witness testified. During that time the parties had worked hard, analyzing the thousands of pages of trial transcripts, deposition excerpts, and documents that had been admitted as evidence. They also reread relevant cases and researched possible new points to make. Prior to appearing in court each side had submitted lengthy written arguments to Judge Walker, drawing attention to key matters of law and important pieces of evidence that we believed supported our position, and challenging the law and evidence on which the opposition relied. Judge Walker had devoted weeks to studying those submissions, as well as his own notes from the trial and those of his law clerks. Before the final arguments were to be presented, he gave each side written questions designed to clarify their positions and views of the evidence, which had been answered in written submissions. By the time June 16 came, we were all more than ready for our moment of truth.

———

As Ted and I walked to court that morning, it was impossible to ignore the enormity of what was about to happen. In a little more than an hour we would ask Judge Walker to do what no judge had ever done—to declare that the right to marry the person you loved, regardless of gender or sexual orientation, was a fundamental right guaranteed by the U.S. Constitution.

We were confident that our team had established an overwhelming record supporting what we needed to prevail in our contention that marriage was a fundamental right, that depriving gay and lesbian Americans of that right seriously harmed them and their children, and that banning marriage equality benefited no one. And I knew that no lawyer was as well prepared to present our case, and to answer what we knew would be the judge's probing questions about it, as Ted. Almost half a century of practicing law, countless oral arguments in state and federal courts across the country—including more than fifty arguments in the U.S. Supreme Court itself—more than four years of reading and rereading every prior case and each element of our evidence, and weeks of writing, rewriting, and practicing the points we would emphasize had prepared him for this moment.

Still, as we made our way through the demonstrators and camera crews that filled the plaza outside the courthouse, we felt the weight of what was at stake. Entering Judge Walker's courtroom, we exchanged greetings with many of the courtroom regulars, whom we had not seen in months. While the opponents of marriage equality were well represented among the demonstrators outside, inside the courtroom most of those who had stood in long lines to get a seat were supporters of our cause. And as would become particularly clear a few hours later, this was as true for the overflow room as for the courtroom itself. (Because people who wanted to be present outnumbered the seats available in his courtroom, Judge Walker had arranged for a closed-circuit video of the argument, as he had during the trial itself, to be transmitted live to another courtroom.)

When Judge Walker took the bench at 10:03 A.M., the courtroom's low hum was immediately replaced by silence. Walker was a commanding but not intimidating presence. Although he had conducted the trial without showing any bias, we could tell that he was skeptical about our opponents' claim that same-sex marriage posed a threat to heterosexual marriage. He did, however, seem open to their concern about society's limited experience with marriage equality. And he was certainly focused on determining the proper role for the courts to play in this whole matter. Because plaintiffs bear the burden of proof, their counsel has the advantage of speaking both first and last. As Ted rose to begin, he spoke not just for the two couples we were representing, or for our team, but for millions of Americans who were suffering from discrimination. Much later a Supreme Court justice would refer to the forty thousand children in California who lived with same-sex couples and ask, "The voice of those children is important in this case, don't you think?" On June 16, 2010, Ted gave those children a voice.

He began by reminding everyone of what was at stake in *Perry:*

> **This case is about marriage and equality. The fundamental constitutional right to marry has been taken away from the plaintiffs and tens of thousands of similarly situated Californians. Their state has rewritten its constitution in order to place them into a special disfavored category where their most intimate personal relationships are not valid, not recognized, and second-rate. Their state has stigmatized them as unworthy of marriage, different, and less respected.**

He then walked the court through the evidence that had been presented at trial from experts in psychology, sociology, economics, and history that detailed the damage done to gay and lesbian couples, and their children, by depriving them of the right to marry, and that demonstrated that marriage equality would not harm the institution of marriage in any way. He also described how the defendants' strategy at the beginning of the trial had been to try to shift away from a blatantly antigay theme and to rely instead on making a case for the supposed harm that same-sex unions would pose to "the institution of marriage." Ted quoted Chuck Cooper as having promised, "Mr. Blankenhorn will testify that [same-sex marriage] will likely lead to very real social harms, such as lower marriage rates and high rates of divorce and nonmarital cohabitation, with more children raised outside the marriage and separated from at least one of their parents." That testimony had not materialized and the defendants had been reduced, Ted noted, to admitting that "they actually had no idea and certainly no evidence that any of their prognostications would come to pass if Proposition 8 were not enacted."

If judges never asked questions, an argument could simply be written and delivered as scripted. But judges do interrupt to dispute or ask for clarification, which, while challenging for lawyers, is good for the process. To prepare for Judge Walker's queries, Ted had spent hours in so-called moot courts being grilled by members of the team who played the role of the court. The importance of that preparation was soon evident, for Ted was only a few minutes into his argument when Judge Walker began to pepper him with questions.

With respect to our argument that the defendants had presented no evidence of any harm done to marriage as an institution, Judge Walker asked, "But it is the plaintiffs, after all, who bear the burden of proof. Do they not, Mr. Olson?"

Ted agreed but emphasized two points. First, in order to justify a discriminatory law, the proponents had to demonstrate that some real harm would occur if that particular law weren't enacted and enforced. Simply believing a harm might occur is not a justification. Second, Ted said, "The overwhelming evidence in this case proves that we do know. And the fact is that allowing persons to marry someone of the same sex will not, in the slightest, deter heterosexuals from marrying, from staying married, or from having babies."

An important question in every case challenging a state law under the due process and equal protection clauses of the federal constitution is how much deference to give to the decision of the state's voters or legislators. Most cases apply the so-called rational basis test: If there is any rational basis, any reasonably debatable proposition, supporting the state law, it must be upheld. However, where a state law adversely affects a group or class that has been historically marginalized and suffered discrimination, a state is required to prove more to justify continuing to discriminate. Judge Walker pressed Ted on this point, asking if there was any support for applying the rational basis test. No, Ted replied. Because of the history of discrimination against gays, Supreme Court precedent required defendants to meet a higher standard. Moreover, even if the lower standard applied, "As the Supreme Court said in the *Romer* case, there has to be a rational objective that the government is seeking to sustain, and that the measure itself will advance that rational proposition"—in short, that the discriminatory provision enacted actually served to accomplish some legitimate goal. Ted reminded the judge that even in a rational basis context, the Supreme Court had ruled in a case involving housing rules affecting disabled persons that "mere negative attitudes, fear or unsubstantiated factors or assertions won't be sufficiently cognizable."

Coming at the issue from a different direction, Judge Walker asked, "Doesn't California accommodate gays and lesbians by providing domestic partnership rights which are essentially all the rights associated with marriage? Why isn't that sufficient accommodation?"

As Kris and Sandy had explained, the status of domestic partners was dramatically different from marriage for them and their children. Simply put, marriage and domestic partnerships were separate and unequal, and that fact was at the heart of our case. As Ted explained:

> Marriage is the most important relation in life. . . . It is the foundation of society. It is essential to the orderly pursuit of happiness. It's a right of privacy older than the Bill of Rights and older than our political parties. One of the liberties protected by the due process clause. A right of intimacy to the degree of being sacred. And a liberty right equally available to a person in a homosexual relationship as to heterosexual persons. That's the *Lawrence v. Texas* case. Marriage, the Supreme

Court has said again and again, is a component of liberty, privacy, association, spirituality, and autonomy. It is a right possessed by persons of different races, by persons in prison, and by individuals who are delinquent in paying child support.

In contrast, Ted noted, domestic partnerships were, and were designed to be, a second-class institution that stigmatized gay and lesbian citizens and their relationships. The very reason this case was so hard fought was that both sides recognized that domestic partnerships were entirely different from marriage.

"Would this case be different," Judge Walker continued, "if California had never permitted same-sex marriage?" Ted replied that a ban on same-sex marriage would still be unconstitutional, but that the case would be different. When the U.S. Supreme Court in *Romer* struck down a Colorado initiative that invalidated local ordinances prohibiting discrimination based on sexual orientation, the Court held that it was significant that Colorado was taking away a right that had been previously granted.

Judge Walker was not convinced. "So," he asked, "the facts are stronger simply because there was a period of time, albeit six months, in which the State of California permitted same-sex marriage?" When Ted replied, "That is correct, Your Honor," and began to explain why, the judge interrupted: "What kind of a constitutional system is it that because of a California Supreme Court decision, which had a shelf life of six months, that that creates a greater entitlement than if that right had never existed in the first place?"

This was complicated territory. Our primary argument was that a ban on same-sex marriage was unconstitutional under the due process and equal protection clauses—and that this was true regardless of whether a state had ever previously permitted those marriages. In the earlier marriage equality case of *Loving v. Virginia*, the Supreme Court struck down Virginia's ban on interracial marriages; it didn't matter that the state had never permitted such marriages. We believed the same principle was true in our case. However, we also believed (as later proved to be true when we reached the U.S. court of appeals) that a court might prefer to decide this case on the narrower ground that, having recognized the right to gender-neutral marriage, California could not then take away that right without justification.

Although we wanted to stay focused on our main argument, we didn't want to deny ourselves any alternatives. Keeping those options in balance is difficult under the easiest of circumstances, which these certainly were not, given Judge Walker's aggressive questioning.

Ted began his response by observing, "The California Supreme Court, I think, would say that we didn't invent that right. We determined, when it was brought to us, that the California constitution, which we are not changing, we are interpreting, contains that right." Previously he had noted that in virtually every major civil rights case, including *Brown v. Board of Education,* the Supreme Court had enforced rights that had previously been denied. The fact that a right has only recently been enforced does not in any way diminish the importance of that right, and in *Romer* the Supreme Court did not think it was relevant whether the rights secured by local ordinances were or were not recent.

Ted summed up our position by arguing that our claim "is a more forceful fact because of the *Romer* case . . . and the taking away of rights," but if we were litigating the issues in another state without California's history we would be making the same basic argument that bans on same-sex marriage, like bans on interracial marriage, were unconstitutional, regardless of a state's prior practices.

Judge Walker also asked about our reliance on *Lawrence v. Texas,* pointing out that the statute involved in that case was a criminal statute. When Ted agreed that was true, Judge Walker said, "The denial of the right to marriage of same-sex couples doesn't have any criminal sanction. There isn't any sanction that attaches to it. It's simply a denial of access to the estate of marriage. That's not a criminal penalty."

The unconstitutionality of discrimination did not depend on whether the discrimination carried with it criminal sanctions, replied Ted. *Brown v. Board of Education* was not a criminal case. While the state law in *Loving* did include criminal sanctions, the Court struck down not only the criminal sanctions but the ban on interracial marriage itself. *Romer,* too, was a civil, not a criminal case. Ted also quoted from the *Lawrence* opinion directly to make his point:

> "Our laws and our tradition afford constitutional protection to personal decisions relating to marriage, procreation, contraception, family relationship, child rearing, and education." That's not a complete list. And then the Court goes on to say, "Persons in a homosexual relationship may seek autonomy for these purposes just as heterosexual persons do."

As I listened to the argument, and to Ted responding to the judge's questions with just the right citations to just the right Supreme Court precedents at just the right time, I thought again how lucky we were to have him presenting our case. Ted is an exceptionally gifted and experienced oral advocate, but an argument in a case like this requires even more: It requires a lawyer who will work incredibly hard (harder than anyone who has not done it at this level can imagine) to do the preparation necessary to fully employ those gifts and that experience. Perhaps only Olympic athletes spend more time preparing (and for a briefer performance) than trial lawyers.

To underscore his points, Ted played excerpts from the video recordings that were made of the witnesses' trial testimony. One of the most dramatic moments of this part of the closing came when he played excerpts from our four plaintiffs' explanations of why they wanted to get married, what the right to marriage meant to them, and how they and their children felt when their right to marry was withdrawn. It was impossible not to be affected by their accounts.

Ted also played key excerpts from the testimony both of our experts and of the defendants' expert David Blankenhorn. He began by noting:

> We are not . . . just talking about the couples who wish to get married. We are talking about their children. In 2005, there were thirty-seven thousand of California's children living in households headed by same-sex couples. The evidence was

uncontradicted during this trial and overwhelming that the
lives of these children would be better if they were living in a
marital household. Even Mr. Blankenhorn, the proponents'
witness, proponents' principal witness, agreed with that proposition.

In further excerpts cited by Ted, Blankenhorn admitted other ways
our clients were harmed by the marriage ban. Finally, Ted presented
the testimony in which Blankenhorn agreed that, given our American
ideals of tolerance, inclusiveness, and equality, "We will be more, emphasize more, American the day we permit same-sex marriage."

Perhaps Judge Walker's most important questions were these:

So, when is it appropriate for the judiciary to weigh in on
legal and constitutional questions that may touch on sensitive
social issues? What are the criteria that a court should look at
in deciding whether or not it should render a decision that a
certain right or lack of right implicates constitutional considerations? When does it become ripe for the court to weigh in on
these issues?

In a sense these questions spoke to the core of Ted's argument: If
you have a fundamental right (to vote, to go to school, to marry), or
even rights perhaps not so fundamental, a state cannot discriminate
against certain of its citizens without an adequate countervailing justification. Here both sides had agreed on the fundamental importance
of the right to marry. The only question was whether California could
limit that right based on gender and sexual orientation.

Once it was established that depriving gay and lesbian citizens of
the right to marry seriously harmed them and their children, and that
such a ban was not justified by any countervailing state interest, the
court was obligated to act. It is why we have a written constitution and
an independent judiciary to enforce it. Ted quoted from a Supreme
Court case from 1886 striking down a San Francisco law prohibiting
Chinese Americans from operating a laundry: "The very idea that a

person would be denied a material right essential to the enjoyment of life"—which certainly applied to marriage—"seems to be intolerable in any country where freedom prevails, as being the very essence of slavery."

Ted also directly addressed the question of whether "we've always done it that way" or "it's the traditional definition of marriage" could be considered an acceptable reason to reject or delay enforcement of a right to marriage equality for gay and lesbian citizens:

> It's not a reason. You can't have continued discrimination in public schools because you have always done it that way. You can't have continued discrimination between races on the basis of marriage because you have always done it that way. That line of reasoning would have prevented the *Loving* marriage. It would have justified racially segregated schools and maintaining subordinate status for married women.

Ted also emphasized that the fact that many people strongly objected to same-sex marriage on religious grounds could likewise not be used as a justification against marriage equality. The Constitution protects their right to their beliefs, but at the same time it forbids them from imposing their religious beliefs on others. Ted noted that in *Loving* "the argument was made that it's God's will that people of different races not be married" and that although in 1967 many people "honestly felt that it was wrong to mix the races," that view could not warrant a state's prohibiting interracial marriage. Returning to California's Proposition 8 ban on same-sex marriages, he concluded:

> The evidence is overwhelming that it imposes great social harm on individuals who are our equals. They are members of our society. They pay their taxes. They want to form a household. They want to raise their children in happiness and in the same way that their neighbors do.
>
> We are imposing great damage on them by . . . saying they are different and they cannot have the happiness, they cannot

have the privacy, they cannot have the liberty, they cannot have the intimate association in the context of a marriage that the rest of our citizens do. . . . If we had a reason, a really good reason for inflicting all of that harm, that might be another matter, but there is no reason. . . . We have improved the institution of marriage when we allowed interracial couples to get married.

We have improved the institution of marriage when we allowed women to be equal partners in the marital relationship. We have improved the institution of marriage when we didn't put artificial barriers based upon race. And we will improve the institution of marriage and we will be more American, according to Mr. Blankenhorn, when we eliminate this terrible stigma.

Ted was followed by Terry Stewart, counsel for the City and County of San Francisco, who supported the case for marriage equality. An experienced lawyer who had spent years fighting for the rights of gays and lesbians and others, Terry was an effective and passionate advocate. She began by emphasizing the harm caused by Proposition 8 and that the extent of that harm had to be weighed in any consideration of whether the ban had a rational basis. To emphasize her point, she quoted a holding from a U.S. Supreme Court case striking down a Texas statute barring undocumented children from attending public schools: "In determining the rationality of the statute, we may appropriately take into account its costs to the nation and to the innocent children who are its victims."

Terry cited the evidence that the public discrimination and stigmatization effectively legitimized by Proposition 8 not only encouraged bullying and hate crimes but caused emotional distress to gay people. She noted that "the rates of suicide or suicide attempts are higher among lesbian and gay youth," that in California schools "over 200,000 incidents of such bullying based on sexual orientation occur year in, year out," and that "hate crimes based on sexual orientation" had been the second-highest category of hate crimes since 1995.

To Judge Walker's question on whether bullying and hate crimes "depend upon motives that the law really can't change," she responded that she did not contend that changing the law would eliminate the problem entirely, but reminded him that the evidence of both experts and public officials at trial had been "that when you have structural stigma" such as Proposition 8 "it does send the message and the message translates into things like hate crimes."

Shortly after Terry finished, Judge Walker took an early lunch break to give Chuck Cooper an opportunity to prepare his response. Cooper faced a difficult task. Ted had been thorough and effective. Though extremely talented, Cooper, who was burdened with a weaker argument, would be hard-pressed to overcome what we had accomplished in the morning. If we had been engaged in, say, a college debate, which is simply a contest to determine the best presentation, my money would still have been on Ted. More important, what mattered most here was who had the facts and law on their side, and the evidence at trial had eviscerated each legal theory the defendants had advanced.

Still, Cooper soldiered on. When it came his turn to make his presentation that afternoon he advanced five basic themes. He began by observing that "until quite recently it was an accepted truth for almost everyone who ever lived in any society in which marriage existed that there could be marriages only between participants of different sex."

Second, he stressed the fundamental importance of marriage, couching his argument in dramatic terms: "Without the marital relationship, Your Honor, society would come to an end." His explanation for the significance of marriage was that it encouraged what he described as "responsible procreation":

> And the historical record leaves no doubt, Your Honor, none whatever, that the central purpose of marriage in virtually all societies and at all times has been to channel potentially procreative sexual relationships into enduring stable unions to increase the likelihood that any offspring will be raised by the man and woman who brought them into the world.

Third, Cooper argued that because a person's sexual orientation was not "immutable," and because gay citizens had political power, all that was required to uphold Proposition 8 was that it have a rational purpose.

Fourth, because same-sex marriages were a relatively recent phenomenon, it was impossible to know how they would ultimately affect the institution of heterosexual marriages. It was therefore rational for a state to wait until more evidence of their consequences was available before permitting same-sex marriage.

Fifth, Cooper argued that courts should not use the Constitution to inject themselves into divisive political debates concerning "social issues."

Notably, he did not dispute that preventing gay and lesbian couples from marrying seriously harmed them and the children they were raising.

The strength—and weakness—of Cooper's closing was that he stuck to his five themes in response to virtually every question Judge Walker posed. His strength was his consistency. His weakness was that none of his themes answered many of the court's questions.

Judge Walker seemed skeptical about the claim that the only purpose of marriage was to benefit society by encouraging responsible procreation. As he put it, "The state doesn't withhold the right to marriage to people who are unable to produce children of their own." When Cooper concurred with that observation, the judge replied, "Well, then, the state must have some interest wholly apart from procreation."

Cooper now disagreed, arguing that the fact that states "haven't required procreation of marital couples in no way eliminates the procreative purpose of marriage." He explained that it was sufficient that the state was increasing the likelihood that children were produced in a relationship where their parents had an obligation to care for them.

Judge Walker later asked, "Why isn't the limitation on marriage for gay couples and lesbian couples similarly at war with their desires to raise children, raise their own children in the context of a marriage partnership?"

Cooper's answer, which was striking but consistent with his themes, was that because only heterosexual couples were likely to engage in "irresponsible procreation," they were the only ones who needed to be "channeled" into marriage. "For a same-sex couple to procreate it, by definition, has to be responsible. It can't be by accident. That's the key point."

This response prompted Judge Walker to ask, "What does the evidence show that the procreative function of marriage was a rationale of the voters in enacting Proposition 8? What's the evidence on that, the evidence in this record?"

Cooper referred in response to some of the official ballot arguments and official advocacy materials used by the ProtectMarriage.com groups that referred generally to parenting and "a loving environment for the raising up of children," but that conspicuously did not mention "responsible procreation" or make the kind of argument Cooper was making in his closing argument. The voters would never have understood it. So Cooper segued instead into his rational basis argument, that he did not need to prove what actually motivated the voters, only that some rational theory might have supported Proposition 8's adoption.

He discussed the factors that lead courts to reject rational basis review and apply a heightened level of scrutiny. "We have never disputed and we have offered to stipulate that gays and lesbians have been the victims of a long and shameful history of discrimination." However, he argued that "a history of discrimination is not by itself sufficient to warrant heightened judicial scrutiny," but immutability and political powerlessness are also required. He noted that "the Ninth Circuit in the *High Tech Gays* case said, unequivocally, 'sexual orientation is not an immutable characteristic.'" (In that case an organization called High Tech Gays had failed to overturn a government policy that barred the hiring of gay workers based on the belief that they could be blackmailed and thereby posed a security risk.) Cooper also disputed the contention that gays lacked political power, "especially as reflected in the extraordinary difference in the legal landscape today and twenty years ago with respect to protections."

Throughout Cooper's argument, Judge Walker asked questions such as "What does the evidence show?" and "Who was the witness who offered the testimony?" and "What's the evidence of that?"

Cooper had difficulty with these questions. When he stated that "responsible procreation is really at the heart of society's interest in regulating marriage," Walker pressed him to point to testimony in the case. Cooper could only identify authorities (including Blackstone, the author of the eighteenth-century law dictionary) who, the judge pointed out, had not testified. "But, Your Honor, you don't have to have evidence for this from these authorities. This is in the cases themselves. The cases recognize this one after another."

The startled judge asked, "I don't have to have evidence?"

Cooper's inability to cite trial testimony underscored the exasperation he must have felt with their trial record. Earlier in the argument, he expressed regret for ever having said "I don't know" when asked months earlier what effect same-sex marriage would have on opposite-sex marriage. "I don't know how many times, Your Honor," he admitted, "I had wished I could have those three words back."

Cooper seemed to get the most traction with Judge Walker with his final theme—that the courts should not inject themselves into the ongoing political debate over marriage equality. Cooper quoted a passage from a California court decision refusing to recognize gay marriages that, he said, went "to the heart of our submission": "It is the proper role of the legislature, not the court, to fashion laws that serve competing public policies. The legislative process involves setting priorities, making difficult decisions, making imperfect decisions, and approaching problems incrementally."

Cooper observed that the political debate concerning the definition and future of marriage, and the effort to balance competing views and considerations, was "at work in this state. And it's at work elsewhere in this country. . . . There is a debate about the morals, the practicalities, and the wisdom of this issue that really goes to the nature of our culture. And the Constitution should allow that debate to go forward among the people."

As Cooper returned to his seat, Ted rose for his rebuttal. He worked efficiently, dismantling Cooper's arguments like an expert shooter hitting one clay pigeon after another. At various points in his rebuttal, he touched on all the key themes. He dismissed the idea that history supported limiting marriage to heterosexual relationships by noting that cases defining fundamental civil rights for African Americans, women, and others had routinely changed what had historically once been acceptable practices. Indeed, in many other respects society had come to recognize that the bias against gay and lesbian citizens, which was at the heart of restrictions on same-sex marriage, was no longer justified. "It's no longer against the law to work for the federal government," Ted pointed out. "Psychiatrists have changed their view about homosexuality. People no longer think it's a disorder, or anything like that . . . and people have begun to understand . . . that all of those horrible taboos are not justified in fact. And the stories, some of which were in the ads which were supporting Proposition 8, are no longer true. So, of course, people are thinking, 'Well, if these are our fellow citizens and they don't present a risk to us, they are not damaging, they are just like us, why shouldn't we start talking about marriage?'"

Responding to Cooper's argument that the purpose of marriage was responsible procreation, Ted reminded Judge Walker that on fourteen different occasions the Supreme Court had ruled that marriage was a fundamental right. "This is an individual constitutional right," he stressed. "And every Supreme Court decision says that it's a right of persons. Not the right of California to channel those of us who live in California into certain activities or in a certain way."

Ted also explored the further implications of Cooper's argument. "If it's the state's interest in procreation that animates the right to marriage, what if the state changes its mind? . . . I don't think anyone here would agree that the state could then cut off the right to marry. Because it is an individual right of privacy, liberty, association. And that's what it is. So the state can't put the switch on and the switch off, because it's not the state's right. It's the individual's right."

During his argument Ted had quoted from Justice Stevens's dissent in *Bowers*. He now cited another portion of that dissent: "'Individual decisions by married persons concerning the intimacies of their physical relationship even when not intended to produce offspring are a form of liberty protected by the Due Process Clause of the Fourteenth Amendment.'"

Ted pointed out that neither of the two exhibits that Cooper had produced in response to the judge's question about whether the procreative function of marriage was a rationale of the voters in enacting Proposition 8 actually mentioned procreation—and neither did the official guide that explained the proposition to voters. He also argued that the *High Tech Gays* case on which Cooper had repeatedly relied had been decided in 1990, and had depended on the Supreme Court's opinion in *Bowers,* which was binding precedent at the time. However, *Bowers* had since been overruled:

> *Bowers v. Hardwick* isn't anything that you can rely on, in the Ninth Circuit or anywhere else. The *High Tech Gays* case was superseded by *Hernandez-Montiel,* which is a 1999 decision. And on page 1093, I'll just read one sentence. "Sexual orientation and sexual identity are immutable. They are so fundamental to one's identity that a person should not be required to abandon them."
>
> If we're going to have a Ninth Circuit precedent that would be guidance for Your Honor, that's the case.

With respect to the argument that permitting same-sex marriage might somehow harm heterosexual marriage, Ted stressed that all of the evidence that had been presented at trial was to the contrary, that the experience of jurisdictions that had adopted marriage equality was to the contrary, and that the defendants could not identify what possible harm there might be, let alone provide any evidence of it. He also observed that the defendants' expert, Mr. Blankenhorn, had admitted that any evidence of a weakening of the institution of marriage in recent decades could be attributed to no-fault divorce and other social developments among heterosexuals. It had nothing to do with the prospect of gays and lesbians getting married.

Ted reminded the Court that *Romer* had held that "'under the lowest standard of review, you have to prove you have a legitimate interest and that the object,' Proposition 8 in this case, 'advances that legitimate interest.'" The defendants had not met, or even tried to meet, this requirement:

> You have to have a reason. And you have to have a reason
> that's real. Not a post hoc justification. Not speculation. Not
> built on stereotypes. And not hypothetical. That's what the Su-
> preme Court decisions tell us.

He also noted that in *Loving* the State of Virginia had made the same
argument, that allowing interracial marriage was "going to change the
traditional definition of marriage. It's going to weaken marriage."

Ted emphasized that you couldn't take away a fundamental right,
and subject citizens to discrimination that everyone conceded seriously
harmed them and their children, on the basis of "I don't know, and I
don't have to prove anything, and I don't need any evidence."

It has always been the courts' responsibility, he added, to protect
the rights of individuals, particularly minorities. "The argument that
Mr. Cooper makes," Ted said, "is, essentially, the same argument that
was made in the *Loving* case":

> The same argument was made to Martin Luther King,
> and to Thurgood Marshall, and to Ruth Bader Ginsburg. We're
> talking about fundamental constitutional rights. We are talk-
> ing about treating people equally. That's not breaking new
> ground. We're talking about allowing people the same freedom
> to marry the person that they love as we have the rest of our
> society.

When Judge Walker asked if there was a political tide in favor of
marriage equality, and if that was an important factor in deciding
whether a court should act, Ted replied:

> I believe, Your Honor, that there is a political tide running.
> I think that people's eyes are being opened. People are becom-
> ing more understanding and tolerant. The polls tell us that.
> That isn't any secret.
>
> But that does not justify a judge in a court to say, "I really
> need the polls to be just a few points higher. I need someone to

go out and take the temperature of the American public before
I can break this barrier and break down this discrimination."

Ted also explained why it was essential for this court to recognize
a federal constitutional right to marriage equality and not wait for the
uncertainty of Californians' somehow changing their minds and re-
pealing Proposition 8 sometime in the future:

> Because if they change it here in the next election in Califor-
> nia, we still have Utah. We still have Missouri. We still have
> Montana. This case is going to be in a court. Some judge is go-
> ing to have to decide what we've asked you to decide.
>
> And there will never be a case with a more thorough presen-
> tation of the evidence. There will never be a case with such
> a wildly crazy system that California has. There will never be a
> case more like *Romer*, where the right existed and then it
> was taken away. There will never be a case against [this] back-
> ground.

The plaintiff's rebuttal is the most difficult part of the closing arguments. The attorney making the presentation has a limited amount of
time, must respond to all of the defendants' key arguments, and has no
time to prepare. Ted had not had even a brief break between the completion of Cooper's argument and the beginning of his rebuttal, but he
had done a superb job. He concluded with an articulate and heartfelt
summation:

> You are discriminating against a group of people. You are
> causing them harm. You are excluding them from an important
> part of life. And you have to have a good reason for that.
>
> And I submit, at the end of the day, "I don't know" and "I
> don't have to put any evidence," with all due respect to Mr.
> Cooper, does not cut it.
>
> It does not cut it when you are taking away the constitu-
> tional rights, basic human rights and human decency from a

large group of individuals, and you don't know why they are a
threat to your definition of a particular institution. . . .

That is not acceptable. It's not acceptable under our Constitution. And Mr. Blankenhorn is absolutely right. The day that
we end that, we will be more American.

Decorum in a federal courtroom while the judge is on the bench is
strict. When Ted resumed his seat, I squeezed his arm and whispered,
"Thank you." The audiences in the overflow courtrooms were not similarly constrained. As soon as Ted turned from the podium to return to
our table, they rose and cheered.

As we reflected on the final argument, and the trial itself, we believed we would win the case. We had established, as a matter of evidence and a matter of law, that Proposition 8 was unconstitutional. In
the course of the trial we had also created a record that would likely
withstand the appeals process. Indeed, we had given Judge Walker so
much evidence and so many points of law that he could offer several
different justifications for striking down Prop 8, and thereby give
higher courts many ways to uphold his ruling.

But a lawsuit isn't like a football game or a basketball game, where
the action ends with a final, quantifiable tally of points earned. In a
district court the outcome ultimately rests with a single individual's
subjective judgment. No one could confidently predict what Judge
Walker would decide.

ELEVEN

Judge Walker's Decision

After the June 16 closing arguments, we spent the following seven weeks anticipating and preparing for Judge Walker's decision. Looking back on the trial, the closing argument, and the judge's questions, we could not help but be cautiously optimistic, but we also knew better than to let our expectations, and the expectations of our clients, get too high. A defeat would be devastating enough.

While we were waiting for Judge Walker's decision, the Field Poll reported on July 20 that California's voters were now tilted in favor of marriage equality by 51 to 42 percent. The following day the Public Religion Research Institute released the results of a survey that indicated that two years after it had passed with a 52 percent majority, only 20 percent of Californians now believed that Proposition 8 was a "good thing." Around the same time a U.S. district court judge in Boston held that the federal government could not deny benefits to same-sex couples who had been married in Massachusetts, even though the federal Defense of Marriage Act ordained that result. (We were quite sure that DOMA would end up at the Supreme Court, but no one could predict when.)

Encouraged by these developments, we were informed on August 3 that we should be prepared to appear in Judge Walker's courtroom at 1 P.M. on Wednesday, August 4, to hear his decision. As we eventually learned, Judge Walker and his clerks had devoted hundreds of hours to drafting, editing, and redrafting the document. The resulting opinion not only settled the Proposition 8 question but comprehensively addressed all of the arguments that had been advanced during the election contest and the trial to justify discriminatory treatment of gays and lesbians.

However, as we flew in from all over to gather at Gibson Dunn's office in San Francisco we had no idea what to expect. As a courtesy Judge Walker's staff distributed his opinion at noon on August 4 to the lawyers for both sides, with an admonition that we were not permitted to discuss it publicly until it was officially released at 1 P.M. Since it was lunchtime, someone ordered pizza. The legal team quickly scanned the remarkable document that we printed and copied as rapidly as our equipment would permit: a 136-page meticulous, comprehensive analysis of the facts, the issues, and the contentions as well as elaborate findings of fact and conclusions of law. Naturally we were anxious to know the bottom line, so we hurriedly turned to the last page. There it was. Everything we could have hoped for:

> **Plaintiffs have demonstrated by overwhelming evidence that Proposition 8 violates their due process and equal protection rights and that they will continue to suffer these constitutional violations until state officials cease enforcement of Proposition 8. . . . Because Proposition 8 is unconstitutional under both the Due Process and Equal Protection Clauses, the court orders entry of judgment permanently enjoining its enforcement.**

To say we were euphoric would be a massive understatement. Here, in an opinion from a respected, experienced chief judge of a federal court, after a full trial and thorough briefing, was, for the first time in history, a ruling completely vindicating of our clients' rights, recognizing their status as equal, fully entitled citizens, and upholding their right to marry the person they loved regardless of gender or sexual orientation. It was a wonderful moment. In page after page the judge laid out and accepted the evidence we had offered and systematically, with logic, fact, and precedent, demolished every contention that our opponents had put forward.

This was something that we simply could not withhold from our clients. We reasoned that the embargo on public comment or dissemination of the opinion until 1 P.M. could not possibly mean that the individuals who brought the suit could not be told the outcome. Keeping most of the assembled crowd—friends, family, supporters—outside the corner conference room in which the legal team had assembled, we invited Kris, Sandy, Paul, and Jeff into the room, cautioned them against shouting, fainting, or screaming, and shared the wonderful news with them. "We won!"

Shock, joy, tears, and hugging. It is impossible to describe how much energy, emotion, prayer, and faith had been poured into this effort by our four wonderful plaintiffs. They were relieved, thrilled, and emotionally exhausted all at once. Nor is it possible to describe how ecstatic we felt in sharing the good news with them.

By then it was one o'clock and we could let the others know, which we did, again to much shouting, embracing, crying, and laughing. We then turned to reading and digesting the balance of the opinion, preparing press statements, and hosting a press conference. It was both literally and figuratively a labor of love.

We reminded everyone that this was just the first decision in a long process that could well end at the Supreme Court, some two or three years into the future. Since appellate courts do not conduct trials, the outcomes in those courts would depend on our advocacy skills and the record set down in Judge Walker's courtroom. Thanks to our clients, our experts, and our legal work, this record was as complete and favorable as it could possibly be. From this point on, the two couples' task would be to interact with the press and the public, serving as the public face of an historic cause.

Judge Walker's opinion included a series of findings that would reverberate both legally and socially, including:

- Individuals do not generally choose their sexual orientation.
- Domestic partnerships lack the social meaning associated with marriage.

- Permitting same-sex couples to marry will not affect the number of opposite-sex couples who marry, divorce, co-habit, or have children outside marriage, nor will it otherwise affect the stability of opposite-sex marriages.
- Children do not need to be raised by a male parent and female parent to be well adjusted.
- The children of same-sex couples benefit when their parents can marry.
- Proposition 8 places the force of law behind stigmas against gays and lesbians.
- Proposition 8 does not affect the First Amendment rights of those opposed to marriage for same-sex couples.
- Public and private discrimination against gays and lesbians occurs in California and in the United States.
- Stereotypes and misinformation have resulted in social and legal disadvantages for gays and lesbians.
- The Proposition 8 campaign relied on fears that children exposed to the concept of same-sex marriage may become gay or lesbian.
- The campaign to pass Proposition 8 relied on stereotypes to show that same-sex relationships are inferior to opposite-sex relationships.

After his careful recitation of his factual findings, Judge Walker concluded that Proposition 8 denied our clients a fundamental right without a legitimate, let alone a compelling, reason. He wrote that the amendment violated the plaintiffs' right to equal protection "under any standard of review," and he determined that the state had no interest in denying same-sex couples marriage equality. "A private moral view that same-sex couples are inferior to opposite-sex couples is not a basis for legislation," he enjoined.

The judge prescribed an order barring the enforcement of Proposition 8 by California officials. However, since the defendants were expected to appeal to the Ninth Circuit Court of Appeals, Judge Walker temporarily stayed the effect of his decision to give our opponents an opportunity to ask the Ninth Circuit to keep in place the California ban on same-sex marriage until the completion of the appeal process, which the Ninth Circuit subsequently agreed to do. However, on an emotional, legal, social, and even spiritual level, the decision was an unmitigated victory that was celebrated by us and throughout the United States.

We held a press conference in San Francisco, surrounded by cheering members of the public, and immediately flew to Southern California, to a joyous, excited, and tearful crowd of supporters in a park in West Hollywood, where we were joined by, among others, Los Angeles mayor Antonio Villaraigosa. Chad Griffin, our plaintiffs, the mayor, and the two of us took turns addressing the large, enthusiastic, cheering crowd. The sun was shining, and the park was filled with people of every conceivable race, age, and background. This was one of those once-in-a-lifetime events that defy simple description. Couples had their arms around one another, families had brought their children and dogs. Everyone seemed to be weeping with joy, appreciation for the judge, the Constitution, the rule of law, and all of us involved in the case. Proposition 8 had been recognized for what it was—a shameful, menacing dark cloud over all of their lives. And it was now one step closer to oblivion. One could not look out at those people, with hope and love in their eyes and hearts—for one another, and for their future—and not ache for them to soon see the day when their dream of freedom and equality would finally and fully be redeemed by their government.

TWELVE

The Appeal

E very lawyer has lost a case. Any lawyer who says he or she has never lost is (a) just starting in the profession; (b) lying; or (c) possessed of a conveniently selective memory. But there is nearly always the opportunity to appeal to a higher court, and the trick is to set oneself up for the next round.

Some of our opponents in *Perry*, however, seemed not able to focus on where they were headed. It is generally counterproductive to attack the trial judge or mischaracterize what has happened in that venue. Yet Andrew Pugno, the lawyer who helped formulate the Prop 8 campaign, and who had often sat with Chuck Cooper at the defense table, publicly attacked Judge Walker, asserting he had "literally accused the majority of California voters of having ill and discriminatory intent when casting their votes for Prop 8."

With the case headed to the Ninth Circuit Court of Appeals, Pugno's acerbic criticism may have felt good, smarting as he may have been from his loss in the district court, or perhaps it was intended to excite his financial backers, but such a provocative statement risked alienating the jurists who would consider the ruling on appeal. All the appeals court judges have a considerable level of respect for their colleagues and for the district court judges whose work they oversee, so assaults on a judge, rather than purely legal arguments, are risky propositions. Our opponents' next step was equally aggressive—and equally risky. But throughout this case our opponents had manifested little hesitation in attacking the judiciary and the judicial process.

Although the Ninth Circuit has a reputation for being relatively liberal, with a majority of its judges appointed by Democratic presidents, one never knows which panel of three judges will be selected at random to handle the appeal in any particular case. The panel selected for the *Perry* case appeal included as the senior most member Stephen Reinhardt, who was widely regarded as one of the most liberal appeals court judges on the court. Also on the panel were Judge Randy Smith, regarded as one of the Ninth Circuit's more conservative judges, and Judge Michael Hawkins, who had a moderate, middle-of-the-road reputation. Pugno, Cooper, and Brian Raum were anxious to get Reinhardt off the panel. They petitioned him to recuse himself on the ground that his wife, Ramona Ripston, had been the executive director of the Southern California American Civil Liberties Union, which had long fought for marriage equality and had wound up supporting our side in this case. (She and her ACLU colleagues had been among the groups urging us not to bring this case but had switched to a supporting position after we filed.) The U.S. Code requires a judge to "disqualify himself in any proceeding in which his impartiality might reasonably be questioned."

The problem for Cooper and his colleagues was that the motion was addressed to and would be acted on by Reinhardt himself. Nothing in his past suggested he would voluntarily withdraw from a case like this. Also, attacking Reinhardt's impartiality could offend his colleagues on the court. Four days before the hearing date he issued a terse rejection, stating that "a reasonable person with knowledge of all the facts would [not] conclude that [my] impartiality might reasonably be questioned. I will be able to rule impartially on this appeal, and I will do so. The motion is therefore DENIED."

By the time he refused to step aside, Judge Reinhardt had had ample time to review the briefs the parties had submitted in the case. Our brief repeated some of the points we had made previously, emphasizing that "class-based balkanization and stigmatization of our citizens is flatly incompatible with our constitutional ideals. . . . There is no legitimate interest that is even remotely furthered by Proposition 8's arbitrary exclusion of gay men and lesbians from the institution of marriage." We concluded our support for Judge Walker's decision by referencing events that occurred *after* the district court ruling that underscored the fact that the quest for equality in matters of sexual orientation was often, quite literally, a matter of life and death.

On September 22 a young Rutgers University student committed suicide by jumping off the George Washington Bridge after being cruelly outed on the Internet by a fellow student. Days later two seventeen-year-old boys and a thirty-year-old man were attacked and beaten severely by a gang who suspected their targets were gay. Incidents such as these are all too common. We wanted to remind everyone who read the brief that discrimination written into our governing laws, as witnesses had explained at trial, can too often lead to shame, humiliation, ostracism, fear, and hostility. The consequences can be, and frequently are, tragic.

Prop 8's defenders disputed virtually every conclusion Judge Walker had reached, from his holding that the state sought through its restriction on marriage to impose a different, second-class status on our clients, to his finding that the evidence established the immutability of sexual orientation. In their view homosexuality is a "complex and amorphous phenomenon," and therefore gays and lesbians did not constitute a specific and identifiable group worthy of special protections. They cited *Bowers v. Hardwick* as a case that they claimed established "binding precedent" to this effect. Remarkably, however, they failed to acknowledge that *Bowers* had been subsequently eclipsed by *Romer* and explicitly overturned by *Lawrence*.

The basic rhetoric in the proponents' briefs was essentially unchanged from the arguments they had made in the district court, but it had darkened in tone and ignored the evidence at trial. The district court, they said, had blinded itself to the genuine animating purpose of marriage. Unable to deal with our proof, including the consistent and unrebutted testimony of our fact and expert witnesses, they fell back on unsupported, conclusory assertions. Our evidence was "feeble," merely "bald assertion." Their strongest argument was that

California's voters did not need to prove anything before excluding gays and lesbians from marriage: They only had to demonstrate a plausible reason for doing so. Quoting from a 1980 decision in *Railroad Retirement Bd. v. Fritz,* they wrote that, as the Supreme Court had explained, "Regardless of what 'reasoning in fact underlay the legislative decision,' so long as 'there are plausible reasons' supporting the legislation, judicial 'inquiry is at an end.'"

———

On December 6 the three-judge panel convened to hear the oral arguments that would augment our briefs. The century-old Beaux-Arts courthouse that is home to the Ninth Circuit in San Francisco is a beautiful public building. Its white granite exterior recalls an Italian palazzo, while its interior, decorated with brass fixtures and carved marble from three continents, leaves visitors awed. Fortunately, the world got a chance to view the remarkable courtroom, and hear the proceedings, because the court of appeals decided to televise our arguments. This time our opponents did not even try to get the Supreme Court to block the telecast.

In a preview to an issue that would come to play a large role in the balance of the case, the early stages of the argument were dominated by consideration of whether the proponents of Proposition 8 had the right to defend it in court. The technical term is "standing," and the judges were eager to explore whether Cooper's clients had standing to defend a constitutional amendment that top officials of the State of California had declined to defend. Article III of the U.S. Constitution describes the functions of the federal courts. In general terms, a case can be brought, or defended, in the federal judiciary only by parties who can show they are directly affected by events or issues in dispute. This is to ensure that judges decide actual controversies between genuine litigants and do not inject themselves into advisory roles on random societal disputes, converting themselves into activist philosopher-kings. California state courts had generally allowed citizens putting forth a ballot initiative to defend their proposals, but federal courts were not bound by state procedures; they were bound by Article III and federal precedent interpreting it. If Hollingsworth and the rest of the defendants couldn't establish standing, since the State of California, while a party in the district court, had chosen not to appeal, the appeals court would be required to simply dismiss their appeal and leave Judge Walker's decision in place, without addressing the facts or points of law directly.

Illustrating the importance of the standing issue, the appellate court had allocated the same amount of time to argue the issue of standing as to argue the merits of our case. In fact, the issue of standing was closely related to the merits of our claim. By the time we reached the court of appeals the importance of marriage and the harm to gay and lesbian citizens and their children from prohibiting same-sex marriage were virtually conceded. The central remaining merits issue was whether the defendants could make a credible case that Proposition 8 preserved heterosexual marriages and that invalidating Prop 8 would thereby cause demonstrable harm.

The issue of standing was whether the defendants could demonstrate that they had personally suffered concrete harm. If so, they had standing. If not, they were out of court. It might be that there would be sufficient plausible harm to heterosexual marriage to support Prop 8 on the merits but that the particular defendants here did not suffer that harm in a sufficiently personal and concrete way to justify standing.

Within our team we had initially mixed views about whether we wanted the defendants to be granted standing. On the one hand, if the defendants lacked standing to appeal, Judge Walker's opinion would stand, and our clients, and everyone in the country's largest state, would have the right to marry the person they loved. On the other hand, that opinion would technically apply only to California and we would not achieve the multistate victory of a Ninth Circuit decision (which, in addition to California, covered the states of Arizona, Alaska, Hawaii, Montana, Idaho, Nevada, Oregon, and Washington, as well as Guam) or the national victory of a U.S. Supreme Court decision.

We ultimately came down firmly on the side of arguing that the defendants lacked standing. We believed they did lack standing under applicable Supreme Court precedents, and that we had an obligation to the court and to our clients to say so. Moreover, while we were confident we were right, a finding of lack of standing avoided the risks inherent in an appellate decision on the merits. And victory in California would, we believed, affect other states and other courts. California itself had more than 10 percent of the country's population and, together with New York, which later achieved marriage equality through legislation, greatly influenced what happened in the rest of the country. Finally, of course, we had an obligation to our individual clients to redeem for them the right to marry. A standing victory overturning Proposition 8 would deliver the result we had set out in the first place to achieve.

Cooper was first to speak. He began by referencing cases from California state courts to claim standing for his clients. When asked if he could name a federal case that would permit his clients to defend Prop 8, he forthrightly replied, "Your Honor, I don't have a case for allowing a proponent Article III standing. I am here advocating that this case be one that allows proponents Article III standing."

David, who appeared first for our side, discussed the many legal and factual reasons why these defendants lacked standing, but the essence of his argument was that "in order to have an ability to invoke the jurisdiction of this court, the appellants here must have a personal, concrete, particularized injury, and they don't." They had not been authorized by California or its officials to take over the role of state officials in defending California laws in court.

Following the standing argument, the court took a ten-minute break and then returned to consider the merits of the case. Cooper was again the first to speak. Within moments each of the judges had challenged his argument. Judge Hawkins pointed out that the Prop 8 ban on same-sex marriage took away a right that courts had previously granted. "Could the people of California reinstitute school segregation by a public vote?" he asked. When Cooper replied that the courts would not permit such an act, the judge countered, "And how's this different?"

Unable to muster a very persuasive answer to that question, Cooper next heard Judge Reinhardt say that the asserted state interest in the welfare of children "sounds like a good argument for prohibiting divorce . . . but how does it relate to having two males or two females marry each other and raise children as they can in California and form a family unit where children have a happy, healthy home? I don't understand how that argument says we ought to prohibit that."

"Your Honor," Cooper answered, "the point and the question is whether or not the State of California has a rational reason for drawing a distinction between same-sex couples who cannot, without the intervention of a third party of the opposite sex, procreate and opposite-sex couples who not only can procreate but can do so unintentionally and create unwanted pregnancies. That is not a phenomenon that exists with respect to same-sex couples."

Cooper was interrupted again. Referring to California's domestic partnerships, Judge Smith asked, "But what is the rational basis for an initiative that when California law really says that homosexual couples have all the rights of marriage, all the rights of child rearing, all the rights that others have, what is the rational basis then? If, in fact, the homosexual couples have all of the rights that the heterosexual couples have? We're left with a word—marriage. What is the rational basis for that?"

Cooper replied, "Your Honor, you are left with a word, but a word that is essentially the institution, and if you redefine the institution, if you redefine the word, you change the institution."

This, yet again, was Cooper's case at its most basic, and tautological, level: If same-sex couples were allowed to marry, the traditional definition of marriage would change. Any change in that institution might have unknown deleterious consequences; he didn't have to specify what they were, and the state could rationally want to avoid any such risk.

As appellate judges the panel was sensitive both to precedent and to the prospect that its work would probably be reviewed by the Supreme Court. That might have explained why the judges seemed particularly interested in the Supreme Court's *Romer v. Evans* decision, which overturned a Colorado constitutional initiative that had withdrawn rights previously granted to gay and lesbian citizens. They mentioned it often in questioning Cooper, who replied that the Colorado law that had been invalidated in that case "became constitutionally objectionable" by going further than Prop 8, changing numerous laws and ordinances, not simply affecting one single relationship, marriage. Cooper also relied on another case in which the Eighth Circuit Court of Appeals in St. Louis upheld a proposition from Nebraska "that contained identical language" to Proposition 8. Those judges had determined that "it was entirely rational for the people in that state to confer and retain the inducements and benefits of the institution of marriage." Of course, no one in Nebraska had previously granted same-sex couples the right to marry, which had been the situation in California, and which was why *Romer* was relevant.

After David addressed the standing issues in the first half of the hearing, Ted dealt with the merits issues in the second phase. Judge Reinhardt immediately returned to his concern about Prop 8's revocation of a right previously granted. Ted was ready, with a reference not only to *Romer,* but also to a 1964 case, *Reitman v. Mulkey,* which involved a California ballot initiative that had stripped minorities of their rights under state fair housing laws. Its proponents had argued that the initiative merely affirmed one's right to sell one's home to the buyer of one's choice. The U.S. Supreme Court found that the measure encouraged discrimination and violated the Fourteenth Amendment.

In further questions Judge Reinhardt pressed to see if Ted would contend that "gay marriage is required by the Constitution of the United States." Ted responded that the issue was the fundamental right to marriage, not something called "gay marriage" or "single-sex marriage," and whether that established right could be withheld from some segment of society based on its members' sexual orientation. "Mr. Cooper talks in terms of the right of society, society's interest in procreation. It is not society's right. The rights under the Constitution are not the rights of California, they are not the rights of voters of California, they are rights of citizens of the United States under the Bill of Rights."

Aware that the appellate court was concerned with issuing a decision based on legal principles and precedents, Ted then stitched together the two most relevant Supreme Court decisions—*Romer* and *Lawrence*—which combined to compel a decision for our clients:

> **The United States Supreme Court has determined that intimate sexual conduct between persons of the same sex is constitutionally protected and the Supreme Court has said . . . marriage is a fundamental right.**
>
> **How can the fundamental right of marriage be taken away by Californians from persons because they're engaged in a constitutionally protected activity?**
>
> **It cannot exist. If you put the *Lawrence* case together with the marriage cases, *Loving* case, and so on and so forth, you cannot take away that right, which is not a right of same-sex persons. It's a right of all citizens and it's a right to be with the person that they love, to have an association that they select, to live a life of privacy . . . a self-identification, as Justice Kennedy talked about in both *Romer* and *Lawrence*. That right cannot be taken away from individuals in this state because of their sexual orientation.**

Later in the same response Ted recalled that Cooper had asserted that Prop 8 was necessary to protect children from exposure to discussions of sexual issues. "That is *nonsense*," he stated, "that you can enact a proposition that walls off the citizens of this state from a fundamental right because you're worried that otherwise children might be prematurely preoccupied with issues of sexuality. That, of course, if that was a justification, it would equally warrant banning comic books, television, video games, and conversations with other children."

The laughter that followed the reference to "conversations with other children" was the kind of spontaneous outburst that relieves the tension but also places a notable emphasis on the point being made. It is nice when it happens that way.

The judges also asked Ted some probing questions about our trial presentations, expressing some skepticism about the evidence of animus toward gays and lesbians that we had submitted. Judge Hawkins observed, "You know, people in popular election campaigns make all sorts of nonsensical arguments." Judge Smith questioned Judge Walker's acceptance of our evidence that same-sex couples can raise children just as well as opposite-sex couples. "All else being equal, children [are most] likely to thrive when raised by [the] father and mother who brought them into this world, [why is that] irrational?"

Ted explained that the trial evidence did not indicate that same-sex parents were less capable than opposite-sex ones. He referred to David Blankenhorn's testimony that "the children in those [same-sex] relationships would be better off" if their parents were permitted to marry. Ted also drew on Judge Reinhardt's earlier observation about divorce: "If a child is a product of a biological relationship between a man and a woman, that's up to that man and that woman to keep them together. I think Judge Reinhardt suggested that a better remedy for that would be to prohibit divorce. But that's not something that Californians are interested in doing."

Before our allotted time was up, Terry Stewart, again representing the City and County of San Francisco, had an opportunity to supplement our argument. She raised a number of key points about the state's regulation of child rearing, which is separate from its regulation of marriage: "The California law continues to recognize that same-sex couples and opposite-sex couples are the same, for purposes of family and child rearing, in every way that matters." She also delivered a most effective counterargument to the other side's attack on our evidence of animus in the Prop 8 campaign: "Proponents say that in order to affirm the district court this court must find that the majority who voted for Proposition 8 are bigots and that is not so. Prejudice . . . is not always born of hatred. It may, as Justice Kennedy said, . . . be the result of simple want of careful rational reflection or an instinct to guard against people that we think are different from ourselves."

———

We again felt cautiously optimistic after the argument. Each of the three judges had expressed genuine skepticism about the constitutionality of

Prop 8. Two of the reporters who had most rigorously covered the trial and appeal agreed with us. Howard Mintz of the *San Jose Mercury News* wrote that the court "appeared generally inclined to support" us. Maura Dolan of the *Los Angeles Times* wrote that the judges "seemed headed toward a decision that could reinstate same-sex marriages."

However confident we were, we knew better than to set our hearts on a specific outcome. The court could choose one of several paths, and no matter which they chose, further appeal was likely. In fact, we had been working all along on possible arguments to present to the Supreme Court in the case of a loss and arguments opposing a further appeal if we won.

What we least expected after the hearing was that the Ninth Circuit would delay its decision and request some assistance on an issue of state law from the California Supreme Court, but that is precisely what happened. Just after Christmas 2010 the federal court asked the state court to rule on whether the Prop 8 proponents were legally entitled, under California law, to defend their initiative against our claims. Judge Reinhardt explained that in the end, the defendants might well have standing to maintain their appeal, and that "the important constitutional question before us may, after all, be decided by an appellate court—ours, the Supreme Court, or both." That said, the panel did want clarification from the state as to the rights of the proponents to take over the role of state officials in defending Proposition 8.

Fearing a long delay while the state court deliberated, we requested that they decline to become involved, since the issue, we felt, was one of federal constitutional law, not state procedural requirements. The justices, however, disagreed and asked each side to submit briefs and argue the issues in September 2011. Considering that the court might then take as long as ninety days to rule, we could envision, to our dismay, another year passing before we could expect the Ninth Circuit's decision.

While we prepared for the California high court, the country continued to move forward on equality for gays and lesbians. Under the leadership of Senator Kirsten Gillibrand from New York, a congressional bill to repeal the military's notorious "Don't Ask, Don't Tell" policy was enacted, which would allow openly gay and lesbian citizens to serve; DADT would end the following September. In late February 2011 the administration announced it would no longer defend the Defense of Marriage Act in court. As Attorney General Eric Holder explained, he and President Obama had determined that DOMA amounted to official discrimination. He added that the government would continue to enforce it until the Supreme Court eventually settled the question of its constitutionality. He referred to a New York case that was likely to be the vehicle for such a decision. It had been filed by Edith Windsor after she was required to pay a $363,000 estate tax after the death of Thea Spyer, whom she had married in Canada. Spyer and Windsor had been together for more than four decades. DOMA meant that their Canadian marriage was not recognized by the U.S. government.

The administration's shift on DADT (whose repeal the administration supported) and DOMA reflected the latest stage in the president's "evolution" on equality for gays and lesbians, and equal rights advocates hailed it as a defining turn in the struggle. That evolution was matched, and perhaps facilitated, by the evolution of the American public. In March, ABC News and the *Washington Post* released a survey that revealed a national majority in favor of marriage equality. Support for same-sex marriage had risen dramatically from 32 percent in 2005 to 58 percent in 2011.

Our satisfaction in the positive developments toward achieving equality was tempered by an unexpected development in the federal district court. In April our opponents asked the judge who had assumed responsibility for Judge Walker's cases (Walker had retired at the end of February) to throw out the *Perry* judgment. The basis for this motion was Judge Walker's status as a gay man involved in a ten-year relationship that, they argued, might eventually result in a marriage. "Such a personal interest in his own marriage," the defendants argued, "would place Chief Judge Walker in precisely the same shoes as the two couples who brought the case."

Coming as it did many months after Judge Walker rendered his decision, and months after our appeal was argued in the Ninth Circuit, the filing might have left the impression that it was based on some new discovery. It was not. In fact Judge Walker's relationship had been well known and widely discussed inside and outside of legal circles for many years. Cooper, Pugno, and Raum could have raised it as an issue at the start of the trial. They chose not to. Moreover, their newly minted theory was based on the notion that a judge cannot hear a case that relates to his or her own life circumstances. Of course, this would imply that no woman judge could be assigned a case about gender discrimination or pregnancy, no black judge could consider a case concerning racial discrimination or affirmative action, and no disabled judge could sit on a case involving the Americans with Disabilities Act.

To us the recusal motion suggested that our opponents were desperate and that they believed (as we did) they were headed for defeat in the appeals court. The hearing on this motion was conducted by Judge James Ware, and from the start both he and Chuck Cooper sounded as though they didn't want to be there. Ware began by saying that he considered the matter a straightforward legal issue and added, "I don't know why we gave you so much time to argue it under these circumstances, but we did. So proceed."

Cooper began rather sheepishly, saying, "We approach the court awkwardly and not in any way welcoming the obligation to make and argue this motion, but nonetheless, here we are. And at the heart, Your Honor, of the concept of due process is the requirement by our Constitution and at the common law that decision be by an impartial tribunal."

After Cooper expressed his objection to Judge Walker's involvement in the Proposition 8 case, Judge Ware pointed out that the rules require recusal when a judge might have a pecuniary interest in the outcome of a case or an otherwise substantial stake in the decision. No one was arguing that Judge Walker had a financial interest in *Perry*, so the matter really came down to a question of whether he had some other substantial interest. Cooper responded that what mattered was Judge Walker's ten-year relationship with another man, which made him "similarly situated to the plaintiffs for purposes of marriage because he, too, was in a serious long-term relationship with an individual of the same sex."

After listening carefully, Judge Ware turned to the speculative part of Cooper's statement. "I'm not sure what you mean by 'for purposes of marriage,'" he said. "What is the fact that you rely upon that Judge Walker was in a relationship for purposes of marriage?"

While expending a considerable amount of energy in his effort to explain how Judge Walker's relationship aligned him directly with our clients, Cooper could offer no evidence that Walker had any intention to marry. Instead, he called for the application of "common sense," arguing that the fact that Walker had not disclosed his relationship would lead a "reasonable objective observer" to conclude that he should have recused himself.

The judge's question to Cooper—here was a lawyer essentially questioning the integrity and impartiality of a fellow judge—was a testy exchange. Ware seemed most exasperated by Cooper's repeated attempts to link the fact of Walker's relationship to a presumed interest in getting married. With exasperation in his voice the judge eventually said, "I think I hear me. I recognize my voice, but I'm not sure *you* hear *you*."

Having devoted serious consideration to Cooper's concerns about Walker, Judge Ware posed a number of questions that punctured his arguments. Should a judge who had been raped never hear a case involving sexual assault? How about a judge who was abused as a child? Should he never hear a case related to maltreatment of a child? Should judges in these circumstances be required to reveal their histories? Would those revelations disqualify them? Cooper had no good answers for any of these questions, because judges are typically presumed to be capable of conducting fair trials and reaching decisions even when they have life experiences and interests related to the general subject matter in the case. Indeed, it is inevitable. Judges get married, divorced, and have children. They are victims of crimes, they have relatives or friends who take drugs, they buy homes and insurance. They live the same lives the rest of us do.

At this hearing our side was represented by Ted Boutrous, who summarized our argument in his opening statement. "This motion is frivolous, offensive and deeply unfortunate," he said. "But I guess it shouldn't come as any surprise, because throughout the history of civil rights litigation in this country, there has always been an attempt by a litigant seeking to stop recognition of equal rights for everyone to challenge judges who are members of the minority group that is litigating. And there is a solid wall of authority dating back decades. Every single time that this kind of issue has been raised, whether it be race, ethnicity, gender, religion, the courts have rejected it."

This court agreed. Less than twenty-four hours after the end of the hearing Judge Ware ruled in our favor, and in favor of Judge Walker. "The fact that a federal judge shares a fundamental characteristic with a litigant, or shares membership in a large association such as a religion, has been categorically rejected by federal courts as a sole basis for requiring a judge to recuse her- or himself," he wrote in his decision. Ware took particular note of Cooper's strained attempt to link Walker's relationship with a disqualifying intent to marry, writing that it was "warrantless." He added that "it is reasonable to presume that a female judge or a judge in a same-sex relationship is capable of rising above any personal predisposition and deciding such a case on the merits."

Though expected, Judge Ware's ruling was not only an important affirmation of the presumption of judicial integrity but also brought us over one more hurdle in the pursuit of marriage equality. The cause received another moral boost a few weeks later when the New York legislature approved a same-sex marriage bill that Governor Andrew Cuomo pledged to sign. By July gay men and lesbian women would be permitted to marry in the Empire State.

The next step in our battle was the California Supreme Court's hearing on the question of whether Prop 8's proponents should be allowed to defend the initiative. Once again we took the position that the proponents lacked standing and that the duty to defend a ballot initiative fell to the governor and attorney general. We argued that nothing in California's initiative process or constitution gave proponents any authority to go into federal court and replace California's chief constitutional officers and their judgment as to what was in the best interest of the persons they had been elected to represent.

The hearing on this matter was conducted in San Francisco in a courthouse that was rebuilt after the Loma Prieta earthquake of 1989. The quakeproof modern facility was constructed behind the historic façade, which had been built in 1922 after an architecture competition. Inside, the seven justices presided in an elegant wood-paneled courtroom with a thirty-foot vaulted ceiling. When we arrived a contingent of supporters occupied the sidewalk in front of the courthouse, holding placards that read, LIBERTY, JUSTICE, AND MARRIAGE EQUALITY and WE ALL DESERVE THE FREEDOM TO MARRY.

As Ted made our argument, he faced almost uniform opposition. Justice Ming Chin expressed obvious skepticism as he asked, "So the attorney general and the governor get to pick the laws that they want to enforce?" The answer, we believed, was yes, within limits. The executive—the governor and attorney general—must have the discretion to execute and enforce laws in a manner consistent with their own judgment as to the best interests of the state and the people they were elected to serve. That is precisely what they are elected to do. That is the separation of powers that our Constitution is founded on.

This question—whether a proposition could be left undefended by state officials—was the crux of the matter. Our opponents asserted that if the government was permitted to decline to defend a ballot initiative, and proponents were barred from taking up the duty, the citizens' power to create their own laws through ballot initiatives would be thwarted. State officials would effectively enjoy veto power over the citizens, and this, they argued, was not what the framers of the state constitution intended when they established the initiative process.

It was our turn to struggle a bit as one justice after another addressed the matter of a governor's and/or attorney general's refusing to support a measure that was the manifestation of the will of the people. The justices distinctly did not like the power vacuum they perceived in our position. Justice Kathryn Werdegar stated, "We have generous, liberal intervention policies, so that irrespective of whether the executive branch in the person of the attorney general is supporting an initiative or not supporting an initiative, either way, we liberally allow intervention so that the courts will have the full benefit of all views in resolving the validity of an initiative." This intervention policy had been applied only to questions arising in state courts under state law, but now that the Ninth Circuit had asked for clarification, the justices seemed ready to extend it wherever a challenge took place—in federal courts as well as in state courts.

It was obvious to us as we packed up and left the courtroom that the court was likely to find that proponents had the right as a matter of California law to defend Proposition 8 in the absence of such a defense by state officials. And just as the courtroom observers correctly foresaw the outcome of the hearing before federal district judge Ware, they were correct in their predictions about the state supreme court's ruling on standing. The journalists, law school professors, and others who commented on the hearing were broadly of the view that the Prop 8 proponents would win, and in November they did. The state supreme court advised the Ninth Circuit that California's constitution implicitly granted standing to proponents to defend a ballot measure they had put forward where state officials decline to do so. While we did not agree that the decision trumped federal law, we were prepared for the decision and glad that we could at last move forward.

On December 8, 2011, almost exactly a year after our first court of appeals argument, the Ninth Circuit brought us back to court to argue two matters. One key issue was the defendants' appeal from Judge Ware's denial of their motion to disqualify Judge Walker, vacate his decision, and start all over again. Chuck Cooper's basic argument was that Judge Walker had concealed that he was in a committed relationship that might have led him to want to marry his partner of ten years, and that "if anytime during his handling of this case, Judge Walker desired to marry his partner . . . he would have . . . stood in precisely the same shoes as the plaintiffs before him." Cooper asserted that this meant that Walker was in effect sitting in judgment on his own case, and should have disqualified himself.

All three judges were skeptical. "So, a married judge could never hear a divorce," asked Judge Hawkins. When Cooper said a married judge could hear a divorce, Judge Smith asked, "Would he have to disclose 'Oh, I've been married . . . for twenty-four years and we have a relationship that is kind of difficult.'?" When Cooper suggested that Judge Walker should have been asked whether he wanted to marry, Judge Reinhardt dubiously inquired, "In what proceeding would he have been asked that question?" Cooper did not have good answers to the judges' questions. And when David rose to argue he seemed to have the wind at his back.

David began by pointing out that the cases were clear that "an interest which a judge has in common with many others in a public matter is not sufficient to disqualify him." He reminded the court that there was no evidence that Judge Walker in fact wanted to marry his partner, and that if he had wanted to he could have done so in the fall of 2008. However, he emphasized that even if Walker had wanted to get married, no court had ever held that that was sufficient to require disqualification. David also noted that the defendants had known about Judge Walker's relationship from the beginning and had never raised a question or concern about it until after they lost the trial and argued their appeal.

Finally, David discussed the danger to the judicial system inherent in disqualifying judges based on interests they might have in common with litigants based on race, gender, religion, or sexual orientation. He pointed out that the rule defendants proposed was "inevitably and by definition targeted at minority judges," and explained:

> Cases seeking to vindicate a minority's constitutional rights typically raise the question of whether it is permissible for a majority to exclude that minority from an institution or activity. Is it, for example, permissible to exclude African Americans from particular educational institutions? Is it permissible to exclude gays from the institution of marriage? The majority

typically defends the exclusion by asserting that the exclusion is desirable to preserve the quality or stability of the institution, that the exclusion is supported by tradition, that the exclusion is based on religious faith. All of these arguments were used to support excluding African Americans from traditionally white institutions. All of these arguments have been used to support excluding gays from the institution of marriage.

David reminded the court that many majority judges, like members of the majority generally, might have an interest in preserving the status quo. Should white judges be able to decide whether to admit African American students to previously all-white schools? Should a Christian judge be able to decide whether to permit Christian symbols on public property? Should Mormon or Catholic judges be able to decide cases involving gay marriage given the position of their respective churches?

If both majority and minority judges were excluded, there might be no one to decide cases.

"But consider," David argued, "how intolerable it would be to rule that the possible interest of a majority judge in preserving the status quo is irrelevant to recusal, but that a minority judge's possible interest in changing the status quo requires recusal. It is for this reason that every court to consider the issue has ruled that an interest that a judge has in common with many others in a public matter is not sufficient to disqualify. That is the law."

That same day we also argued the defendants' appeal from Judge Ware's decision to make public the videos of the trial. Cooper's main argument was that Judge Walker had promised that the videos would not be made public but used only for the purpose of deciding that case.

Ted responded that the public had a great interest in access to the actual evidence at trial in a case of this importance, there was no prejudice to anyone in making the videos public, and the court should defer to Judge Ware's exercise of discretion after hearing all of the evidence.

After the arguments were completed, the judges adjourned without a decision, and without mentioning the issues of standing or the merits of our underlying claim. The only arguments the court had set for December 8 were on defendants' applications to seal the videos and disqualify Judge Walker, so it was not unexpected that the other issues were not discussed. However, we wondered whether the court would want us at some point to argue the implications of the California Supreme Court opinion it had solicited.

The issues we argued on December 8, 2011, were soon decided. The court unanimously denied defendants' effort to disqualify Judge Walker and ruled that the videos would remain sealed. However, the issues of standing and of the merits that we had argued in early December 2010 remained undecided.

All this waiting was frustrating to us lawyers and even more trying for our clients. Almost everyone who is thrust into the judicial system is surprised by the slow pace of justice in America. Generally speaking, courts at all levels are overburdened and understaffed. Where particularly difficult issues are at stake, the wheels may grind especially slowly. Motions pile on top of motions, appeals are followed by appeals, and judges may ask for additional briefings in order to advance their deliberations. Years pass. Expenses mount. Emotions are frayed.

In our case, Sandy, Kris, Paul, and Jeff developed a philosophical approach to the waiting. They came to rely on our assurances and were nearly able to put the case in the back of their minds during the long periods when it seemed as if nothing was happening. And even when something *did* happen, they understood that progress was incremental. One court's decision could be overturned by the next, and the process would not be over until the U.S. Supreme Court determined that it was over.

The Ninth Circuit opinion, finally delivered on February 7, 2012, and written by Judge Reinhardt, agreed with the California Supreme Court that the proponents had the right to appeal Judge Walker's decision. On the merits, they affirmed Judge Walker's decision on the relatively narrow ground that under the *Romer* decision, a constitutionally granted right could not be taken away from a minority group without "at least a legitimate reason." No legitimate reason existed in the case of Prop 8, the court said, and thus the court was "left with the inevitable inference" that the initiative was "born of animosity." Judge Reinhardt concluded by declaring that in approving Proposition 8 "the people of California violated the Equal Protection clause." Judge Walker had been correct. His decision was affirmed. Judge Smith dissented.

While the outcome was a victory—it overturned Proposition 8—the reasoning of the court, relying as it did on the granting and then removal of the right to marry, applied only to California and did not address all the issues that Judge Walker had considered and decided. It left unanswered important concerns about the overall rights of gay and lesbian Americans to enjoy equal access to marriage under the Constitution whether or not such a right had previously been recognized in a state.

We rejoiced in the decision notwithstanding its narrow scope. It dealt a fatal blow to Proposition 8—the goal that we had set for ourselves from the beginning. The decision striking down Proposition 8 was stayed pending a petition by our opponents to the Supreme Court. Another episode of waiting was upon us.

THIRTEEN

The Supreme Court

A petition for a writ of certiorari is the formal document a lawyer submits to the U.S. Supreme Court seeking review of a case that has been lost in a lower-level court. *Certiorari* is a Latin word meaning "to be informed of." The writ is issued by a superior court to a subordinate court asking the latter to send its record to the higher court for review. The Supreme Court receives as many as nine thousand of these requests per year, and most are screened out as obvious nonstarters by the justices' clerks. Only a small percentage of these petitions are distributed to members of the Court for closer consideration, and only about seventy-five are accepted for review each year.

Four justices must agree to accept a case, which will then be briefed and argued before the entire Court. Nearly all of the grants fall under the Court's three principal areas of concern: important federal questions on which the federal circuit courts of appeals are divided; certain lower-court decisions that conflict with Supreme Court precedent or where a federal statute has been declared unconstitutional; and important unresolved questions, especially involving constitutional law, that have not been but should be settled by the Court.

The request for "cert" filed on July 30, 2012, by Charles Cooper argued that the Proposition 8 case dealt with the "profoundly important question of whether the ancient and vital institution of marriage should be fundamentally redefined to include same-sex couples." Cooper quoted the lower court's finding that the issue was "currently a matter of great debate in our nation" and urged the Supreme Court to move to correct an "error" with "widespread and immediate negative consequences." The petition went on to assert a "gross misapplication" of *Romer v. Evans* and other "manifest errors in disregard of this Court's precedents." It also dismissed the Ninth Circuit's findings regarding animus toward gays and lesbians in the Prop 8 campaign as "untrue" and "unfair."

There was much to dispute in Cooper's assertions, including his basically unsupported declarations that Proposition 8 served a "legitimate governmental purpose" in precluding gays and lesbians from marriage and did not "dishonor" gay and lesbian Californians. However, there was no dispute that the issues involved were of pressing national importance and had not been, at least since *Lawrence,* addressed by the Supreme Court.

Amicus curiae (friend of the court) briefs were filed to support Cooper's petition by a number of religious and conservative social organizations, including the National Association of Evangelicals, the Church of Jesus Christ of Latter-day Saints, and the Eagle Forum, a national group founded by the longtime activist Phyllis Schlafly, who described her activities as "pro-family" and, though best known for her opposition to abortion rights and feminism, had in recent years turned her turrets on same-sex marriage.

Determining how to respond to Cooper's cert petition was complicated. On one hand we had to urge the Court to reject the petition. We had won in the lower courts, and Proposition 8 would finally be removed from the lives of Californians if the high court did not intervene. On the other hand, if the Court did take the case, we would have an opportunity to advance a powerful argument that all citizens in all states were entitled to marriage equality. We finally determined to assert broadly that the lower courts had properly applied *Romer* and other relevant precedents and that our opponents did not have standing under Article III of the U.S. Constitution to appeal Judge Walker's decision and therefore had no right to seek Supreme Court review. To satisfy Article III of the Constitution, we argued, "a party must establish, among other things, that it has suffered an 'injury' that is 'personal, particularized, concrete, and otherwise judicially cognizable,'" a statement of the law in the Supreme Court's 1997 decision in *Raines v. Byrd,* rejecting a challenge by members of Congress to a law granting the president a line-item veto. We argued that the proponents did not qualify for standing as a matter of federal court jurisdiction, even if the state supreme court in California had ruled that they could defend the measure in California courts under California law. Standing in federal courts under Article III of the Constitution involves the power of the federal judiciary, and we argued that the Ninth Circuit had erred when it simply accepted the California Supreme Court's analysis of standing to appear in California courts.

However, we also noted that if the Supreme Court were to take this case, it presented an ideal vehicle for the Court to decide the broader marriage equality constitutional question in light of the trial and the comprehensive findings of fact by Judge Walker.

Anyone who had followed the case closely would have recognized much of what we argued in our reply. However, in the time that had passed since the Ninth Circuit's decision, David Blankenhorn had given us an unexpected gift that we used to buttress our submission. In an op-ed titled "How My View on Gay Marriage Changed" published in the *New York Times* on June 22, 2012, our opponents' star witness acknowledged that he had modified his previous position on marriage equality as a result of his growing respect for the couples who sought it and what marriage would mean to them.

"For me, the most important [thing] is the equal dignity of homosexual love," he wrote. "I don't believe that opposite-sex and same-sex relationships are the same, but I do believe, with growing numbers of Americans, that the time for denigrating or stigmatizing same-sex relationships is over. Whatever one's definition of marriage, legally recognizing gay and lesbian couples and their children is a victory for basic fairness. . . . So my intention is to try something new. Instead of fighting gay marriage, I'd like to help build new coalitions bringing together gays who want to strengthen marriage with straight people who want to do the same."

Blankenhorn's reversal was notable for its sincerity and its practical good sense. He recognized the sea change in public opinion and admitted to his "deep regret" that "much of the opposition to gay marriage [seemed to him] to stem, at least in part, from an underlying anti-gay animus." Difficult as it may have been for Blankenhorn to write these words, it must have been all the more painful for him to acknowledge that many of his previous erstwhile allies had in fact been motivated by antipathy toward or discomfort with same-sex relationships.

As we read Blankenhorn's about-face and cited it in our brief, we couldn't help but think that his turnabout had begun in Judge Walker's courtroom. No one who was present during David's cross-examination of Blankenhorn would forget their sometimes sharp exchanges regarding family structure, child rearing, and marriage throughout history. But Blankenhorn's time on the stand was especially notable for the way in which he first resisted but eventually embraced views that revealed the better side of his own nature.

Although the justices of the Supreme Court weren't likely to give weight to a Blankenhorn conversion, referencing it reminded everyone of the remarkable change in public opinion that was under way.

———

As reported in the press, expert opinion on whether the high court would take up the Prop 8 appeal was mixed. It seemed certain that Edith Windsor's challenge to the federal Defense of Marriage Act, which was pending at the Court at the same time, would be accepted for review. After all, it dealt with a lower-court decision finding a federal statute unconstitutional. However, in our case, the justices faced many options, and it was difficult to predict which among them might vote to consider it, and why. Rejecting the petition would leave the Ninth Circuit decision intact and provide a major victory for marriage equality—the defeat of Proposition 8—although the impact would be limited to the state of California and other states that might have granted and then withdrawn a comparable right to marry.

If the petition were denied it would almost certainly be denied without any explanation. With few exceptions—an occasional written dissent from denial—a petition for certiorari that is denied is simply listed as such without any elaboration. This meant that if the Court declined to hear Cooper's appeal, none of us would know what that implied for the next case.

Even as we waited, the tide of public opinion was continuing to change rapidly. In November 2012 voters in Maine, Minnesota, and Maryland approved referenda that legalized same-sex marriages. Prior to these elections no state in the Union had approved a comparable measure by popular vote. A month later, on December 6, 2012, *USA Today* and the Gallup organization released the results of a new poll that found that nine out of ten gay men and lesbians felt their communities had become more accepting of them than ever before. The same poll showed that 51 percent of all Americans as a whole expected same-sex marriage to be legal across the country in the near future. Among adults under the age of thirty, almost three-quarters said they supported same-sex marriage.

On the day after the poll was published, the Supreme Court announced that it had granted petitions and would hear arguments on the *Windsor*/DOMA case *and* in our Prop 8 case. Considering the Court's calendar, we anticipated that both would be heard in March. Decisions on both were likely to hinge on whether the Court found that DOMA and Prop 8 discriminated against same-sex couples in violation of the Fourteenth Amendment. However, the Court asked the parties in each case to brief the issue of standing (the attorney general of the United States having declined to defend DOMA, as his counterpart in California did with Prop 8).

Some analysts speculated that the Court had granted Cooper's request for cert because some of the justices wanted to use the case as a means of reinforcing the power of states to set their own rules for marriage. Others believed that some of the justices were interested in going the other way—recognition of same-sex marriage nationwide. While we certainly hoped for the latter outcome, we didn't spend any energy speculating about it. That was out of our control—above our pay grade, as the saying goes. Our task was to prepare the best brief we could. We also began preparations for the hearing itself, which the

Court ultimately set for March 26, 2013 (argument was set in the *Windsor* case for March 27).

Our opponents submitted their brief on January 22, with a light blue cover, as required by Court rules. (The Court sets strict guidelines for every item it receives from attorneys. Word limits and type size are specified, and an array of colors is used to identify the type of document submitted. This is simply a way for the justices to recognize immediately which side a brief is supporting.) Cooper's brief—representing the petitioners—addressed the two main questions the Supreme Court sought to answer: first, whether the proponents (now petitioners) had standing under Article III of the Constitution to have appealed Judge Walker's decision; second, whether the Fourteenth Amendment prohibited the State of California from limiting marriage to the union of a man and a woman.

The blue brief opened by observing the broad public debate over same-sex marriage, including the three pro-equality referenda that had been approved in the November elections. Cooper wisely used those developments to his advantage as support for his argument that our issues were being addressed in the political sphere and should be left to state officials or the voters and not be usurped by the judiciary. "No precedent or established constitutional precept justifies federal judicial intervention into this sensitive democratic process," Cooper argued. "This is not a case, like *Lawrence v. Texas,* where the State has punished as a crime 'the most private human conduct, sexual behavior, and in the most private of places, the home,' or sought 'to control a personal relationship that, whether or not entitled to formal recognition in the law, is within the liberty of persons to choose without being punished as criminals.'" He argued there was no "warrant in precedent" for the judiciary to take on this issue and that the Court should allow the public debate regarding marriage to continue through the democratic process, both in California and throughout the nation.

The brief went on to press many by now familiar arguments. It stated, for example, that Prop 8 was not a badge of discrimination but rather a protective measure written to prevent changing the time-immemorial definition of marriage. The brief rejected *Romer* as a controlling precedent, and asserted that the people of California could withhold the nomenclature of marriage from gay and lesbian couples because the state had a legitimate interest in encouraging heterosexual couples to reproduce in stable families. This "animating purpose of marriage," Cooper stated, was established in distinguished and respected sources dating back to the famous eighteenth-century British jurist William Blackstone, who wrote that the relationship between husband and wife was "founded in nature, but modified by civil society: the one directing man to continue and multiply his species, the other prescribing the manner in which that natural impulse must be confined and regulated." The Cooper legal team had obviously done thorough historical research. This was important to them, since so much of their case rested on history and tradition—in short, the way things have always been.

As expected, Cooper's brief was well researched and well written. What it lacked, including any discussion of how the lives of flesh-and-blood human beings would be affected by the outcome of this case, and little in the brief evoked any genuine emotion, was rooted in the weakness of his side of the case and the strengths of our trial record. For our part, we wanted to ensure that the case would be seen through the lens of human rights—an issue that had a real impact on the lives, dignity, and self-respect of millions of people.

Our red brief was drafted by several members of our team, with special attention by Ted and David to the introduction and conclusion, which focused on Jeff and Paul, Sandy and Kris. We reprised our now familiar standing arguments, but our brief primarily focused on the merits of our cause. The word "love" appeared four times in the first three pages, as did the word "commitment." We described marriage as an "officially sanctified" relationship and recalled from the trial how Jeff had said he wanted to marry Paul because marriage has a "special meaning" that would affect how their relationship was viewed by their families and others. We called for a decision that would protect the marriage rights of all gay and lesbian citizens, arguing that equal treatment under the law required nothing less.

As we presented our side of the ledger—where the pain and hurt experienced by our clients under Prop 8 was recounted—we reminded the Court that "with the full authority of the State behind it, Proposition 8 sends a clear and powerful message to gay men and lesbians: You are not good enough to marry. Your loving relationship is not equal to or respected enough to qualify to be called a marriage." Then we let Kris Perry speak, as she had during the trial: "If Prop. 8 were undone," and gay and lesbian "kids . . . could never know what this felt like, then . . . their entire lives would be on a higher arc. They would live with a higher sense of themselves that would improve the quality of their entire life."

Some of our brief was allotted, naturally, to responses to Cooper's assertions. With respect to his reference to the three pro-equality ballot initiatives recently approved in Maine, Minnesota, and Maryland, we reminded the Court that prior to 2012, gays and lesbians had lost thirty state referenda votes in a row. We pointed out, "Those recent results . . . do not alter the discrimination that gays and lesbians have faced, and continue to face, nationwide—and do not affect the applicability of heightened scrutiny to laws targeting gays and lesbians." When we turned to the proponents' claim that states could bar same-sex marriage as a means of promoting family stability and child welfare, we showed that it was at base an illogical concept: "The surest and most direct impact of Proposition 8 on children is not to increase the likelihood that they will be raised in stable and enduring family units, but, instead, as the district court found, to make it 'less likely that California children will be raised in stable households' by reducing the number of families who can be married."

Our most important arguments were those that drew upon bedrock American ideals. "This case is also about equality," we said in the first page of the brief. Proposition 8 placed "the full force of California's constitution behind the stigma that gays and lesbians, and their relationships, are not 'okay,' that their life commitments 'are not as highly valued as opposite-sex relationships,' and that gay and lesbian individuals are different, less worthy, and not equal under the law." In explaining the effect of this discrimination we borrowed a line from *Brown v. Board of Education* that noted that official discrimination "generates a feeling of inferiority . . . that may affect their hearts and minds in a way unlikely ever to be undone."

At the end of our brief we asked the Court to uphold the Ninth Circuit and overturn Prop 8 because "it denies gay men and lesbians their identity and their dignity; it labels their families as second-rate. That outcome cannot be squared with the principle of equality and the unalienable right to liberty and the pursuit of happiness that is the bedrock promise of America from the Declaration of Independence to the Fourteenth Amendment, and the dream of all Americans. This badge of inferiority, separateness, and inequality must be extinguished. When it is, America will be closer to fulfilling the aspirations of all its citizens."

As Supreme Court briefs go, ours was more emotional than those submitted in cases involving patents or antitrust matters. This was a civil rights case, a case about the effect of a discriminatory law on people, families, children. We hoped not only that the justices would be touched by the impact on the individuals concerned, but that our brief itself would stand as a document that might be read, remembered, and quoted as offering both a legal and a human rationale for our cause.

There was an overwhelming outpouring of support for marriage equality in the form of "friend of the court," or amicus, briefs filed in the U.S. Supreme Court. Fifty-four amicus briefs, with more than six hundred signatories, were filed in support of our position in the Court. More than the sheer volume of submissions, it was the breadth of the support—from state governments, scores of leading corporations, and well-known conservative leaders—that was truly staggering. Perhaps the most important brief was filed by the United States, which took the bold step of urging the Supreme Court to invalidate Proposition 8 and to apply a heightened level of judicial scrutiny to all classifications discriminating against gay men and lesbians—a dramatic shift from the federal government's position until the 1970s that gays and lesbians were unfit for any government employment and its position until 2011 that they were unfit to serve openly in the military. One hundred companies—including Apple, Facebook, Morgan Stanley, AIG, Nike, Intel, Verizon, Google, eBay, Cisco Systems, Oracle, Panasonic, Barnes & Noble, Office Depot, and Alaska Airlines—also submitted a brief, emphasizing that marriage equality is not only a moral imperative but also a business imperative. As the brief explained, "By singling out same-sex couples for unequal treatment, laws like Proposition 8 can impede business efforts to recruit, hire, and retain the best workers in an environment that enables them to perform at their best."

Ken Mehlman and 130 other prominent conservatives, including Jon Huntsman, Mary Cheney, Tom Ridge, Christine Todd Whitman, and Paul Wolfowitz, also joined a brief in support of our position. Taking issue with one of our opponents' primary grounds for defending Proposition 8, these conservative leaders wrote that "it is precisely because marriage is so important in producing and protecting strong and stable family structures that *amici* do not agree that the government can rationally promote the goal of strengthening families by denying civil marriage to same-sex couples." Other notable submissions included a brief from the State of California urging the Court to invalidate its own ballot initiative, a separate brief from thirteen other states—Massachusetts, Connecticut, Delaware, Illinois, Iowa, Maine, Maryland, New Hampshire, New Mexico, New York, Oregon, Vermont, and Washington—and the District of Columbia, as well as briefs from a coalition of religious organizations (including bishops of the Episcopal Church in California and the Union for Reform Judaism), the AFL-CIO, the American Psychological Association, the California Teachers Association, the Southern Poverty Law Center, and NFL players Chris Kluwe and Brendon Ayanbadejo. In quantity and, far more important, in quality, these briefs dwarfed the submissions supporting our opponents and left no doubt that the tide of public opinion had shifted dramatically in favor of marriage equality.

Since we hoped to communicate with a broad legal community and even the public, we were pleased that our brief received considerable attention. People were actually reading it. The well-regarded Lyle Denniston, dean of the Supreme Court reporting corps, posted his reaction on the Web site SCOTUSblog. It was entitled "All-out assault on

Proposition 8." It noted that while we had taken a "sweeping approach," we might have made it easier for the Court to give us a win, if only by upholding the Ninth Circuit's decision affecting just the State of California. The *Los Angeles Times* likewise noted the scope of our argument and said it would have the effect of "ratcheting up the pressure on the Obama administration" as well as on the justices.

We had hoped that our brief would help influence the White House and the Justice Department to support us in the Court and, as noted above, the United States did file a supporting brief. As deadlines for amicus briefs arrived, Solicitor General Donald Verrilli first filed a brief against DOMA and then, a week later, against Proposition 8. Echoing our own arguments, the Verrilli brief on Prop 8 affirmed that "prejudice may not be the basis for differential treatment under the law." The administration also stated that marriage "conveys a message to society that domestic partnerships or civil unions cannot match."

We were delighted to receive the administration's support, which added to the momentum favoring our position. And we were also delighted to learn, on the same day, of the Mehlman brief. Mehlman, former chairman of the Republican National Committee, had been involved in political campaigns that were hostile toward gays and lesbians. In 2010 he publicly acknowledged he was gay and repudiated the policies he had previously advocated.

From the beginning we had tried to convey that our cause was not a liberal or conservative issue, or a Republican or Democratic case, but a matter of human and constitutional rights. Nothing could have made that point better than the amicus briefs filed by the administration and prominent Republicans.

Win or lose, we all felt immensely enriched and inspired by a movement that kept gaining momentum and acceptance, crossed political lines, and built an irreversible case for greater equality, respect, decency, caring, and tolerance.

FOURTEEN

Days to Go

Ted rose, walked to the lectern, set down an open file, and commenced the Supreme Court argument that we had been working toward for over three years.

After beginning with the customary, "Mr. Chief Justice, and may it please the Court," Ted immediately addressed the way that Proposition 8 harmed our clients, and all gay and lesbian Californians, as both private individuals and public citizens. The amendment, he said, enshrined in the California constitution the notion that a union between gay or lesbian partners "is second class, unequal, and not okay," a law that was "unreasonable, irrational, and stigmatizing [to] a class of Californians based on their status."

As typically happens, the panel interrupted Ted's opening statement to ask questions and express their own positions on the issues. One justice asked, "You're not saying, are you, that there could not have been millions of Californians who voted on the basis of a different reason, one that is *not* bias?"

The reason is not as important as the outcome, Ted thought, and he replied with this in mind. "The outcome [was the product of] what the proponents said in their materials." The materials in question included advertising, public presentations, and letters that clearly appealed to prejudice. These had been presented at the trial and were part of the record, as well as the videos that went as far as linking marriage equality to pedophilia, incest, and even terrorism.

Another question came from the bench. "Marriage is just a word, a name, isn't it?"

"So is the word 'citizen,'" Ted responded.

"But what's to keep them from just *calling* themselves married?" asked the same justice. The inference being that gay and lesbian couples could start simply using the term "married."

"They could call themselves Martians, too," answered Ted. "But the state says [that a marriage between them would not be] valid. I respectfully suggest the testimony of the plaintiffs be read, and reread. What does it mean to be married? Well, there's a reason people do not celebrate domestic partnerships with flowers and parties."

From another side of the bench came a pointed question about the propriety of the Court's stepping into a controversy that was still being debated heatedly around the country. "Mr. Olson, the trend has already been shifting in your favor," noted a third justice. "Wouldn't it be better to let the people and their representatives decide this rather than have their position determined by judicial fiat?"

The question framed a central issue related to our democratic process. In the American system power rests with the people, and policy decisions should be made by citizens, localities, states, and finally the federal government, and not, except as a last resort, by the courts. Supreme Court justices, like all federal judges, are unelected and therefore not directly accountable to the people. Justices are sensitive to this issue and know that critics are always ready to protest that they have overstepped their bounds and become activist jurists. This was the complaint raised by opponents of the *Roe v. Wade* decision, which legalized abortion rights in 1973 but did not put to rest the bitter fight over the issue. Justice Ginsburg had revealed her sensitivity to the activist charge in February 2013, telling an audience at Columbia Law School that the Court may have "moved too far too fast" in *Roe*. She added, "The Court made a decision that made every abortion law in the country invalid, even the most liberal. . . . Things might have turned out differently if the Court had been more restrained."

But just as courts need to be careful not to overstep and usurp issues that belong in the political arena, they need to be sure that they are vigilant in protecting those fundamental rights that the Constitution guarantees that no political majority can infringe. Ted reviewed the historical circumstances in which majority rule, as expressed by voters or legislatures, failed to safeguard, and occasionally ran roughshod over, fundamental individual rights. The so-called tyranny of the majority was the main concern that the framers had in mind when they drafted the Bill of Rights. Several subsequent amendments to the Constitution also focused on equality and the protection of individual rights. The Fourteenth Amendment is particularly important in this regard, providing that no state may "deprive any person of life, liberty, or property, without due process of law; nor deny to any person within its jurisdiction the equal protection of the laws." Over time this protection has been affirmed and amplified by the Court to cover evolving conceptions of individual rights and discrimination. Perhaps the most famous of these decisions was the 1954 ban on "separate but equal" education for the races in *Brown v. Board of Education*.

"You could have said the same thing about integration of the schools or the decision to end the prohibition on interracial marriage," said Ted in response to the question from the bench. "What do you say to the citizen who happens to live in a state that's a long way from granting equal rights? Justice delayed can be justice denied." And in California, Ted added, gays and lesbians would have their previously established rights as married couples and parents "taken away" if Proposition 8 was allowed to stand.

"You keep saying 'taken away,'" protested one of the justices. "They never had these rights in the first place."

"But they *did* in California," Ted replied. "Eighteen thousand people were married when they were allowed to."

"But that's a state's right."

"Not when it's a matter of privacy, liberty, free association."

This exchange took place not in the actual court but rather in a conference room at Gibson Dunn's Washington, D.C., office, where tables and chairs had been arranged to approximate the setting in which in a week's time our arguments would be made to the actual Supreme Court. Along the back wall, seated behind a table facing the

audience, were David Boies, Matt McGill, Ted Boutrous, and Gibson
Dunn attorneys Andrew Tulumello and Thomas Dupree, playing their
roles as Supreme Court justices. Each had put substantial effort into
studying not only the case itself but the Court's justices and how they
might be thinking about it.

During this moot court session, which was one of several we held as
part of our preparation, each of the participants, in their own way, attempted to channel the individual justices, including particularly Justice
Antonin Scalia, whom everyone expected to offer the greatest resistance
to our position. As a self-described originalist, Justice Scalia considered
it his duty to determine and be guided by the intentions of those who
drafted and voted on the Constitution and its amendments. He resists
the popular notion that the Constitution is a "living document" subject
to new interpretations based on changing times. Justice Scalia can find
no support in the Constitution for many rulings that have established
"new rights," like the right to abortion ("judicially invented," in his
words), which was established by the Court in 1973 in *Roe v. Wade*.

Perhaps imagining what Justice Scalia might ask, Matt McGill
challenged Ted on the notion that gays and lesbians deserved extra
protection—heightened scrutiny—as a minority that suffered discrimination and the loss of fundamental rights under Proposition 8.

"It used to be that [gays and lesbians] could not get a federal job,"
explained Ted. "You could get arrested. The Internal Revenue Service
even denied tax exemptions to organizations that supported gay rights
on the ground that such groups permitted immoral activity." Such
forms of discrimination demonstrated, in our view, that gays and lesbians were entitled to careful judicial scrutiny when their rights were
being infringed.

Switching issues, one of the "justices" raised the point that the state
had an interest in restricting marriage to heterosexuals because only
opposite-sex couples could create children. "Do you deny the biological differences?" he asked.

"Marriage is not about having children," answered Ted. "Justice
Scalia made that point in his dissent in *Lawrence v. Texas*."

Our typical procedure for Supreme Court arguments is to have members of our team assemble assessments of each of the justices in order to evaluate how they might approach the upcoming case, what questions they might ask, how they might see the issues, and to preview as much as possible their ultimate take on the case. This time, rather than have one lawyer prepare the analysis, we parceled the job out to nine different evaluators, each of whom was responsible for drafting a memo on a single justice. There was no guarantee that this extra effort would result in unique insights, but it would at the very least give us more thoroughgoing analyses than we might expect from assigning only one or two people to handle all the assessments. The evaluation memos that the team produced were filled with important background information.

The results of this process were somewhat predictable. While we continued our efforts to find a way to persuade all nine justices, we felt that on the merits, as opposed to the standing issue, we would have most difficulty with persuading Chief Justice Roberts and Justices Scalia, Thomas, and Alito. Our most receptive audience, we believed, would consist of Justices Breyer, Ginsburg, Sotomayor, and Kagan. The critical vote, we felt, as did most commentators, would be Justice Kennedy.

Justice Kennedy had written for the majority in *Romer* and *Lawrence*, showing sensitivity to the rights of homosexuals and concern over acts that discriminated against them as a class. But he had also manifested in his jurisprudence a strong respect for federalism and the rights of states. How would he balance his presumptive understanding of the impact of Proposition 8 on gays and lesbians with his respect for the rights of California and Californians to determine for themselves who could be married?

No one attempted overtly to impersonate Justice Kennedy (or any of the other justices) during the moot court sessions, but one of our participants did make a rather Kennedyesque observation when he noted, "You are binding forty-nine other states to one circuit court's decision."

"That's what happens when you make a Fourteenth Amendment decision," answered Ted. "You do that all the time without going state by state."

With its due process and equal protection clauses, the Fourteenth Amendment has supplied the rationale for a host of Supreme Court decisions that have benefited minorities and imposed sweeping change upon the nation: integrated schools, interracial marriage, access to abortion, rights of aliens, for example. Less substantial Fourteenth Amendment remedies were, as Ted pointed out, handed down frequently. But this regularity didn't make a broad Fourteenth Amendment decision concerning marriage equality any easier for justices concerned about overstepping the role of the Court. We would have to provide powerful arguments to support a far-reaching decision and provide reassurances that the justices would not be embarking on a slippery slope that would have unintended consequences as to states' rights and reasonable state restrictions on the right to marry, such as age of consent to marry and marriage between family members.

Because this was a moot court, the participants and observers were expected to comment and advise us when the formal session came to an end. One of the first to speak was Terry Stewart. "I think when you are asked the question about why the Court should act now," she suggested, "it's important to say that there are many states where it's unlikely that anything good will happen for a very long time." This seemed like good advice, but when Terry moved on to the subject of polygamy, where Ted explained that he wanted "a quick answer that keeps me out of quicksand," the issue became more complicated.

"Polygamists are not denied the right to marry," noted Terry. "They are just denied the right to marry again and again." At first blush this sounded like a perfect quip, both amusing and true. But such facile responses often backfire in the Supreme Court. This was an issue that would have to be handled carefully.

Ted concluded that if pressed he would argue that the government has a right to police polygamy because courts had held that polygamy "fosters a patriarchal society" that endangered the rights and welfare of women, that it created immense problems with respect to children, child custody, divorce, and property rights, and that limits on polygamy restricted conduct, not a person's status.

As we debated other questions that might be asked by the justices,

David kept reminding everyone that the "full majestic stop" for each of our answers should be a reference to one of the landmark cases— *Brown, Loving, Romer, Lawrence*—that led inexorably to a decision in our favor in this case. And Ted referred to the Supreme Court decision in 1940 upholding a state law requiring Jehovah's Witnesses to say the Pledge of Allegiance. The Court reversed itself shortly thereafter when it became apparent that the earlier decision led to bullying and discrimination. That is what we felt could happen here with an erroneous decision.

Minersville School District v. Gobitis had gone pretty much the way we remembered it. A local school board in Pennsylvania had expelled William Gobitis's four children after they repeatedly refused to say the pledge due to their faith, which forbids any oath sworn to an earthly power. An eight-to-one decision against the family was followed by more than a thousand acts of violence against Witnesses or their property. In 1943 the Court reversed itself in *West Virginia State Board of Education v. Barnette*, in which Justice Robert Jackson wrote, "If there is any fixed star in our constitutional constellation, it is that no official, high or petty, can prescribe what shall be orthodox in politics, nationalism, religion or other matters of opinion."

In our series of moot courts, we rehearsed the full range of issues we might expect to encounter in the Supreme Court. In fact, we went far beyond that. We wanted to try to be ready for whatever happened, however unlikely. It is impossible to predict everything that might be asked, but there is no excuse for not trying to get as close as possible. Moot courts were attended by lawyers from the Boies Schiller and Gibson Dunn firms as well as by outsiders with expertise in a particular area. One especially useful session was held at Georgetown University's law school, where we were hosted by Irv Gornstein, executive director of the university's Supreme Court Institute. The Georgetown University Law Center contains a beautiful approximation of the real Supreme Court chamber, right down to the red drapes that hang behind the justices and the old brass clock, complete with Roman numerals, suspended from the ceiling. The center hosts moot courts for a substantial portion of the cases the Supreme Court hears every year. The staff there is very, very good at helping an advocate prepare for the real thing.

Our Georgetown moot court panel included: Pamela Harris, a prominent appellate lawyer who served in government; Christopher Landau, who heads the appellate practice at the Washington office of Kirkland & Ellis; and Maureen Mahoney, another brilliant and experienced Supreme Court litigator, who practices at Latham & Watkins. Mahoney had represented the University of Michigan in *Grutter v. Bollinger* (2003), in which the Court upheld admissions policies that included race among the factors considered as part of student applications to the university's law school in order to foster a diverse student body.

Although we intentionally restricted attendance at most of the moot sessions, we did open one at Gibson Dunn to a handful of interested parties, including AFER members and our clients Sandy, Kris, Paul, and Jeff. Their presence served as a vivid reminder that this case was not merely about abstract legal concepts but rather the lives of tens of millions of individual Americans who were harmed by Proposition 8 and similar laws and regulations.

Like other important moments from the early beginnings of this case, these sessions were captured by award-winning photographer Diana Walker, who moved quietly around the room photographing the scene. As always, she worked so unobtrusively that it was easy to forget she was there, clicking away. Thirty years of capturing images in the corridors of power, including as *Time* magazine's White House photographer, had endowed her with both an impeccable eye and a flawless manner. What was even more impressive was her graciousness and enthusiasm. Tirelessly, she approached every moment that appeared in the lens with her full attention, as if no one—not even the many presidents and world leaders she had recorded for posterity—could be more important than the people she was photographing in the present.

In the years we devoted to this case, Diana made thousands, if not tens of thousands, of images. In the same period we, as a group, participated in hundreds of interviews for print articles, broadcast pieces, and reports on various Internet sites. It was vitally important that we get our message of equality and acceptance out to as many people as possible. At other moments, like when we secreted ourselves away from the world to focus more intently on our work, we forced the media attention into the background and concentrated on the central purpose of our mission—to win for our clients and others the right to get married. This required single-minded focus, and that meant building a defense against distractions.

Nevertheless, outside our self-imposed insular bubble, influential individuals and groups continued to attempt to influence the Court and public opinion. The Catholic archbishop of San Francisco made a statement outlining his reasons for supporting Proposition 8, as did a team of advocates whose argument was published by the Heritage Foundation think tank in Washington, D.C. They raised the by now familiar specter of polygamy as well as the "anthropological evidence" that children require opposite-sex parents.

On the other side of the ledger the American Academy of Pediatrics declared its support for marriage equality, noting that there was no evidence that children were harmed in any way by being raised by gay or lesbian parents, nor were children adversely affected by life in households headed by same-sex couples. Republican senator Rob Portman of Ohio changed his view and announced his support after heart-to-heart conversations with his gay son. Some hailed Portman, while others criticized him for abandoning his earlier convictions. The senator's GOP brethren, meanwhile, announced a $10 million "inclusion campaign" intended to persuade gays and lesbians as well as members of ethnic and racial minorities that the party was not insensitive to them or their needs.

Republicans and Democrats alike were conscious of national opinion polls. Days before our argument, the *Washington Post* and ABC News released the results of a survey that found that an astonishing 58 percent of Americans supported marriage equality. Three years earlier, when we started this case, only 47 percent supported this position. And just nine years ago, fewer than a third of those surveyed said they approved of state-sanctioned marriage for lesbian and gay couples. Polling experts couldn't recall when the country had changed its mind so thoroughly, and in such a short time, on any issue of comparable importance.

The press made a great deal out of the poll findings and spotlighted every prominent person—athlete, entertainer, politician—who took a stand. The vast majority of those announcing positions lined up behind us, for a variety of reasons ranging from personal morality to a desire to be on the right side of history. Even though this all took place in the court of public opinion, and therefore not in the court that ultimately mattered the most to us, the tide that was running so strongly in support of our clients was both gratifying and exciting. But however much we might have wanted to join the discussion of the issues taking place in the mass media, we determined that it was in our clients' best interest for us to maintain a low profile in the days before the argument. It would be seen as unseemly, we felt, by the justices to do otherwise. The one exception we made was for the Sunday morning news program *Meet the Press*. When producers asked for an interview, we agreed that David would sit for a one-on-one discussion with its host, David Gregory, so that we might respond to the legitimate public interest in the case in a respected, mature forum.

This turned out to be a good decision, especially as we watched some of the guests who appeared on the program before David mangle the issues and distort the facts. Ralph Reed, a political operative of the Christian conservative movement, declared as an uncontested fact of social science that biological parents were the gold standard of family life. Reed also claimed that the polls showing majority support for marriage equality were "within the margin of error."

Waiting in the wings, David knew he wouldn't have the chance to correct all the boldly stated but erroneous points made by others. He also understood that he would be pressed to prognosticate about the outcome of the upcoming argument. In an age of twenty-four-hour news competition in which everything was presented as if it were a horse race or a prizefight, David Gregory would naturally feel obliged to ask for a prediction about the Court's decision. That kind of speculation wouldn't serve us well, no matter how carefully it might be crafted. Supreme Court justices undoubtedly ignore such things. They are used to it, after all. But why take a chance that something like that might rankle a justice or seem presumptuous?

To his credit, Gregory opened the segment with a serious discussion of the case's merits, allowing David to offer a capsule version of the key points. David explained the hard work that had already been accomplished at the trial court level. He began with the short summary of what was at stake that had worked so well before. "At the very beginning of this case, we said we needed to prove three things. We needed to prove, first, that marriage was a fundamental right. And I think we did that, and even the defendants agreed with that, because the Supreme Court has ruled that [it is] fourteen times in the last one hundred years. Second, we needed to prove that depriving gay and lesbian citizens of the right to marry seriously harmed them, and seriously harmed the children that they were raising. And we proved that too, not only through our witnesses but through the defense witnesses."

After these ninety-seven words, which amounted to a rather long statement by television standards, the host couldn't resist interrupting to ask, "Are you saying that you want gays and lesbians to be treated as a protected class, like African Americans? So in other words, the burden is so high to discriminate against them?"

This was an important but delicate issue, and David was glad to have the chance to discuss it. But instead of carrying the entire burden himself, he let the president, whose solicitor general had by then filed the brief for the United States in our support, bear a bit of it. As he told Gregory, "That's exactly what the administration's brief says. But we believe that even if you simply apply the rational basis test, there is no rational basis to justify this ban. And that's because of the third thing that we proved, which was that there was no evidence, none, that allowing gays and lesbians to marry harms the institution of marriage or harms anyone else."

Eventually, the host shifted to the predictable line of questions about how we thought the justices might rule. "Handicap this," said Gregory. "Do you remember the *Time* magazine last summer about Justice Kennedy, that he is the decider? How do you think this goes?"

David knew better than to predict, out loud, what individual justices might do. After some back-and-forth he responded as diplomatically as he could and as optimistically as he thought appropriate.

"What I've said is I think we're going to win. I don't think we're going to win five-four. I think this is a basic civil rights issue, I don't think that this is the kind of issue that's going to divide the Court the way some other issues divide the Court."

———

Our team went silent after that. With less than forty-eight hours to go before our appearance before the Court, Ted spent all day Sunday at his home in the Virginia woodlands twenty miles northwest of the District of Columbia. In his quiet study there he surrounded himself with books and papers and rereviewed again and again the argument he had made before but would now make in the most important and most challenging forum.

On the dozens of occasions when they have lived through a Supreme Court argument, Ted and his wife, confidante, and sounding board, Lady, have found themselves contentedly lost in the details and anticipation. Few occasions invite this kind of sustained focus on such challenging issues, and they cherished the chance to discuss the facts, the merits of various arguments, the precedents, and the perspectives of the men and women of the Court.

Having witnessed many arguments and spent time with a number of the justices, Lady may have been one of the most informed Supreme Court observers in the country. But like almost everyone else on our side, she had become so fully persuaded that the merits favored us that she struggled to understand why anyone would decide against us. The way she saw it, even the most skeptical should have to realize that the Fourteenth Amendment, which allows for the Court to continually revisit the concepts of equal protection and due process, supported the idea that we live under a constitution that is at least informed of changing science and expanding wisdom of who and what we are as a people. No longer could we see gays and lesbians as deviants, outcasts, threatening, or alien. We had to embrace them as our equals.

We resisted letting our hopes rise too high; imagining a decision for our clients signed by at least five justices felt as far as we dared go. On the day before the argument we spent hours sharpening our points—like Ted's Number 2 pencils—on the chance that something we might offer would tip the balance. Ted's private office at Gibson Dunn, behind an unmarked door, became the war room for the day. Ted Boutrous, Matt McGill, Amir Tayrani, and others scurried in and out with comments and critiques while Ted's notes for the argument were constantly being refined to the absolute essence. By the end of the day, we were ready, and there wasn't much that any additional group effort might contribute.

Ted went home to Virginia, where, as he opened the door on the eve of the argument, he was greeted by the homey aroma of a barbecued chicken dish that Lady had been cooking slowly throughout the afternoon. She had wanted to recall for Ted the cozy home life he knew growing up with a mother who had delayed her teaching career while her children were young in order to provide nightly home-cooked meals. A quiet evening was followed by an early bedtime, but no one on the team slept very soundly—adrenaline was surging in all of our hearts.

FIFTEEN

March 26, 2013

In Virginia Ted arose before 4 A.M., slipped out of bed, and dressed for the momentous day to come. Concerned that the justices focus on what he said and not what he was wearing, he put on a sober black suit with a soft white pinstripe, a serious white shirt, and a muted gray tie, and selected ladybug cuff links. Into a pocket went a laminated picture of the Archangel Michael, who defeats Satan in the book of Revelation, a somewhat whimsical good-luck talisman his late wife, Barbara, had slipped into his pocket without his knowledge the morning he went to court to argue the *Bush v. Gore* case.

While Ted made the twenty-mile drive to his office in the predawn darkness, Paul, Jeff, Kris, and Sandy were each giving up on getting any more sleep. In their hotel rooms in Washington they switched on lights, coffee makers, and televisions, which were showing newscasters already positioned in front of the Supreme Court. The argument was the top story of the day on every channel. Soon the team from AFER would call for them, and they would begin a whirl of press briefings and interviews, all before the session at court.

Meanwhile, on her early morning bus ride to Gibson Dunn, Ted's assistant Helen Voss, who had worked with him for over twenty years, contemplated the incredible effort that had brought our team to this day. As she considered all of the people who would be affected by what we were about to do, her eyes filled with tears.

None of us had ever worked on a case that meant so much, so

deeply, on a personal level to so many people. The Proposition 8 case was not about politics, but about love and identity, and it was this reality that so moved Helen. Knowing Ted was already at the office, she sent an e-mail asking if he wanted her to stop on the way in and pick up a coffee. At his desk, inside the windowless refuge with the unmarked door, Ted typed out a quick reply—"Got one, thanks." He had been lucky; the coffee shop next to the office had opened early and he already had his latte reinforced with an extra shot of espresso—not that extra caffeine was needed that morning.

Ted focused yet again on the first words for the Court that he had carefully crafted. That was all he might reasonably expect to get out before being interrupted by questions from the bench. Each side in a Supreme Court argument is usually allowed only thirty minutes—and that very short time is almost always interrupted frequently by questions from the jurists. The justices almost always begin a salvo of questions and comments as soon as the lawyer who has begun to argue takes a breath—often before that. Interruption is part of the game, and it is a practice accepted by all, so it is prudent to make your best effort at delivering a forceful point in that first breath. The proceedings would be recorded, and the audio and print transcripts posted on the Internet within hours of the argument, which was scheduled to start at 10 A.M. Millions of people would access these recordings as soon as they were available, and the world press would rely on them for quotes. An opening line delivered clearly, briskly, and with as little interruption as possible would be our one best chance at expressing in compact form what we believed the case was all about that would be played over and over again on television, radio, and the Internet. In the war for the hearts and minds of the American public, a memorable encapsulation—sound bite—was invaluable.

The key sentiment, which Ted continued to refine with his pencil, addressed the unconstitutional effects of Proposition 8. He wanted to make clear, as succinctly as possible, that real people with normal aspirations and dreams were being brutally harmed by the discrimination carved into their state's constitution. To convey this he relied on straightforward, simple words, not legalese, and a single clear, hopefully memorable sentence: "Proposition 8 walls off gays and lesbians from marriage, the most important relation in life according to this court, thus stigmatizing a class of Californians based upon their status and labeling their most cherished relationships as second-rate, different, unequal, and not okay."

The structure of that sentence, composed carefully to convey its full oratorical force, would enable him to conclude that message with a powerful cadence ending with a resounding four-beat measure. The last three words—"and not okay"—were the kind of easily understood phrase you might hear in any regular conversation, but if communicated in just the right tone, those words conveyed the depth of pain experienced by people whom society repeatedly stigmatizes. "Not okay" would set the tone for the argument in a way that felt right to Ted as he sat at his desk and read it over, and then over again. It was inspired by the official ballot measure arguments placed in voters' hands by the proponents of Proposition 8. The measure was necessary, they argued, so that Californians, especially children, would not be taught that homosexuals and marriage between persons of the same sex were "okay." The message was clear. These people are not okay, they are not you. They are different. You must protect yourself and your children from "them." This same message was repeated by our experts and by our plaintiffs during the trial. Being gay, society was telling them, was different, wrong, not okay.

When Helen arrived at the office, she saw that her boss was deep into his usual preargument routine—reviewing, editing, rewriting—and left him alone to make the final corrections on the notes he would carry to the Supreme Court. There were only four key pages. Three, which were stapled together, took care of the main points of the argument, including the opening statement, the established right to marriage, and the status of our plaintiffs as parties worthy of constitutional protection. On a fourth sheet Ted had finalized his "Key Answers," which anticipated issues that were likely to be interjected in questions. None of this was really necessary, of course. Ted knew the material backwards and forwards. He had been preparing for this moment for years. But the process of constantly reviewing and distilling was part of his routine. He wasn't going to change it now.

Ted had written on his notes a reference to Martin Luther King Jr.'s famous 1963 *Letter from Birmingham City Jail*, which paraphrased Gladstone: "Justice too long delayed is justice denied." The letter, later published as a book, is a foundational text of the American civil rights movement, and its answers and arguments applied as forcefully to the cause of marriage equality as they did to the cause of equal rights for African Americans in the 1960s.

As Helen took this work from Ted's hand to make him a fresh, edited copy, David arrived for a last-minute run-through. At eight o'clock the team, which included Ted Boutrous, Matt McGill, and Amir Tayrani, headed for the elevators and rode down to the lobby. Outside the sky was cloudless, and sunlight reflected from the windows of the buildings along Connecticut Avenue. The weather was a dramatic change from the previous three days, which had been cold, overcast, and wet.

After everyone piled into a waiting SUV, driven by Chris Arborn, David's longtime assistant and a former New York City police officer, we set out for the Court along a route that took us past the White House, the Washington Monument, various government departments, and the U.S. Capitol. More power and history resided along this route than along any other stretch of road in the western hemisphere, a fact that's hard to ignore on your way to the Supreme Court to argue a history-making case.

The Court occupies a city block just east of the Capitol. We arrived at the north, Maryland Avenue side of the building, where counsel and Court officers usually enter through a side door. However, construction had closed the entrance, so we walked to the front of the courthouse, where more than two thousand people had gathered like opposing armies, waving banners and chanting slogans on both sides of First Street NE. We heard cheers, shouts, and a few jeers as we crossed the granite plaza and entered the court on the ground level, where we would pass through security, greet Court officials, and await the proceedings.

Outside the crowd of demonstrators continued to grow as the clock ticked toward ten. Most came walking up First Street from Union Station, where the Human Rights Campaign had posted greeters at the train escalators and doorways and on the sidewalks. The ones in the station building held little American flags and offered cheery good-mornings as they handed out cards announcing, "Today is a wonderful moment in history!" Anyone who feared that the Proposition 8 oral arguments would bring an unruly crowd of demonstrators would have been reassured. The greeters practically glowed with kindness, and their information cards urged their friends and allies, "If you encounter those opposed to our point of view, be respectful." The final two words were printed in red.

Despite the size of the crowd and the intensity of the passion on either side of the issue, police would report no arrests, and the few conflicts that did arise never escalated beyond an exchange of words. Many of the homemade signs carried by our supporters addressed the issue in personal terms. One woman dressed in a red wool coat and matching hat held a piece of cardboard on which she had written, YOU CALLED ME NAMES. BULLIED ME. NOW GIVE ME JUSTICE. Another sign playfully announced, MY GAY AGENDA. 6 AM—WAKE UP. 6:30 AM— WALK DOG. It wasn't until 7:45 P.M. that the agenda included the item, BREAK UP A HETEROSEXUAL MAN/WOMAN MARRIAGE. Religious messages predominated among the supporters of Proposition 8, along with dozens of identical signs declaring, KIDS DO BEST WITH A MOM AND A DAD. The Prop 8 supporters were less vocal than the opponents, but they did cheer loudly when a few hundred people paraded onto the scene behind heraldic banners emblazoned with the words TRADITION, FAMILY, and PROPERTY.

For the most part the placards of the Prop 8 supporters were polite expressions of their point of view, printed on slick cardboard stock. The exceptions were the sadly familiar, hand-painted messages of hate displayed by the provocateurs of the Westboro Baptist Church of Topeka, who are infamous for spreading hateful dogma at every sort of public event, from military funerals to the sites of mass shooting tragedies. Their GOD HATES FAGS posters have unfortunately become familiar emblems of bigotry.

By 9:45 A.M. the Supreme Court chamber was filled to its capacity of roughly three hundred, including those who had taken seats behind interior columns. The press corps, which included quite a few nationally known journalists (Nina Totenberg, Pete Williams, Adam Liptak, Jan Crawford, Jeff Toobin), crowded into a section on the justices' right. To the justices' left sat spouses and guests of the Court itself. Attorneys presenting arguments sit at small tables that flank a wooden lectern that is positioned directly in front of Chief Justice Roberts. Some attorneys, who are aware of a little cranking mechanism that will raise or lower the lectern, make ceremonious adjustments to signal that they are veterans of the Court. Everyone knows that a little white light on the podium will come on five minutes before a lawyer's allotted time will expire. When a red light illuminates, time is up, and you must stop talking.

Ceremony is an important part of the Court's proceedings and sets a solemn tone. For example, the justices' arrival is announced at precisely ten o'clock as the marshal cries, "The Honorable Chief Justice and the Associate Justices of the Supreme Court of the United States. Oyez! Oyez! Oyez! All persons having business before the Honorable, the Supreme Court of the United States are admonished to draw near and give their attention, for the Court is now sitting. God save the United States and this Honorable Court." They file in and are seated with the help of four young attendants. Except for the chief, who always occupies the center chair, the justices' positions on the bench are determined by seniority, with the longest-serving member at the chief's right hand. Above them, carved into friezes over the draperies, are portraits of history's great lawgivers, including Moses, Cato, Justinian, Blackstone, and Charlemagne. Suspended between two great marble columns fifteen feet above the chief's head, the faded red hand of a distinctive brass-framed clock records the passing minutes.

In every case the arguments commence when the chief justice calls the attorney for the petitioner, who always begins, as Chuck Cooper did that day, with the words, "Thank you, Mr. Chief Justice, and may it please the Court." With the formalities covered, Cooper spoke quickly, saying, "New York's highest court, in a case similar to this one, remarked that until quite recently, it was an accepted truth for almost everyone who ever lived in any society in which marriage existed—"

That was as far as Cooper got with his prepared remarks before the chief justice stopped him to ask, "Mr. Cooper, we have jurisdictional and merits issues here. Maybe it'd be best if you could begin with the standing issue."

Chief Justice Roberts spoke firmly, signaling that the justices were in full control and would focus on the issues they wanted to hear addressed. As usual, this would mean rapid-fire questions and pointed follow-ups whenever a justice was unsatisfied with an answer or chose to make a particular point. With the game on, Cooper dropped his prepared remarks and tried to get into the flow.

Beginning with a little throat-clearing phrase that gave him a moment to think—"I'd be happy to, Mr. Chief Justice"—Cooper then replied, "Your Honor, the official proponents of Proposition 8, the initiative, have standing to defend that measure before this court as representatives of the people and the State of California to defend the validity of a measure that they brought forward."

Cooper's claim was not based on any federal rule, law, or precedent, a point that Justice Ruth Bader Ginsburg made as she now interrupted to ask, "Have we ever granted standing to proponents of ballot initiatives?" Everyone in the room knew Cooper would have to answer, "No," and after he did, Justice Ginsburg said that once the proponents had gotten their referendum onto the California ballot, their special interest in it was finished. "It's law for them just as it is for everyone else," said the justice. "So how are they distinguishable from the California citizenry in general?"

As she stated her view of the facts, Justice Ginsburg spoke in a steady but quiet voice that carried barely a trace of her native Brooklyn. The justice is a slight woman who wears her brown hair pulled back into a professorial bun. Her blue eyes are framed by big glasses, and her black robes are always adorned with a lacy collar. Having reached the age of eighty just eleven days prior to our argument, the justice was a woman whose frail appearance belied enormous strength. During her time on the Court she had worked while receiving treatments for both colon and pancreatic cancer, twice beating the odds to survive. Other justices might speak more loudly and rapidly, but no one was tougher in mind or spirit, and no one was more admired. She *always* knew the facts and history of the case and the pertinent case law, and her questions were always focused and penetrating. With her question she had pointed to a modest way out of the case for the Court. If the justices determined that Hollingsworth et al. were not the right parties to appeal the decision striking down Proposition 8, their standing could not be established, their appeal of Judge Walker's decision would have been ineffective, and that decision, overturning Proposition 8, would be final.

Chief Justice Roberts and Justice Elena Kagan also expressed concern about the prospect of unofficial actors, rather than state officials, coming to the Court with various issues whenever the actual authorities declined to take them up. As further concerns were raised by Justices Sotomayor and Breyer, Cooper reminded the justices that the California Supreme Court had found that his clients were entitled to defend their proposition because they had authored, financed, and sponsored it. Then he made the point that citizens should have the right to defend a voter-enacted proposition when authorities declined to do so. Otherwise, he argued, a governor, attorney general, or president could defy the will of the people whenever he or she chose by simply choosing not to defend a law.

The debate on standing went on for more than nine minutes, taking up much of Cooper's limited half hour—and everyone in the courtroom could hear the tension in his voice as the clock ticked away. Finally the chief justice rescued him, saying, "Counsel, if you want to proceed to the merits, you should feel free to do so."

Visibly relieved, Cooper resumed his opening reference to shifting public attitudes on same-sex marriage. "The question before this court," he said, "is whether the Constitution puts a stop to that ongoing democratic debate and answers this question for all fifty states."

This was a crucial issue. Should the Court rule against Proposition 8 and then apply its decision to all fifty states, ending once and for all the practice that Cooper called tradition and we regarded as discrimination? This kind of question has arisen in many civil rights cases. Those who resist change in the practices being challenged urge that the body politic should be given the chance, state by state, or community by community, to change. Those who feel oppressed or discriminated against rail against having to put their rights to a vote. Why, they ask, should anyone be denied a basic freedom because he or she happens to live in a particular part of the country? People have been born, lived, and died while waiting for such wrongs to be righted. The Court had certainly found itself in precisely this kind of situation in previous cases. In cases like *Loving*, which was decided when a majority of Americans steadfastly refused to accept the idea of interracial marriage, the Court intervened, and within a very short time it became hard for most Americans to imagine why interracial marriage had ever been forbidden, indeed criminalized.

The justices pressed Cooper on the issue of whether the government could have any rational basis for banning same-sex marriage. In response, Cooper raised the by now familiar rationale that the state had a legitimate interest in fostering heterosexual marriage because it contributed to responsible procreation and stable family life. "The state's interest and society's interest in what we have framed as responsible procreation is—is vital," he argued, "but at bottom, with respect to those interests, our submission is that same-sex couples and opposite-sex couples are simply not similarly situated." At the same time, he added, gays and lesbians did not deserve protection as a minority group because, unlike blacks or other recognized minorities, their status "does not qualify as an accident of birth."

Cooper kept stressing that "it is impossible for anyone to foresee" what real-world harms to heterosexual marriage might result from same-sex marriage. He noted that only nine years had passed since Massachusetts had legalized same-sex marriage, and the outcome was as yet unclear. It would be reasonable, he said, "to hit the pause button and await additional information from the jurisdictions where this experiment is still maturing."

Justice Sonia Sotomayor asked one of the most insightful questions in the dialogue: "Outside of the marriage context, can you think of any other rational basis reason for a state using sexual orientation as a factor in denying homosexuals benefits or imposing burdens on them?" Cooper's answer, it seemed to us then and now, was as damaging to his case as his "I don't know" early in the case: "Your Honor, I cannot." He thus conceded, we felt, that gays and lesbians were a class that could not be denied equal rights. But then why deny their right to marry?

Cooper was in trouble and Justice Scalia tried to help him out. "Mr. Cooper, . . . let me give you . . . one concrete thing. I don't know why you don't mention some concrete things. If you redefine marriage to include same-sex couples, you must . . . permit adoption by same-sex couples, and . . . there's considerable disagreement . . . among sociologists as to what the consequences of raising a child in a . . . single-sex family, whether that is harmful to the child or not. Some states . . . do not permit adoption by same-sex couples for that reason."

Justice Ginsburg, never reluctant to tangle with her more forceful and aggressive colleague (and her close friend off the bench), pounced. "California does," she interjected. And in fact, between their own biological offspring and adopted kids, same-sex couples in the state were parenting roughly forty thousand children.

Seeming not to hear his colleague, Justice Scalia continued. "I don't think we know the answer to that. Do you know the answer to that, whether . . . it harms or helps the child?"

"No, Your Honor. And there's—" said Cooper.

"But that's a possible deleterious effect, isn't it?" said the justice.

"Your Honor, it—it is certainly among the—"

Here again, Justice Ginsburg spoke up, this time a bit more

forcefully. "It wouldn't be in California, Mr. Cooper, because that's not an issue, is it? In California, you can have same-sex couples adopting a child."

"That's right, Your Honor. That is true. And—but—but, Your Honor, here's—here's the point."

Now it was Justice Scalia's turn to volley. "I—it's true, but irrelevant," he persisted, allowing his voice to rise a bit with exasperation. "They're arguing for a nationwide rule which applies to states other than California, that every state must allow marriage by same-sex couples. And so even though states that believe it is harmful—and I take no position on whether it's harmful or not, but it is certainly true that—that there's no scientific answer to that question at this point in time."

"And—and that, Your Honor, is the point I am trying to make," agreed Cooper, "and it is the respondents' responsibility to prove, under rational basis review, not only that—that there clearly will be no harm, but that it's beyond debate that there will be no harm."

As we watched Cooper interact with the justices, we noted how quickly time was passing. Although we certainly did not feel sorry for him, we knew it was going to happen again when it was Ted's turn, and it was easy to imagine the frustration he must have been experiencing being stuck on this single issue. Justice Kennedy seemed to give Cooper a few points when he agreed that society's experience with families headed by same-sex couples was limited and noted that "we have five years of information to weigh against two thousand years of history or more."

But if Cooper thought he had an ally in Kennedy he was disappointed when the justice went on to call the Court's attention to all the children left in limbo by Proposition 8. "There are some forty thousand children in California, according to the red brief, that live with same-sex parents, and they want their parents to have full recognition and full status. The voice of those children is important in this case, don't you think?"

The red brief was, of course, our written submission to the Court defending the decision by the lower courts striking down Proposition 8. Justice Kagan focused on our arguments refuting the procreation rationale, questioning Cooper about whether states could legally deny the right to marry to couples over the age of fifty-five. "Would that be constitutional?" asked Kagan. Cooper answered, "No, Your Honor, it would not be constitutional." He then raced ahead to suggest that Kagan's example was flawed. "Your Honor, even with respect to couples over the age of fifty-five, it is very rare that both couples—both parties to the couple are infertile, and the traditional—"

Unable to resist, Justice Kagan interrupted to say, "No, really, because if the couple—I can just assure you, if both the woman and the man are over the age of fifty-five, there are not a lot of children coming out of that marriage."

This was as tough an issue for Cooper as it had been when the same line had been pursued by Judge Walker. And with Justice Kagan's retort, laughter bubbled out across the courtroom. Even Chuck Cooper smiled. Not to be outdone, the famously humorous Justice Scalia interjected, "I suppose we could have a questionnaire at the marriage desk when people come in to the marriage—you know, 'Are you fertile or are you not fertile?'" The crowd laughed again, and he continued, "I suspect this court would hold that to be an unconstitutional invasion of privacy, don't you think?"

Finally, after a bit more commentary from Mr. Cooper, Justice Scalia cited the one reference to enduring fertility that would cause anyone in Washington to smile. "Strom Thurmond," said Justice Scalia "was—was *not* the chairman of the Senate committee when Justice Kagan was confirmed." (The now deceased senator from South Carolina had famously fathered a child at age seventy-four.) Cooper hesitated briefly before finally saying, "Very few men—very few men outlive their own fertility." A minute or two later, after an impenetrable assertion that the "marital norm [is] designed . . . to make it less likely that either party . . . [to a] marriage will engage in irresponsible procreative conduct outside of that marriage," Cooper yielded the podium. The chief justice said, "Thank you, Mr. Cooper," and Cooper ceased speaking. The time, according to the clock over the bench, was about 10:35 A.M.

⸺

Outside the courthouse, where thousands of people still stood, a group from HRC had set up a portable sound system and presented a series of speakers who offered inspiring stories and encouraging words. One of the first to stand at the microphone was David Frum, a former speechwriter for George W. Bush. In the 1990s he had been a fierce and vocal opponent of same-sex marriage, warning of an apparent slipping away of tradition and values due to the rise of individualism and radical autonomy. At that time he said, "Those of us who oppose gay marriage . . . believe that these new values are not changing the family—they are destroying it, and harming those within."

An articulate and outspoken advocate for his own positions, David is also rigorous and intellectually honest. As he followed the issue he began to note data showing that in the years since 2003, when gays and lesbians began winning marriage rights, American families had actually grown a bit stronger. In 2011 the facts, along with the logic of the equality argument, had moved him to the other side. Outside the Supreme Court on March 26, he received a warm welcome that demonstrated just how far the equality campaign had come. He was followed by NFL linebacker Brendon Ayanbadejo and then Gene Robinson, the first openly gay bishop of the Episcopal Church in America.

While hundreds of people cheered these presentations, others in the crowd were carefully monitoring their smartphones, reading the early reports from inside the court by a reporter for SCOTUSblog. The first entry was not encouraging for our side: "There are not five votes to strike down Prop. 8 and recognize equal right to SSM [same-sex marriage] at this time."

However, anyone disappointed by that dispatch might have taken heart from the next two:

BREAKING—Key vote Kennedy VERY uncomfortable striking down Prop 8. suggests dismissing case. Would leave in
place 9th Cir. Pro SSM ruling

BREAKING—Prop 8 unlikely to be upheld: Either struck
down or SCOTUS won't decide case.

It is a testament to our instant-information age that reports on the
proceedings were being issued as they were taking place. However,
these bursts of information were the product of a reporter who, with
words like "unlikely to be upheld," trafficked more in speculation than
fact. Predicting the outcome of a Supreme Court case in the middle of
an argument is like picking a Kentucky Derby winner as the horses
make the first turn. No one can make such a call with an expectation
of being right beyond what chance allows. And way too much can be
read into an individual out-of-context question or remark.

Inside the courtroom it was Ted's turn to argue. He felt completely
focused as he waited for Chuck Cooper to settle in his chair. On the
one hand, it is great to go first in a Supreme Court argument. On the
other, there are advantages in following one's opponent, knowing what
he has said and what the justices have revealed about their thinking.

Chief Justice Roberts said, "Mr. Olson?"

Ted rose and took his place at the lectern. From Cooper's experience Ted knew he was going to be pulled into the standing issue, but
he very much wanted first to state for the Court and the world what
this case was all about: human life, marriage, discrimination, and
equality. He sensed that he might get away with one real sentence. He
was right, and it was important.

"Thank you, Mr. Chief Justice, and may it please the Court: I know
that you will want me to spend a moment or two addressing the standing question, but before I do that, I thought that it would be important

for this court to have Proposition 8 put in context, what it does. It walls off gays and lesbians from marriage, the most important relation in life according to this court, thus stigmatizing a class of Californians based upon their status and labeling their most cherished relationships as second-rate, different, unequal, and not okay."

As anticipated, Chief Justice Roberts seized the moment. "Mr. Olson, I cut off your friend before he could get into the merits."

"I was trying to avoid that, Your Honor."

"I know."

It was a warmly human exchange, and the crowd in the courtroom responded with laughter. Noting that "it's only fair," Chief Justice Roberts asked Ted to halt his discussion of the merits of the case and instead address the question of standing. Our brief had, of course, argued that Hollingsworth and his proponent colleagues were not the proper parties to bring the case to the Court. Justice Samuel Alito and others on the bench had said they were concerned that if interested citizens were denied standing, elected officials could thwart the will of the people by declining to defend duly adopted referenda and legislation. We knew that if we won the standing argument, the appeal would be dismissed and we would win the case. Proposition 8 would fall. Ted pointed out that state executives who didn't want to pursue a particular case could appoint individuals to do so.

This kind of arrangement is well known. For example, so-called special prosecutors are sometimes named by presidents so that a controversy can be handled in a manner independent of White House influence. As many people in the courtroom were aware, in the 1980s Ted had resisted a special prosecutor's subpoena in a case related to his work in the Reagan administration. Back then he had argued that these appointed prosecutors, if compelled by Congress, usurped the power of the executive and were unconstitutional. He had prevailed until the case reached the Supreme Court, where he ultimately lost. (Justice Scalia dissented.) But by then the investigation was over and the special investigation was dropped. But this case was different. Here executive officials would appoint a surrogate volitionally.

For those who did remember this case, the thought of Ted Olson now suggesting that an appointed special prosecutor, or "independent counsel," could be helpful was ironic. Amid scattered chuckles, Ted explained, "The government of the State of California frequently appoints an attorney where there's a perceived conflict of interest." But he also acknowledged that the decision the Court had to make on this question was "a close one." In fact, if we lost on standing, the case would proceed on the merits. That was, after all, what we had been preparing for from day one.

When he was allowed to resume presenting the merits of our case, Ted began by reminding the Court of its own record. "As I pointed out . . . at the outset, this is a measure that walls off the institution of marriage, which is not society's right. It's an individual right that this court again and again and again has said, the right to get married, the right to have the relationship of marriage is a personal right. It's a part of the right of privacy, association, liberty, and the pursuit of happiness. . . . The procreation aspect, the responsibility or ability or interest in procreation, is not a part of the right to get married."

What Ted was saying was that the Supreme Court had declared marriage to be a fundamental right more than a dozen times, and whenever it had been extended—as it had been in the case of interracial marriage—it was done not with procreation in mind but in the spirit of liberty, privacy, and equality. In a country founded on the principles of liberty and the pursuit of happiness, these values are fundamental. Procreation and family stability may have underpinned the institution of marriage at the time of its origins as a religious sacrament, but they were not a requirement for marriage anywhere in the United States. When questioned, Ted expressly noted, "The California Supreme Court decided that the equal protection and due process clauses of the California constitution did not permit excluding gays and lesbians from the right to get married."

Here Justice Scalia jumped in, as if he had been waiting for the right opening. "You've led me right into a question I was going to ask," he said. "The California Supreme Court decides what the law is. That's what we decide, right? We don't prescribe law for the future. We . . . decide what the law *is*." With this last word, the justice paused for a moment to emphasize the point he wanted to make. "I'm curious . . .

when did it become unconstitutional to exclude homosexual couples from marriage? Seventeen ninety-one? Eighteen sixty-eight, when the Fourteenth Amendment was adopted? . . . Sometime after [the Court's decision declining to address the issue in] *Baker,* where we said it didn't even raise a substantial federal question? When—when—when did the law become this?"

As Justice Scalia spoke, Ted listened carefully. This was what the case was all about. He had not heard this question in precisely those terms at any of the moots, but it was precisely the core of the case. He knew the question in some form was coming, and he was eager to answer.

It was not possible to answer the question with a precise date in time. Things did not happen that way. Ted answered the only way he thought he could, and pointed the inquiry right back to the heart of the matter: "When—may I answer this in the form of a rhetorical question? When did it become unconstitutional to prohibit interracial marriages? When did it become unconstitutional to assign children to separate schools?"

"It's an easy question, I think, for that one," answered Scalia. "At—at the time that the equal protection clause was adopted. That's absolutely true." He then allowed himself to sound a bit perturbed, and added, "But don't give me a question to my question. When do you think it became unconstitutional? Has it always been unconstitutional?"

Courts decide there are constitutional rights when they have before them a case that presents the issue, and when they know—and society knows—enough about the issue to make informed decisions. "When the California Supreme Court faced the decision, which it had never faced before," Ted responded. "Does excluding gay and lesbian citizens, who are a class based upon their status as homosexuals—is it—is it constitutional?"

"That's . . . not when it became unconstitutional," replied the justice. "That's when they acted in an unconstitutional matter. . . . When did it become unconstitutional to prohibit gays from marrying?"

"They did not assign a date to it, Justice Scalia, as you know," Ted replied. "What the court decided was the case that came before it—"

"I'm not talking about the California Supreme Court. I'm talking about your argument."

What the justice wanted to know was, when, in Ted's view, did the country come to the view that denying marriage to gays and lesbians should be considered unconstitutional? Ted's answer depended on identifying when it was that Americans had generally come to accept that one's sexual orientation is not chosen, but inborn. He answered, "There's no specific date in time. This is an evolutionary cycle." The point was not that the Constitution had changed but that we had come to know that homosexuality was a characteristic inherent in an individual—immutable—as we had learned from the experts, and that it therefore became class discrimination to exclude them from rights because of that characteristic. Americans had come now to understand the overwhelming evidence that gays and lesbians constituted a genuine class of people whose right to equality deserved consideration and protection.

Seated in the quiet but keenly attentive audience, Lady Olson tensed as she listened to Justice Scalia bore in about the moment when banning marriage for gays and lesbians became unconstitutional. Although she knew the justice was almost always conscious of the framers' original intent and habitually raised this type of concern, she had hoped that Scalia would ease off of Ted's apt response to the rhetorical question: his adverting to the unanimous *Brown v. Board* and *Loving* decisions, which finally ended state-sponsored racial discrimination ninety-nine years after passage of the Fourteenth Amendment.

Instead, the justice now began pressing even harder, asking, "So it would be unconstitutional even in states that did not allow civil unions?"

"We do, we submit that," answered Ted. But then he quickly added, "You could write a narrower decision."

"Okay. So I want to know how long it has been unconstitutional in those—"

"I don't—when—it seems to me, Justice Scalia, that—"

"It seems to me you ought to be able to tell me when. Otherwise, I don't know how to decide the case."

"I—I submit you've never required that before," replied Ted. "When you decided that . . . separate but equal schools were impermissible, a decision by this court, when you decided that that was unconstitutional, when did that become unconstitutional?"

Again, this was the whole point of the case. The plaintiffs had sued in district court to establish their constitutional rights in the forum the Constitution created for this purpose. The Court was being asked to affirm this claim based on a current understanding of human beings, society, and morality. The fact is that our knowledge of human nature *does* change over time, as the end of slavery and then segregation in America established, and our reading of constitutional protections consequently evolved to accommodate changes in understanding, such as concepts of privacy with the invention of imaging devices, cell phones, GPS devices, and advanced DNA technology. No reasonable person would argue that this process was in error, and a similar process was under way in the instance of marriage equality.

The Court has never inquired, nor could it establish a precise moment in time, when it became unconstitutional to require students to recite the Pledge of Allegiance, or to pray in school, or to use different drinking fountains. Those decisions are made when the Court reaches them. And the Court sometimes gets them wrong before it gets them right—as with school segregation. The point of this colloquy from our perspective was that the time for the Court to reach this issue and decide it was now.

Intervening to end what threatened to become a robust but endless debate between Ted and Justice Scalia, Chief Justice Roberts moved the questioning to the need for gays and lesbians in California to access marriage rights, given that they were already permitted to form civil unions, raise children, and live, for all intents and purposes, like married heterosexual couples. "It's just about the label in this case," he said.

"The label 'marriage' means something," answered Ted. "Even our opponents—"

"Sure. If you tell . . . a child that somebody has to be their friend, I suppose you can force the child to say, 'This is my friend,' but it changes the definition of what it means to be a friend. And that's, it seems to me, what the—what the supporters of Proposition 8 are saying here.

You're—all you're interested in is the label, and you insist on changing the definition of the label."

That point had validity only insofar as one accepted that "marriage" is a social term that has little meaning beyond the label, with no social, cultural, and legal status, like "friend." But the opposite was clearly true. We were arguing that the word "marriage" confers legal and cultural status—a status codified in more than a thousand laws, rules, and regulations—that is aptly compared to the word "citizen." As Ted told the chief justice, "It is like you were to say you can vote, you can travel, but you are not a citizen. There are certain labels in this country that are very, very critical. You could have said in the *Loving* case what—you can't get married but you can have an interracial union. Everyone would know that was wrong, that . . . marriage has a status, recognition, support."

Ted had thereby elevated the question about the word "marriage" above the idea of "friendship" for children and other words used casually as labels, and into the realm of equal rights under the law. Certainly the chief justice hadn't intended, with his question, to equate the two, but had just reached for an easy analogy. In his reply Ted had shifted the conversation to the vastly higher ground, that marriage had a special, particular significance, and with his next response he reminded the Court that it had already established "that marriage is a fundamental right."

Whenever possible, Ted directed the justices back to the fact that the Court itself had determined that right in any number of cases. Hearing this, Justice Sotomayor asked, "What state restrictions *could* ever exist?" Reasonable regulations such as age limits as well as bans against incest, bigamy, and plural marriage all restrict access to marriage across the country. The most pernicious criticisms of the right to marry someone of the same sex had often extended to absurd "slippery slope" concepts such as legalizing incest, plural marriages, and unions of people and animals. Justice Sotomayor didn't go as far, but she did ask, "What's left?" to reasonably regulate.

Fortunately, here again, we had carefully prepared for this line of questioning, and were able to refer to the meaningful record the Supreme

Court had established determining that plural marriage can be regulated when parties are affected by "exploitation, abuse, patriarchy, issues with respect to taxes, inheritance, child custody. . . . [And] if a state prohibits polygamy, it's prohibiting conduct." However, if a state "prohibits gay and lesbian citizens from getting married, it is prohibiting their exercise of a right based upon their status. It's selecting them as a class, as you described in the *Romer* case and as you described in the *Lawrence* case, you're picking out a group of individuals to deny them the freedom that you've said is fundamental, important, and vital in this society, and it has status and stature, as you pointed out in the VMI case."

The "VMI case" (*United States v. Virginia*) involved women's suing to gain access to the Virginia Military Institute, a state-operated, single-sex male college that had barred women for more than a century. Ted was familiar with that case. He had been the lawyer for *Virginia* (VMI) and had lost. After that decision traditionalists predicted a terrible outcome at the institute. Instead the officers, faculty, and male cadets adapted, evolved, and moved on. VMI has maintained its standing as a serious and respected military academy, and women who submit themselves to the rigors of enrollment at VMI do succeed.

Winding up his argument, Ted ended with a remark intended to respond to those who might be reluctant to take the step we were urging, especially Justice Ginsburg, who had recently expressed her reservations about the Supreme Court's overreaching on controversial issues like abortion rights. We strongly felt that the Court should not wait to grant marriage equality, and Ted, drawing from his weeks of preparation, concluded with a sentence that succinctly summarized where society had come on this issue:

> I respectfully submit that we've learned to understand more about sexual orientation and what it means to individuals. I guess the language that Justice Ginsburg used at the closing of the VMI case is an important thing. It resonates with me:
>
> "A prime part of the history of our Constitution is the story of the extension of constitutional rights to people once ignored or excluded."

One has to be careful reciting the specific words of a justice to end an argument. But in this instance Ted chose to do exactly that, because Justice Ginsburg's words in that case were so perfect.

Chief Justice Roberts now summoned Solicitor General Donald Verrilli to present his argument in support of our case. With just ten minutes of the thirty minutes allotted to our side to speak, Verrilli was able only to sketch the outlines of the federal government's case, though he did get into a telling exchange with Justice Alito, who raised the question of our nation's relatively short-lived experience with marriage equality in the states that then allowed it.

"Traditional marriage has been around for thousands of years," said the justice. "Same-sex marriage is very new. I think it was first adopted in the Netherlands in 2000. So there isn't a lot of data about its effect. . . . You want us to step in and render a decision based on an assessment of the effects of this institution which is newer than cell phones or the Internet? . . . Why should it not be left for the people, either acting through initiatives and referendums, or through their elected public officials?"

Verrilli, who is a very good lawyer and accustomed to his role before the Supreme Court, offered counterpoints that suggested that experience with gay and lesbian couples who headed families was fairly conclusive and positive. More important, he noted, the proponents of Proposition 8 had not themselves taken a wait-and-see stand. "California did not through Proposition 8 do what my friend Mr. Cooper said and push a pause button," he added dramatically. "They pushed a delete button. This is a permanent ban. It's supposed to take the issue out of the legislative process."

After Verrilli's testimony Chuck Cooper was permitted a few minutes to rebut, during which he defended the "pause" reference, pointing out that California voters could always reamend the constitution and undo Proposition 8 if they wanted. He countered our comparisons to *Loving v. Virginia* by saying the state could have a legitimate public policy interest in restricting marriage to heterosexuals, who can procreate, that did not exist when it came to interracial marriage. Finally, he implored the justices to leave this issue up to the people, rather than ceding it to the courts. "It is an agonizingly difficult, for many people, political question. We would submit to you that that question is properly decided by the people themselves."

With that the red light came on at the podium, signaling that time had run out. It was over. The chief justice said, "Thank you, counsel. The case is submitted."

The sound of the gavel signaled that the session was closed, and the justices departed. We rose from our seats. Lady Olson stepped forward from her seat behind Ted in the section of the Court reserved for members of the Supreme Court bar. As Ted turned and locked onto her eyes, he read her facial expression with the wordless understanding that comes with years of marriage. With no need for further explanation, he said simply, "We were not going to get his vote anyway," referring to Justice Scalia.

We all felt exuberant about how the morning had progressed, and when we emerged from the courthouse and entered the sunlit plaza on First Street the cheer that went up from the crowd pushed our moods even higher. We strode arm in arm to the bank of TV cameras that had been set up for the usual postargument news conference. Pressed to offer his assessment, Ted said, "They listened, they heard, they asked hard questions."

"What do you think the Court will do?" came a question shouted from the pack.

One *never* gets ahead of the justices in response to a question like this. Ted answered, "Based on the questions the justices asked, I have no idea."

That assessment was true for all of us.

It was not that our cautious optimism had faded or that the argument had not gone well. It was simply that it now seemed clear that on the merits we had four votes for and four votes against with Justice Kennedy the tiebreaker, and several justices had expressed doubts as to whether they should have ever granted cert.

SIXTEEN

Waiting

After the argument and the press conference, we gathered with our entire team and a number of supporters for a celebratory lunch, a post–Supreme Court argument tradition at Gibson Dunn. We were all feeling the combination of exhaustion, elation, excitement, and anticipation that accompanies any case that has been prepared as assiduously as this one. We had finally made our argument before the highest court in the land, though real finality would still have to wait for the justices to deliberate, write, and publish their opinions. This process would take months, but would be done by the end of June.

Sensing that we all needed to absorb and share what we had experienced and decompress, Ted stood as salads were being served and asked the seventy or so people seated in a private room at a downtown restaurant to each stand and speak for a moment. David used his time to praise our clients for "what you have done for our country to bring us toward the goal of eliminating prejudice." He described the legal struggle as a "dogfight" and offered a judgment, in the privacy of that room, that he had withheld from the press: "With one or two exceptions I don't think anyone on the Court really wants to decide this case against us, but they are struggling to find the basis to decide the case for us."

David's evaluation was founded on the fact that during the argument, Chuck Cooper could not offer a single example of how the proponents of Proposition 8 had suffered any particular harm attributable to the ruling against them in the lower courts or to overturning Proposition 8 in general. Indeed, when Justice Sotomayor asked, "How does it create an injury to [your clients] separate from that of every other taxpayer to have laws enforced?" Cooper replied that the issue "is not the injury to the individual proponents; it's the injury to the state." But as everyone knew, officials in California had not determined that the state was being at all harmed. If the chief elected officials of California had found harm to the state or its citizens from eliminating Proposition 8, they would have defended the measure themselves.

When David finished speaking, Ted began to move from table to table, asking for perspective, memories, and feelings. On one wall of the room, a large television screen displayed C-SPAN's coverage of the case, including portions of the transcript, which were displayed in large type. Diana Walker, camera in hand, slid between tables and chairs to photograph the speakers.

When she was asked to make a statement, Jeff Zarrillo's mother, Linda, stood and said simply, "I can't wait to be a mom-in-law."

Film producer Bruce Cohen, who had helped found AFER with Lance Black and Rob Reiner, playfully noted that the classical frieze set high on the courtroom wall behind the chief justice depicted a few naked men among the clothed. After Bruce spoke, Rob Reiner, who with his wife, Michele, had so long ago initiated the effort to overturn Prop 8, said he was proud "to be part of something that will change the world." Noting that he and Michele did not have gay children, he added, as he had said at the very outset of this venture, "But we are in the gay-adjacent community," and "I love Chad Griffin."

Cleve Jones, who created the Names Project, which memorializes people who died of AIDS, and who had been extremely close to murdered San Francisco supervisor Harvey Milk, brought us back to a serious note as he recalled that as a young gay man, "I was illegal. I was sick." He said he left home in the Midwest after his father told him that he should undergo electroshock treatments because of his sexual identity. He had hoped for society to change but didn't know how or when it would. "Now," he said, "I feel I am going to live long enough to see it all happen."

Something of an elder statesman in the LGBT rights movement,

Cleve occupied a special place in the hearts of many in the room. He reminded us of the long struggle for equality and the days when it wasn't so easy for gays and lesbians to find allies. When it was his turn to speak, Chad Griffin turned toward Cleve and recalled the years of effort that he and others had devoted to fighting bigotry through moments like the Stonewall riot and the AIDS crisis, which brought out the worst in some people. "Cleve was there when it was really hard to be there," he said, emotion filling his voice.

Heartfelt, warm, deeply personal, and almost reverential, these were the kinds of moments that a typical lawyer almost never experiences in his or her professional life. Most practices are dedicated to serving private (and often corporate) clients whose needs are more abstract and far less concerned with issues like human rights and equality. But here we listened to people recall suffering under prejudice and even friends who had committed suicide because they couldn't bear the bigotry any longer. Still, the overall tone of the gathering was optimistic because, as Chad reminded us, "Four years ago, many of us didn't even know each other, but today we are family."

In four years this family had rallied to challenge a terrible election defeat in the courts. As it had in previous cases like *Brown* and the famous Scopes Trial, the judicial process had helped to educate the American people. No one can say for certain, but it would be hard to argue that all the publicity associated with our efforts, especially reports on the victory in the federal district court in San Francisco, hadn't contributed in a material way to the sweeping change in public opinion and to the newly enlightened sentiments of many prominent Americans regarding the issue of marriage equality. It was this evolution in the nation's consciousness that moved Ted to say, near the end of the celebration, "We will not lose. It is not possible. We have changed the world already."

What, though, could we reasonably expect from the Court? Most of the postargument analysis offered by editorialists and experts was quite equivocal. No one seemed to think that the justices had offered a clear signal of their intentions during the argument itself. Jeff Toobin of the *New Yorker* and CNN observed that the justices had not rejected any of their options, including a dismissal on the grounds that they had improvidently accepted the case for review. On the merits Toobin counted four votes against us, and four votes with us, with Justice Kennedy occupying his usual swing position.

Political advocates fell into place along the expected partisan lines. The *Wall Street Journal,* for example, urged the Court to rule as narrowly as possible "by letting the people decide" on a state-by-state basis. Maureen Dowd of the *New York Times* wrote, "The Supreme Court should know that civil rights are not supposed to be determined on the whims of the people."

On the day after our argument, the parties in the contest over the constitutionality of the Defense of Marriage Act got their turn in front of the nine justices. DOMA had originally been enacted in 1996 as a response to a state court decision in Hawaii that spawned the marriage equality debate. At that time only a few countries in the world had any significant experience with anything approaching marriage equality. Denmark had legalized registered domestic partnerships and other Nordic states had approved civil unions for gays and lesbians, but no American state other than Hawaii had even come close to creating an option at all comparable to marriage. With little experience or social science to consider, and the prejudice against homosexuality still relatively strong among many of their constituents, members of Congress and President Clinton acted in what they believed were the best interests of the country and, not incidentally, a cynic might observe, in their own political interests. And painful as it was for gays and lesbians, DOMA did seem to settle a controversy, if only temporarily.

The lower courts had deemed DOMA's marriage definition unconstitutional, a ruling with which the Obama administration agreed and that caused the attorney general to join suit with Edith Windsor and against DOMA. A complex struggle then took place as certain Republican members of the House of Representatives sought ways to defend the law in the courts. Ultimately the Justice Department sought a

Supreme Court resolution of the matter (with the intent of supporting Edith Windsor) and certiorari was granted to review the case. Of course, this action did not eliminate all the complex standing issues in the case. To help them resolve those aspects, the Court had asked Harvard law professor Vicki Jackson for an independent analysis. In her brief she said that neither the Department of Justice nor the members of Congress had standing. She would argue this point in person, adding an extra half hour to the proceedings.

The crowds that gathered to demonstrate support for and opposition to Ms. Windsor were just as large and just as loud as the ones that had greeted us the prior day. At the hearing Professor Jackson spoke first and did a credible job of arguing that the president should not have been permitted to ask the Court to hear the case, because the government was not seeking a remedy to any injury it may have suffered and was instead merely seeking judicial permission to stop enforcing portions of DOMA—not something the Court does.

Although Jackson made a coherent argument, the justices seemed to disagree with her generally, almost as if they were eager to resolve the DOMA issue. On the conservative end of the panel, Justice Alito seemed to say that it was perfectly reasonable for the president to assert that a law purports to impose on him a duty to do something unconstitutional—in this case, to discriminate against legally married gays and lesbians—and that he wants the Court to tell him to stop. Other justices compared the government to an official of a trust, carrying out the requirements of the trust even as it goes to court to argue that the dictates of that trust are illegal.

In this, as in all other cases, the justices were not only taking into consideration the specific matter before them but also the broader context of precedents—including the *future* effects of anything they might decide—and more general constitutional concerns. Lurking in the background of the DOMA case were serious questions about how the president responded to acts of Congress.

Justice Scalia challenged the Obama administration's objections to the part of the act that denied Edith Windsor equal treatment under the tax code. Wondering aloud whether "we're living in this new world" where the executive can pick and choose among the provisions of a law, he said, "I don't want these cases like this to come before this court all the time."

When they got to the actual merits of the case, a majority of the justices seemed to voice real skepticism about a federal law that denies legally married people more than eleven hundred federal benefits on the basis of their sexual orientation. In contrast with our case, where conservatives could argue that the federal government should leave the question of barring gays and lesbians from marrying to the states, the conservative argument in DOMA could assert that the federal government had no business interfering with states that *had* bestowed marriage equality on its citizens. "The question is whether or not the federal government, under our federalism scheme, has the authority to regulate marriage." This point, or some variation of it, was made more than half a dozen times by Justice Kennedy and others.

The most pithy remarks in the DOMA hearing, quoted repeatedly by the press and broadcast in the justice's own voice thanks to recordings released that day, came from Justice Ginsburg. She observed that under DOMA, gays and lesbians who were legally wed or involved in a domestic partnership were expected to accept that their nation was recognizing two kinds of marriage, "the full marriage and then this sort of skim milk marriage." Earlier in the hearing she had noted that under DOMA gay and lesbian couples are allowed "no joint [tax] return, no marital deduction, no Social Security benefits; your spouse is very sick but you can't get leave; . . . one might as well ask, what kind of marriage is this?"

After the argument Edith Windsor was greeted outside the courthouse by a roar of cheers and applause from thousands of supporters. She noted for the press that she had climbed forty-four steps to reach the entrance of the Supreme Court building, one for each year that she and her late partner, Thea, had been together. She also said she was optimistic about what the justices would decide.

Legal experts who assessed the arguments against DOMA and Prop 8 seemed confident that Edith Windsor would prevail, but mainly on the basis of states' rights and not necessarily on the principle of equal protection, a broader proposition that some justices might want to delay for another case. The states' rights, or federalism, issue was problematic for the *Perry* case because it implied that every state could make its own decision. Our argument was that because of the due process and equal protection clauses they could not. Relying on states' rights and not reaching equal protection or due process could doom our claim.

Although the parties involved primarily with DOMA seemed more certain about what the Court might decide, no one can reliably predict the outcome of any argument. People who don't know how the Supreme Court functions often claim that so-called insiders must get advance word on the deliberations of the jurists. Surely, they insist, all the clerks, administrative aides, and even security guards must be aware of the discussion taking place among the justices. Considering the thousands of friends and family the justices know, information must leak out of the Court in the same way that it leaks out of every other government office. In fact, anyone who asserts that he knows where the Court is headed in a particular case, let alone what the justices are saying to one another, should not be given even the benefit of the doubt. There may be no more secretive body in America, or the world, than the Supreme Court.

The Court's procedures are established partly by the Constitution, partly by statute, and partly by custom. For example, the law requires the Court to sit for specifically stipulated terms, which always begin on the first Monday in October. In the four brief paragraphs of Article III, the Constitution also sets out the Court's mandate and its powers, including its role as the highest court in the land. Custom sets the rhythm of activity at the Court, which includes alternating two-week periods for arguments and recesses between October and the end of April, with decisions released periodically during the term, ending by the last days of June. During the breaks between argument sessions, the justices study the matters before them and draft opinions with the help of their clerks. Absent an inexcusable breach of faith, no clerk would ever divulge what he or she has heard inside the Court.

Drawn from the nation's pool of recent law school graduates and numbering roughly thirty-six at any given time (not including clerks assigned to retired justices), the clerks know more about the inner workings of the Court than anyone save for the justices themselves. Discreet in the extreme, they are bound by a strict code of conduct that requires, among other things, that they burn draft opinions and marked-up briefs. Their commitment to secrecy is legendary, and transgressions are so rare that on the occasions they do occur the repercussions have been great. In the 1970s, for example, journalist Bob Woodward seemed to have gotten some clerks, or former clerks, to supply information for his book *The Brethren*. Those who were suspected of leaks were ostracized by individual justices and others in the legal community. Thereafter, the clerks were subject to tighter rules, including a ban on visitors at their weekly cocktail hour. Alcohol can dissolve the safeguards that inhibit loose talk.

While the clerks are notably discreet when talking to outsiders, they do play a serious role in the Court's functioning. Frequently tasked with researching issues and even preparing early drafts of portions of decisions, these key aides to the justices can help in varying degrees to shape the work done by the Court. This influence can be direct, as clerks lean toward one side of an argument or another, or inadvertent. As they work long hours in chambers and conference rooms with their young clerks, the justices establish relationships that give them glimpses of the world beyond the Court and their own experiences, which may be narrowed by the limits of their work, their office, or their age. At minimum what the justices know of their clerks, and their lives, becomes at least a small segment of the context for their thinking and provides them with an important view of a changing society.

Where our case was concerned, we knew that in recent decades at least eighteen openly gay and lesbian clerks had served the Court, and as of early 2013, liberal and conservative justices alike had selected gay men or lesbians to be their clerks. This was a far cry from 1986, when Justice Lewis Powell, while deliberating a challenge to the state of Georgia's antisodomy law (*Bowers v. Hardwick*), reportedly remarked that he didn't think he had ever met a homosexual. At the time no clerk had ever come out, but as later reports revealed, Powell may actually have been protecting the privacy of one of his clerks, whom he may have known to be gay. In fact, one witness is said to have reported that Justice Harry Blackmun answered Powell by saying, "Look around your chambers."

Despite the urgings of his gay clerk C. Cabell Chinnis, Powell cast the deciding vote upholding the Georgia law. Chinnis would recall in 2013 that Powell had listened to what he had to say about how much he valued being able "to make love to the person I love," in the context of another case, but ultimately supported a decision that was one of the great disappointments of Chinnis's career in the law. However, the give-and-take Chinnis revealed illustrated well the dynamic relationships inside the Court, which can influence outcomes, if only subliminally.

Supreme Court justices have followed the same basic decision-making process for many generations. They begin to consider specific controversies when they work on petitions for certiorari and deliberate further as they receive briefs. Some observers believe that justices become fixed in their views on a case prior to arguments and that their questions in open court are framed to help one side or the other make salient points, to influence their colleagues, or to communicate their beliefs to the public. These assumptions may apply to some of the justices, some of the time, but it would be wrong to believe they are invariably true.

A striking example of the Court's ability to surprise arose in the challenge to President Obama's health reform measure, the Affordable Care Act. (Opponents dubbed it "Obamacare," a pejorative initially opposed and later embraced by the president—and later less willingly.) In that case (*National Federation of Independent Business v. Sebelius*) the petitioners argued that Congress lacked the authority to require citizens to buy insurance or suffer a civil fine. The president maintained that the commerce clause in Article I of the Constitution, which allows the federal government to regulate interstate and foreign trade, permitted the mandate because the insurance system is national in scope.

Because their complaint rested on what they charged was overreaching by federal authorities, Obamacare's opponents believed they had a winning argument as they faced a Court with five justices who favored individual freedom and limited government. When the ruling was published, some TV reporters who scanned it quickly announced that the petitioners had won because the decision stated that the mandate could not be justified under the commerce clause. "The Federal Government does not have the power to order people to buy health insurance," wrote Chief Justice Roberts for the majority.

For a moment news watchers at the White House believed they had indeed lost. But minutes later the journalists corrected their mistake. Later in the opinion, the chief justice actually upheld the law by identifying the penalty attached to the mandate as a tax. In a highly creative way the chief justice had managed to confound the world and enlist the agreement of four other justices who supported the outcome, if not every word of the reasoning. Nothing in his history had suggested that Chief Justice Roberts would come to such a decision, apart from his reputation as a thoughtful jurist who listened objectively to all arguments.

In the long months between the argument and the Court's decision, Sandy, Kris, Paul, and Jeff did their best to return to their normal lives and control their feelings of anticipation. Waiting is a challenge for anyone who comes before the Court, but it is especially difficult for individual citizens like our clients who through extraordinary circumstances find themselves at the center of an historic case. During down times, while the justices are deliberating over their decision, it can feel as if the world has suddenly gone silent.

Through the long years of our litigation, each of our clients learned to adjust to the on-off nature of the publicity, legal activity, and intense public interest. Kris may have put it best, after the Supreme Court argument, when she said she was eager to get home to California and tend to the gardens around her pretty house in Berkeley. "It's one of the things I want to do first," she said. "I gardened before all this happened. I gardened all through it. And I'm going to garden when it's all over."

As lawyers we were more accustomed to the often glacial rhythms of the justice system, where long stretches of time are taken up with research, writing, and decision making. We also had plenty of our other work to do.

Along with his already full caseload, David took on the task of serving as cocounsel for subscribers in a massive lawsuit against Blue Cross Blue Shield health insurance programs. The case, being heard in federal court in Birmingham, Alabama, consolidated more than a dozen lawsuits filed against the insurers by subscribers and health care providers who alleged that the defendants had divvied up regions to avoid competing with one another. Blue Cross Blue Shield had argued that the suits lacked merit, but a judge allowed the case to go forward. David was chosen from among many leading litigators to handle a job that was as profoundly important as it was complex. On behalf of an American citizen who was injured and whose son was killed in a terrorist bombing in Israel, he also took on a case suing Iran and the Bank of China for facilitating terrorism. The terrorist cell responsible had been financed by Iran through an account in the Bank of China, and the bank had kept the account open even after it was on notice that it was being used to finance terrorism.

Ted became involved with cases on behalf of the State of New Jersey and of the oil company BP, which was involved in litigation related to the compensation program for its *Deepwater Horizon* oil rig accident and subsequent spill. New Jersey wanted to legalize sports gambling and engaged in litigation involving the strictures of a federal law, the 1992 Professional and Amateur Sports Protection Act (PASPA), that sought to restrict the spread of sports betting beyond places, mainly Nevada, where it already existed. In late winter a district court judge had ruled against the state and in favor of various sports leagues that had opposed the effort. The Third Circuit Court of Appeals in Philadelphia was scheduled to take the matter up on June 26. Ted's arguments revolved in large part around a long-established anticommandeering doctrine that limited the federal government's ability to force states to act as regulators pursuant to federal directives.

As we tried (not entirely successfully) to concentrate on other work and to put the impending *Perry* decision out of our minds for certain stretches of time, the country and the world continued its trend toward acceptance of marriage equality. Overseas, the British government moved toward approval, without much rancor, while France did the same, though accompanied by a surprisingly bitter public debate and clashes in the streets over the legislation. In the end the French did decide to permit gays and lesbians to marry, though the ferocity of the struggle came as a shock to outside observers. Days after President François Hollande signed the bill on May 18, a far-right French historian who was a leading public opponent of the cause posted a long screed about the issue and then went to the Cathedral of Notre Dame in Paris and shot himself to death.

In America several more states embraced equality more peacefully. State legislators in Rhode Island, Delaware, and Minnesota approved bills that legalized same-sex marriage, and governors promptly signed them into law. By June 1, 2013, twelve states and the District of Columbia supported full marriage equality. These thirteen jurisdictions accounted for nearly one-fifth of the U.S. population. Only four years before, when our suit was filed, just three states—Massachusetts, Connecticut, and Iowa—permitted marriage equality.

Minnesota's journey to equal rights for gays and lesbians provides an inspiring case study that illustrates the change in attitudes that has swept the nation. In 1997, inspired by DOMA, that state had adopted a statute restricting marriage to heterosexual couples. In 2003 then state senator Michele Bachmann proposed an amendment that would have included this restriction in the state constitution. A devout and outspoken evangelical Christian, Bachmann has argued that God wanted gays and lesbians to be barred from marrying. Although her supporters chanted outside the state capitol, Bachmann's plea to be heard in the last minutes of a contentious 2004 Senate term was gaveled into oblivion as exhausted legislators fled to their districts. However, various comparable measures were approved in a dozen states as social and religious conservatives, emphasizing the Massachusetts Supreme Court decision establishing marriage equality, used the issue to rally voters to the polls.

After Bachmann had left the St. Paul statehouse for Congress, her conservative colleagues took up the cause with the same results in 2006, 2007, and 2009. Then in 2011 they succeeded in putting the restriction on the ballot. At first, as Catholic bishops and others promoted the amendment with advertisements that stressed a supposed danger to schoolchildren, a majority supported the measure. But as the vote in 2012 drew near and a marriage equality campaign picked up steam, the polls began to shift. Shortly before the election, support for the amendment hovered just below 50 percent. When ballots were cast, voters rejected the ban and turned some of its backers out of office. Six months later, amid cheers from the galleries, both houses of the state legislature voted to legalize same-sex marriage. "Today, love wins," declared sponsor Senator Tony Lourey as the bill went to the governor, who pledged to sign it.

This remarkable turn of events and victory in Minnesota sometimes seemed part of an inexorable tide, but we knew it would take court victories and a great deal more change in some parts of the country before the nation as a whole could be put into the "love wins" column. A dismayed Michele Bachman had remarked, "I have a friend from Eden Prairie who's already packed everything she owns into her car and is driving out to Montana as we speak. These are very scary times. I don't want my family to be the last ones out."

The possibility that a politically polarized country might remain divided long into the future when it came to the right of loving couples to marry, just as it had been divided before *Loving*, concerned us. What would happen, we worried, if the Court failed to act with the same moral sense that it had shown when it outlawed racial discrimination in marriage? We felt strongly that this was a national issue—that all our citizens, wherever they lived, should be treated equally. Was a lesbian in Georgia any less equal than one in Minnesota? Was a gay man in Massachusetts somehow more equal than one in Texas?

In addition to the matter of justice on the issue of marriage, we also hoped that the Court would take into account the larger message it would communicate with its decision about what makes us a nation of equals. Discrimination, whether codified by legislation, court decisions, or constitutional amendment, can effectively function as a green light to prejudice, separateness, the legitimacy of discrimination. Certainly the racism and segregation condoned by law in our not so distant past encouraged the dehumanization of African Americans and others and enabled in many ways cruelty, hostility, even violence. The mind-set that gave rise to lynching was fostered in part by laws that identified African Americans as lesser beings. Gays and lesbians have faced similar dangers, and they continued to be the target of hate crimes. Several tragic episodes reminded us of this during our wait for the Proposition 8 decision.

On May 18 two young gay men out walking in the New York neighborhood of Greenwich Village were accosted by Elliot Morales, who shouted a few slurs and, according to police, taunted them with a question: "You want to die here?" A pistol was fired, and thirty-two-year-old Mark Carson died almost instantly after being shot in the head. Morales was arrested and charged with a hate crime murder. Two more antigay attacks occurred in New York on the day that a rally was held to call attention to Carson's death and the problem of antigay violence, which was occurring in the city at more than double the rate of the previous year.

In Orange County, California, crimes against lesbian women and gay men almost doubled in a one-year period. At the end of May, a coalition of antiviolence groups issued a report lamenting a national increase in hate crime murders of lesbians and gays. The most optimistic analyses of the spike in violence regarded it as a "storm before the calm," or a brief homophobic backlash against the backdrop of the larger movement toward equality. One could only hope that was true.

The most encouraging sign that America is headed in the right direction in the matter of unity and equality may be found among the nation's young. We experienced this while appearing together at the University of New Hampshire School of Law commencement in late May. We jointly stressed the value of reaching across the political divide and reminded the soon-to-be lawyers that they must practice in a spirit of fraternity, not enmity. "We are all colleagues," noted David. "We are all servants of justice." Speaking of Ted, he added, "I admire him as much when he is on the other side as I do when he's on my side."

For his part, Ted urged the graduates not to be constrained by labels like "conservative" and "liberal," "pro-business" and "pro-labor." He got a big laugh when he recalled that during a pro football players' strike, David, the supposed liberal, "took the side of management, while I took the side of the beleaguered workers." The strike was characterized as the millionaires against the billionaires, but the point was taken.

Turning to a serious topic, Ted recalled that during *Bush v. Gore* he had sometimes found himself nodding in admiration when David made an especially compelling point. He mentally applauded his adversary in the same way that Michael Jordan admired a creative shot scored by Larry Bird. "We were professional adversaries in the presidential recount case," he added, "but we were not enemies." Ted explained, "The practice of law can be strenuous, stimulating, and rewarding. But there is no place in it for hostility, rancor, or incivility. Keep it out of our profession—*your* profession." Nodding in David's direction, he added, "Reach out to your colleagues on the other side of your cases. They will be among your grandest friends."

Four days later, David spoke at a much larger commencement in Yankee Stadium. New York University grants thousands of degrees every year, and the crowd of well-wishers was so big that it filled half the stadium. Announcements were made through a booming public-address system more typically used to introduce Derek Jeter as he steps up to the plate. Recent years had seen NYU commencement addresses from Justice Sotomayor, Hillary Clinton, and the actor Alec Baldwin. This year the university wanted to recognize the progress being made in the civil rights cause of our time. Edith Windsor was chosen to receive the annual Presidential Award; David was awarded an honorary doctorate and asked to be the main commencement speaker in recognition of our legal and public campaign for marriage equality. Some opponents of marriage equality expressed outrage over David's selection, and some students undoubtedly would rather have heard from Alec Baldwin again.

After NYU president John Sexton hailed Windsor's courage and accomplishments and described her as "our beloved graduate," he placed a gold medal around her neck, after which she waved to the cheering crowd. When David came to the podium he discussed the struggle that had brought Edith and the country to a moment of decision. After noting that "it's a little intimidating to be here, at Yankee Stadium, at second base," he went on to urge students to take platitudes seriously.

"Keep learning, change the world, don't be afraid to fail: It's too easy to dismiss platitudes," he said. Platitudes gain currency, and become platitudes, he insisted, because they contain real truths. He urged students never to dismiss principles such as "All people are created equal, and every person has an unalienable right to life, liberty, and the pursuit of happiness" as merely platitudes. He concluded:

> We are engaged today in a civil rights struggle to try to end the last official bastion of discrimination in this country where the government discriminates against its own citizens. There are many areas of social discrimination that we need to address. We've made enormous progress since I was born, in a time when blacks and whites couldn't go to school together or drink from the same water fountain or eat at the same diner. Where women had few rights, could be legally raped by their husbands, couldn't control their own property. Where gays and lesbians were hunted down and subjected to horrific violence.
>
> When I was a senior in high school, President Dwight David Eisenhower issued an executive order that prohibited the federal government from employing any gay or lesbian citizen in any capacity. You could not be a clerk typist, you could not be a mail carrier. You could not be a government lawyer.

We've come a long way since then, but we have a long way still to go. . . . I can't tell you today how the Supreme Court is going to rule in June. But what I can tell you is that if we don't win it in *Perry* we will continue the fight until we do win it.

No civil rights struggle proceeds in a straight line. There are reverses, and there have been many reverses in this struggle already. But fundamentally we are right because as everyone knows, at the platitude stage, everyone is entitled to equal protection, and we have as a society only succeeded in ignoring that because we have been able to characterize people—women, African Americans, people of different religions, and people of different sexual orientations—as different. They are not. We know it. They know it. And someday the United States Supreme Court will recognize it. Hopefully in June, but if not in June, there will come a day.

Congratulations, and join us in trying to make platitudes real.

David's speech sparked long applause, because it described the argument, the sentiment, and the moral foundation of our cause in a way that was both simple and true. Rare is the moment when a people face a choice that can be framed so sharply. Clearly, we faced one now.

SEVENTEEN

Love Wins

In mid-June Ted began to haunt the Supreme Court, arriving there on Monday and Thursday mornings, so he could be present at the 10 A.M. sessions at which decisions were released. These announcements are conducted in a formal way, with the nine justices taking the chairs they occupy during arguments. Those present are reminded that they should refrain from demonstrative reactions to the decisions. Then the chief justice calls on those of his colleagues who have authored opinions set for release to read both a description of the particular case and a summary of their decision.

Ted's appearance in the courtroom was not absolutely necessary. Thanks to the Internet, anyone can access the news of an opinion seconds after it is announced via SCOTUSblog, the only source for real-time news about the Court. But being present in the courtroom does make one feel more connected to history, as well as to a grand civic tradition. The proceedings are almost sacred in their seriousness and authority. Few proceedings in our civil society inspire more awe and respect.

On some of the opinion mornings we were able to obtain seats for our clients or members of our team. But as the month wore on, tickets grew scarce, as the number of remaining cases yet to be announced dwindled and the profile of the remaining cases increased. The toughest, most contentious cases are almost invariably the last ones to be released in June as the Court's term comes to an end. The less radioactive cases tend to come earlier. On Monday, June 17, for example, the Court sided with Oklahoma in its dispute with Texas over water rights. It also struck down regulations on trucks imposed by the Port of Los Angeles, which sought to reduce pollution in the area around its docks and warehouses. In that case the justices found unanimously that federal rules on pollution and interstate trucking superseded the Port Authority's regulations.

Many people are surprised to learn that unanimous opinions are quite common for the Court, coming in roughly half of the cases decided. Casual observers don't realize that the law governing many controversies is often quite clear at the end of the day and the justices agree (9–0 or 8–1) more often than not. They may disagree sharply with one another when they hear difficult cases like Prop 8, but for the most part they work harmoniously. Friendships among the justices cross ideological differences and make it possible for them to cooperate as they hear arguments, work in conference, and write opinions.

The conferences, which typically occur on Wednesdays and Fridays when the Court is sitting, give the justices a chance to discuss petitions for certiorari and the arguments they have heard. These sessions are held without clerks or other aides present, which enables the justices to have frank conversations. However, the conferences are not so much forums for intense debate as opportunities for the sharing of opinions. They also allow for the chief justice to poll his colleagues on the cases they have heard. The chief justice assigns principal responsibility for writing the Court's opinion if he is in the majority. If not, the seniormost justice in the majority has that responsibility. Individual justices may then take it upon themselves to write concurrences or dissents, in which they can express ideas and points of view that aren't found in the official result in the case, the opinion for the Court.

Confidentiality is the hallmark of the Court's work; the justices do not divulge what happens in conference until sometimes many years later, perhaps in notes or diaries that come to light after a justice's death. It is known, however, that draft opinions are circulated among the justices and critiques are offered. Sometimes a justice will switch his or her vote as an opinion is written, edited, and rewritten, and the actual outcome may change. When this is the case, which is rare, a justice may publish an especially strong dissent, which might suggest that a justice who started out writing for the majority suddenly found him- or herself in the minority. Strong dissents are also often seen where differences are particularly keen, or where the Court is departing in some way from a prior decision.

One noted example of such a signaling dissent was offered by Justice William Rehnquist in the 1985 case *Garcia v. San Antonio Metropolitan Transit Authority*. In that case, in which Ted gave the government's argument in the first of two argument sessions, the majority under Chief Justice Warren Burger allowed the federal government to impose federal labor rules on state and local governments. In his bluntly written four-sentence dissent, Rehnquist wrote, "I do not think it incumbent on those of us in dissent to spell out further the fine points of a principle that will, I am confident, in time again command the support of a majority of this Court."

Rehnquist was referring to the principle that the Constitution limits Congress to specific "enumerated" powers and reserves the rest for the states. This was an essential tenet of his conservative judicial philosophy and one that stood against an expansion of federal power that had been ongoing since the New Deal era of Franklin Delano Roosevelt. Later, as chief justice, Rehnquist led the Court to correct what he saw as overreaching by Washington with a series of opinions that slowed and sometimes stopped the enlargement of federal authority. His confidence in a future Court was borne out.

In the October 2012 term, which included the first six months of 2013, the Court heard arguments in some significant controversies besides Proposition 8 and the Defense of Marriage Act. In *Shelby County v. Holder* the justices were asked to determine whether certain localities were obliged to continue to clear changes in voting laws with the Justice Department under the 1965 Voting Rights Act. In *Fisher v. University of Texas,* they considered, again, whether a state university could consider race in its admissions process. Such "affirmative action" practices have been subject to periodic judicial tests since 1978, when the Supreme Court, in a 4–1–4 decision, suggested that affirmative action to achieve a "diverse" student body might in some circumstances be permissible. Since then, as society in general has debated the continued need for programs to redress discrimination, affirmative action has been limited in certain ways. In *Fisher*, as in so many others, advocates for each side disagreed fervently. Critics of affirmative action said it was a race-based preference that was intrinsically discriminatory—and thus not only unfair but unconstitutional—and had outlived whatever usefulness it may have had. Supporters urged that minorities still suffered the effects of racism, and continuing affirmative action would make for a fairer, more diverse, and therefore better society.

Shelby and *Fisher* dealt with vital political concerns, and they attracted almost as much interest as the marriage equality cases. As June progressed, the Court deferred announcing opinions on each of these "big four" cases—these two cases, plus *Perry* and *Windsor*.

On Thursday, June 20, with seventeen opinions outstanding, Justice Elena Kagan was called upon to read first. Aware of the crowd, and the major cases yet to be announced, she got a laugh when she announced, "This is a case about ACCA, the Armed Career Criminal Act, possibly not what you're here for this morning." Justice Kagan's opinion ruled in favor of a criminal defendant who sought to overturn elements of his sentence that had been enhanced under the ACCA. Kagan added that the law itself was "not very well written [and] it takes up a lot more of our time than we'd like."

Only one of the June 20 opinions made national news. Written by the chief justice, who speaks last at the decision sessions if he has an opinion to announce (decisions by justices are announced in reverse order of seniority, with the chief justice last), it held that private agencies receiving federal money to combat AIDS abroad could not be required to adopt policies opposed to prostitution. By a six-to-three vote, the Court found that the law requiring this policy, which was approved by Congress in 2003, violated the First Amendment's freedom of speech provision by demanding that recipients "pledge allegiance" to a policy that could alienate host governments and impede their mission.

For those of us who were waiting to hear two of the big four opinions, *Windsor* and *Perry,* it almost seemed as if the justices might be getting some satisfaction by prolonging our agony. This wasn't the case, of course, and it was far more likely that those who were writing opinions were laboring over them carefully. As Ted knew from his long experience at the Court, the drafting and editing might occasionally continue right up until the day before an opinion is rendered.

With each passing Monday and Thursday, the crowd of journalists at the Court grew larger, the speculation grew more intense, and even sensible observers began to sound more like soothsayers than legal analysts. The *Washington Post*'s Robert Barnes examined the opinions that had been handed down by the middle of June and speculated that based on the justices who had authored opinions so far, the remaining majority opinions—including the one in our case—were likely to be written by one of the more conservatives justices: Chief Justice Roberts, and Justices Scalia, Kennedy, and Alito.

Calling his method "Supreme Court bingo," Barnes noted that Justice Kennedy was lagging behind his peers in opinion output. (Kennedy's four majority opinions in the term represented just half the number authored by Justice Ginsburg.) This led him to suggest that Kennedy must be working on at least one of the more controversial cases.

Our own handicapping was done by Ted, who kept track of the Court's actions on one of his yellow legal pads, which he recorded with a reliable Number 2 pencil. In carefully drawn columns he listed the names of the cases, the month when arguments had been presented, the vote tally, and the initials of the justice who authored each opinion. By the final Monday in June he had a fairly accurate sense of the flow of the Court's work and saw that three justices were not represented among the group that had written on cases heard in the month of March, when Prop 8 was argued. Of those three, Alito, Kennedy, and Chief Justice Roberts, Alito was the least senior. Given the magnitude of our case, and the fact that it was likely to be a five-to-four vote, it was reasonable to conclude that the opinion on Proposition 8 was going to come from Kennedy or Roberts, and the *Windsor* opinion by the other of the two.

On that last Monday of the month, an early heat wave brought ninety-degree temperatures and extreme humidity to the nation's capital, and as Ted and Lady, David and Mary climbed the steps to the Supreme Court, just a hundred or so observers braved the conditions on the completely unshaded Supreme Court plaza to await history. A gay couple from Massachusetts stood with their infant son, who had been born after we had argued the case. They hoped to hear that men like them could be married in California. Across the street a middle-aged man, the lone opponent of marriage equality present, stood with a hand-lettered sign that featured the phrase THE WAGES OF SIN, which he raised to catch the attention of passing cars.

On that day the Court again delayed issuing the Prop 8 and DOMA opinions, but an extra day session was announced for Tuesday. As we scrambled to our cars, accompanied by our clients Paul and Jeff, we avoided the reporters who shouted questions. By this point we were hoping for the best and knew that we were near the end of our wait. In private, though, we hoped that all remaining opinions would be delivered on Tuesday the twenty-fifth. Ted had to be in Philadelphia on Wednesday the twenty-sixth for the Third Circuit argument in his New Jersey sports gaming case.

Instead, the next day the justices took their seats beneath the brass clock and decided everything but the two marriage cases and one other. By a five-to-four vote, the Court struck down a formula in the Voting Rights Act that identified states and localities that had to obtain the Justice Department's approval before making any changes in their voting rules. In his opinion Chief Justice Roberts acknowledged the remarkable success of the act, which had helped to dramatically increase voter registration among blacks and other minorities. However, as he took pains to note, the criteria that determined which areas would be subject to the act had not changed since it took effect in 1966. The Court had warned of this problem four years earlier. With his opinion Roberts threw the issue to Congress, noting that the House and Senate could devise a new formula "justified by current needs."

The one that had been in place treated the states unequally, however, and was therefore unconstitutional.

The five-to-four vote on *Shelby County v. Holder* broke down along the liberal and conservative lines that people often use to assess the Court. Justices Breyer, Kagan, and Sotomayor joined a sharply worded dissent written and read aloud by Justice Ginsburg. She cited the "massive" record compiled by Congress during more than twenty different hearings as it had recently renewed the Voting Rights Act in sweeping fashion. Signed by then president Bush, and supported by a remarkably bipartisan majority, the renewal was, in Ginsburg's view, evidence that the legislative branch had considered every aspect of the law, including the formula, and found it acceptable.

In any other term of the Court, we might have been captivated by the drama of the Voting Rights Act decision. However, we found it difficult to focus on anything but the fact that the Court had once again put off the marriage equality opinion. It was now certain to come on Wednesday, June 26, however, because the Court announced yet another special session at which opinions would be rendered in *all the remaining cases.* This was good and bad news for us. The good news was that the waiting was all but over. The bad news was that Ted could not be present to hear it because of his case in Philadelphia. The one day he could not be in the Supreme Court was to be the day it decided the case we had been developing and nurturing for four and a half years.

It is one of the agonies of the profession that justices and judges set the schedules for their courts, and attorneys must adapt to their demands. In this instance the State of New Jersey required Ted's representation in its effort to legalize sports betting in Garden State casinos. Ted had to be there. And so it was that he was 138.9 miles away from our clients, our colleagues, and all of our key allies at the moment when the Court made history. He would likely be studying his preargument file, determined to focus on the case about to be considered. If he got the news from Washington before 11 A.M. as he waited to argue in the court in Philadelphia, he wouldn't have much time to digest it.

Nor would he be able to celebrate or commiserate with the rest of the team. But at least the wait would be over.

———

At dawn on Wednesday, June 26, 2013, dozens of men and women had already gathered outside the Supreme Court. Temperatures had climbed to a sultry ninety degrees by the time the Court convened at 10 A.M., but the crowd kept growing, undeterred. Pushing babies in strollers and waving placards and signs, supporters of marriage equality filled the sidewalk and crowded an encampment of network TV crews. Nervous, excited, and hoping to celebrate, they were observed by a lone supporter of Proposition 8 on the other side of First Street NE, who was pacing in the shade of a leafy magnolia and holding up a sign that referenced scripture.

Four years and seven months had passed since California voters had repealed and eliminated the marriage rights of same-sex couples. In that time the issue had been fiercely debated in state and federal courts and in the public arena. The members of our team had devoted hundreds of days to legal work, and the work of opening hearts and minds to the concept of equality for gays and lesbians. With the latest polls averaging 58 percent to 36 percent in favor, marriage equality seemed inevitable someday in many states, whether granted by the courts or won through the political process on a state-by-state basis.

David, Mary, Lady, Ted Boutrous, Sandy, Chris, Jeff, and Paul arrived at the Court just after nine o'clock, accompanied by Chad Griffin and AFER president Adam Umhoefer. The opinion on DOMA came first, at 10:01 A.M. Written and read by Justice Kennedy, it found that "the federal statute is invalid" and that the relationships of legally married gay and lesbian couples could not be denied federal recognition simply because they were of the same sex. Indeed, Kennedy noted, the law served to "disparage and injure those whom the State, by its marriage laws, sought to protect in personhood and dignity. By seeking to displace this protection and treating those persons as living in marriages less respected than others the federal statute is in violation of the [equal protection and due process components of the] Fifth Amendment." (Our case was based on these protections in the Fourteenth Amendment, which limits the powers of the states. The Fifth Amendment, the Court has held, imposes comparable limits on the federal government.) Justices Ginsburg, Breyer, Sotomayor, and Kagan joined him in the majority.

For Edith Windsor the decision was a personal triumph that meant she would recover $363,000 in estate taxes, plus interest. For more than 650,000 legally married same-sex couples—and many more to come— the end of DOMA meant that their relationships would be honored fully under the federal laws.

Ten years earlier to the day, the same Justice Kennedy had read aloud his landmark opinion in *Lawrence v. Texas,* which overturned "antisodomy" laws against consensual sex by gay men and lesbians. (Strictly speaking, many of these laws also outlawed similar heterosexual acts.) In that case, Justice Kennedy wrote that the laws violated individuals' rights of due process, and that the two men who brought the challenge were "entitled to respect for their private lives. The State cannot demean their existence or control their destiny by making their private sexual conduct a crime."

In *Lawrence* Justice Scalia had released a stinging dissent, acerbically writing that the Court was possessed by an "anti-anti-homosexual" bias and had sidestepped the democratic process to create new rights. In the DOMA case he took a similar heated stand against Justice Kennedy's opinion. At twenty-six pages, the Scalia dissent was as long as the majority opinion. But in emotional tone, it far exceeded it. Among other characterizations, Justice Scalia charged that the Court's action was a "jaw-dropping" assertion of "judicial supremacy over the people's Representatives in Congress" and described the majority's reasoning as full of legalistic "argle-bargle," a century-old Scottish term meaning "disagreement." (It was likely the first time the word had appeared in a Supreme Court document.) Justice Scalia also wrote:

[Because he believed the Court had no standing to hear the case because of the attorney general's abdication of its defense,] we have no power to decide this case. And even if we did, we have no power under the Constitution to invalidate this democratically adopted legislation. The Court's errors on both points spring forth from the same diseased root: an exalted conception of the role of this institution in America. . . .

There are many remarkable things about the majority's merits holding. The first is how rootless and shifting its justifications are. . . . Moreover, if this is meant to be an equal-protection opinion, it is a confusing one. The opinion does not resolve and indeed does not even mention what had been the central question in this litigation: whether, under the Equal Protection Clause, laws restricting marriage to a man and a woman are reviewed for more than mere rationality.

Dissenters to a majority opinion have often complained that the Court has overstepped its authority, and they also tend to accuse the other side of generalized fuzzy thinking, muddled writing, and failures in judgment. Scalia's dissent went much further. He objected to the idea that DOMA's supporters were some sort of "wild-eyed lynch mob" taking a "hate your neighbor" stand. Instead, he wrote, DOMA's supporters had acted to "codify an aspect of marriage that had been unquestioned in our society for most of its existence—indeed, had been unquestioned in virtually all societies for virtually all of human history."

Justice Scalia also took issue with Justice Kennedy's assertion that the DOMA ruling did not resolve the issue of same-sex marriages. Recognizing that the majority opinion actually created a road map that would guide those who would challenge the law in states that banned same-sex marriage, Scalia wrote, "I have heard such bald, unreasoned disclaimer[s] before." Indeed, he had read the same disclaimer in Justice Kennedy's *Lawrence* opinion, only to see it go on to invalidate every antisodomy law in the nation and be used to challenge bans on same-sex marriage (including by us).

On this last point—that the DOMA opinion would have a sweeping effect—we agreed. As Terry Stewart noted, Justice Kennedy *had* established a foundation for new challenges to the state DOMA laws. "I think Scalia is correct," said Terry after the opinion was issued. Referring to the *Lawrence* case she said, "Scalia was right before, and he's right again."

The DOMA opinion was followed by a unanimous decision in a fairly ordinary case called *Sekhar v. United States*. Saying, "I'm sorry," Justice Scalia acknowledged the tension in the room. Then, at 10:26, Chief Justice Roberts began reading the opinion in *Hollingsworth v. Perry*.

Joined by an unlikely group—Justices Scalia, Ginsburg, Breyer, and Kagan—Chief Justice Roberts gave us, and the country, a victory that would echo throughout history. After a careful and concise recitation of the issues he bluntly declared that the petitioners "did not have standing to appeal the District Court's Order." Proposition 8 was dead. Judge Vaughn Walker's meticulously rendered decision, which established for the record the protection of equal rights for gay and lesbian Americans, had been left in place. Since it had not been lawfully appealed, it was upheld.

Everyone on our side had to contain their excitement as the chief justice read through his opinion. He noted that Hollingsworth and the other Proposition 8 proponents had not demonstrated that they were "agents of the State" who had been officially authorized to petition the Court. They had also failed to show that they had a "'personal stake' . . . that is distinguishable from the general interest of every citizen of California." The law on this question was well established, he said. "We have never before upheld the standing of a private party to defend the constitutionality of a state statute when state officials have chosen not to," wrote the chief justice. "We decline to do so for the first time here."

———

Few acts in civic life have the authoritative finality of a Supreme Court decision. It would have been great if the Court had gone further and announced a constitutional right to marriage equality for the entire nation, expanding the Walker decision to all states. But it was un-equivocal in its holding that the Walker opinion was now the end of the line for Proposition 8, and it meant that our clients, and all other same-sex couples in California, would be able to marry. This had been our goal from the first day. But we got more. The opinion left in place Judge Walker's record, which would prove immensely valuable to any-one seeking to challenge restrictions on marriage across the country. With the addition of California, 30 percent of Americans from that point forward would live in states with marriage equality, and with the *Hollingsworth* decision, the other 70 percent had more reason than ever to hope that they would soon join them.

Thanks to SCOTUSblog and social media, the world knew of the opinion almost immediately after the chief justice began reading it. By the time our plaintiffs and our legal team (except for Ted Olson) walked out of the cool confines of the Court and into the blazing heat, the crowd on the sidewalk had begun to celebrate. There were chants of "Thank you! Thank you!" as the team made its way to the cameras set up on the marble plaza. David spoke first, noting the victory in *Lawrence* ten years earlier. He then explained that the two decisions announced that day paved the way for marriage equality "to be the law of the land." And of course, our clients would "get to go back to Cali-fornia and, together with every other citizen of California, marry the person they love." David also said that we had achieved our three other major goals: We had established that marriage is a fundamental right. We had demonstrated that depriving gays and lesbians of marriage harmed them and their children. And we had established that allow-ing "everyone to marry the person they love" could not harm anyone.

During our long legal odyssey our three major arguments had been affirmed by the courts. These were the policy points that attorneys and legal analysts would study in the future, and they would form the foundation for the campaigns that, we hoped, would eventually bring marriage equality to the entire country. However, nothing that David could say that day could communicate the significance of our victory to our clients as well as the sheer joy evident on their faces. Paul, Jeff,

Kris, and Sandy glowed visibly as they flanked David, and when their turns came, they spoke from the heart. Kris, always an advocate for kids, reminded the world that her goal had been "to send a message to the children of this country that you are just as good as everybody else, no matter who you love." She expressed tearful joy at the prospect of going home, marrying Sandy, and living as "equal to every other family in California."

As Kris stepped back from the microphone and bit her lip, Sandy came forward, overflowing with gratitude. As she spread her thank-yous around, she may have been the first petitioner ever to thank the Constitution for an outcome at the Court. She also reminded everyone of the children of gay and lesbian parents in places like Texas and Chad Griffin's home state of Arkansas, who still lived in communities where their families were not yet equal. As she expressed it, "We really, really want to take this fight and take it all the way, and get equality for everyone."

Finally, under the glare of the sun and the gaze of the cameras, Jeff and Paul spoke of the love that resided at the heart of our effort. They said they looked forward to getting married, calling each other "husband," and growing old together. Paul declared, "We are gay, we are Americans, and we will not be treated as second-class citizens." He then reminded everyone that our purpose had always been to add strength to the institution of marriage, not diminish it.

"So today is a good day," Paul added, turning to his right, where Jeff stood. His voice shook with emotion as he touched Jeff's shoulder and said, "Today, I finally get to look at the man that I love, and finally say—'Will you please marry me?'" His eyes brimming with tears, Jeff answered him with a hug.

Epilogue

The euphoria on the plaza in front of the Supreme Court after the Court released its decision reached its zenith when Chad Griffin, in the midst of an on-camera interview with the plaintiffs, received a call on his cell phone from Air Force One. "It's the president," Chad called out, and viewers throughout the nation were able to hear Barack Obama's message of congratulations and support.

After the celebration in Washington, the excitement moved to California. David, Chad, Ted Boutrous, the plaintiffs, and other members of our team flew to Los Angeles from Washington. Lady traveled by car to Philadelphia to meet up with Ted, who had just finished his Third Circuit argument, and Matt McGill, and the three of them boarded a flight to California.

We all converged before a large outdoor crowd in a West Hollywood park. Cheers, laughter, and joyous chants greeted us and Los Angeles mayor Antonio Villaraigosa, as it began to sink in to all of us that this was the real thing—our four-and-a-half-year journey from the meetings at the Reiners' home and the marriage license rejections in clerks' offices was about to end.

Just forty-eight hours later, on Friday, June 28, the Ninth Circuit lifted the stay on Judge Walker's decision overturning Proposition 8. In Northern California, Sandy and Kris hurriedly prepared for their vows and traveled to City Hall in San Francisco. California attorney general Kamala Harris sped to San Francisco from her office in

Sacramento to perform California's first lesbian wedding since that day in November 2008 when the voters of California had made them illegal. It was fitting that this was taking place where San Francisco mayor Gavin Newsom had set the process in motion with his authorization for the issuance of marriage licenses nine years earlier. In a happy coincidence, Ted Boutrous was at that same moment arguing a case in the same San Francisco federal courtroom in which the *Perry* case had been tried before Judge Walker. He raced to City Hall and joined Sandy and Kris and throngs of well-wishers as they exchanged the vows that finally—and legally—formalized their marriage.

Thanks to a helpful call from Attorney General Harris, Jeff, Paul, and Mayor Villaraigosa overcame the initial reluctance of a Los Angeles county clerk who had not been informed of the Ninth Circuit's decision and received a marriage license, fulfilling their own dream of marriage.

All over California gays and lesbians joyfully followed Kris, Sandy, Paul, and Jeff into marriage, as did thousands of gay and lesbian couples in the days, weeks, and months afterwards. Many of these couples had been together for decades, and most had never dared to dream that one day they could be married. Proposition 8 and its painful memories were gradually receding into history.

Proposition 8, and the battle to overturn it, will be memorialized in books, videos, court decisions, and law school classes. Onstage it will be relived in performances of the play *8*, created by Dustin Lance Black for local, college, and high school theatrical groups everywhere. The HBO documentary by filmmakers/directors Ryan White and Ben Cotner, *The Case Against 8*, chronicling the entire journey from inception to denouement, was greeted by cheering crowds at the Sundance Film Festival in January 2014 and released in homes and theaters later that spring. It captures elegantly and poignantly the lives, frustrations, hopes, and loves of Kris, Sandy, Paul, and Jeff. No one who sees it can help but be deeply moved and full of admiration and respect for these two couples.

Marriage equality was the law in three states when the *Perry* case was filed. As this book goes to press, it has become legal in seventeen states and the District of Columbia, whose total population constitutes 38 percent of the nation. Five other courts (Utah, Oklahoma, Virginia, Texas, and Michigan) have overturned laws discriminating against marriage for gays and lesbians, decisions that are on appeal. Suits are on file against similar laws across the country in venues such as Virginia, where we, along with outstanding Virginia lawyers, have won a district court case on behalf of four plaintiffs striking down that state's restrictive laws. One or more of these cases are virtually certain to wind up in the Supreme Court—probably sooner than anyone would have expected when the Court released its two marriage equality decisions in June 2013.

Similar change is occurring internationally. When we started trial in January 2010, the Netherlands was one of the few places in the world where gays and lesbians could marry. As we completed this book, Scotland's parliament had just voted overwhelmingly (105–18) to allow same-sex marriage, making it the seventeenth among a rapidly growing number of countries to do so. The roll included, as well as the Netherlands (the first to do so, in 2001), England and Wales, France, Brazil, Uruguay, New Zealand, Iceland, Norway, Sweden, Denmark, Belgium, Spain, Portugal, South Africa, Canada, Argentina, and parts of Mexico.

A tide is clearly sweeping the world. In the United States public opinion polls showed national sentiment against same-sex marriage by an average of 17 percentage points in May 2009. By 2014 a rough average of polls indicated that people approved of the right of gays and lesbians to marry by 8 to 10 or more points. Seventy percent or more of sample groups under the age of thirty support marriage equality. Those young people are the spirit, sense, and sentiment of the future.

Public support for marriage equality has shifted more dramatically and more rapidly than for any other major public political issue in our lifetime. What was a "wedge" issue in the 2004 presidential election is now, just ten years later, becoming widely accepted by the public and politicians alike.

Another phenomenon is complementing the progress in the courts and public opinion polls: We are becoming more open and accepting of differences in sexual orientation as a nation. As more gays and lesbians shed their fears and come out, as more people realize that their sons, daughters, sisters, brothers, coworkers, neighbors, and friends are gay—and have been all along—as gays and lesbians are seen as normal, loving, decent members of our lives and our communities, prejudice toward gays and lesbians is melting away in all walks of life. We are becoming truer to our American ideals of equality, freedom, and inclusion.

———

We are extraordinarily proud to have been a small part of this journey at a pivotal point in history. We are grateful to have been entrusted with bringing the Proposition 8 case in our courts, with arguing the case for our clients and gays and lesbians everywhere, and with making their case to the American public.

We feel that this journey has been the most rewarding, enriching, and satisfying chapter in our professional lives, as it has given us the opportunity to work together; to learn in depth about sexual orientation, marriage, and discrimination; to make progress toward marriage equality in this country; and to tell this story in our courts and to the public through the media and this book.

Acknowledgments

It would be impossible for us properly to acknowledge all of the invaluable assistance we have received in the course of producing this book. To those we have failed to mention, it is not out of lack of appreciation for the many hours of ideas, inspiration, and sage advice we have received along the way. We are truly grateful to those we name here and countless others who have helped us bring this project into existence.

We start with our wives, Mary and Lady, who have invested many, many hours of encouragement, support, prodding, editing, patience, and love. This book could never have been started, much less finished, without them.

The *Perry* case itself, and thus this chronicle of the case, was the product of dedicated, outstanding, and selfless assistance from innumerable lawyers and staff members of our respective firms as well as substantial financial contributions from the two firms. At Gibson Dunn, special thanks to firm chairman Kenneth Doran for putting the resources of the entire firm at our disposal and for authorizing it to contribute a large proportion of the legal services pro bono. Extraordinary contributions to the case in the form of outstanding lawyering were made by Theodore J. Boutrous Jr., Christopher Dusseault, Matthew McGill, Ethan Dettmer, Amir Tayrani, Theane Evangelis, Joshua Lipshutz, Enrique Monagas, Abbey Hudson, Sarah Piepmeier, and many more. Special thanks to Ted's assistant of more than twenty years, Helen Voss, for her time, energy, commitment, and patience during, after, and before normal working hours, as well as weekends. We're also particularly deeply in debt to all the lawyers and staff in Gibson Dunn's San Francisco office, who gave us everything we asked—and more—during all phases of the case, at all times of the day and night, but in particular during the trial and various other hearings in San Francisco.

At Boies, Schiller & Flexner, special thanks go to Bob Silver, Jeremy Goldman, Steven Holtzman, Ted Uno, Rosanne Baxter, Beko Reblitz-Richardson, Josh Schiller, Meredith Dearborn, Rick Bettan, and Dawn Schneider.

Throughout our work on this book, we received energetic, enthusiastic, and invariably cheerful efforts from Michael D'Antonio, who provided invaluable help with research, collection of information, and ideas.

As recounted in these pages, this case began with an inspiration and suggestion from Kate Moulene. Thank you, Kate, for suggesting the initial call to Ted and for planting the seed and providing the idea that started it all.

The federal challenge to Proposition 8 was conceived by Rob and Michele Reiner and Chad Griffin and driven by their fierce determination, intense commitment, and passionate dedication to equality for gay and lesbian Californians. They were the spark and the fuel that got this case going and propelled it every step of the way. Their energy and passion, their enthusiasm, and their idealism are contagious and inspirational. They were at conferences, meetings, in court, at press conferences and fund-raisers. They were everywhere. They are great Americans and true heroes. Chad is now president of the Human Rights Campaign. The LGBT community could not have a more effective leader.

As we commenced work on the *Perry* case, we created the American Foundation for Equal Rights (AFER), a 501(c)(3) nonprofit organization, to receive contributions and supervise the funding of the litigation. Its board of directors consists of Chad Griffin (president), Michele and Rob Reiner, Dustin Lance Black, Bruce Cohen, Kristina Schake, Ken Mehlman, and Jonathan Lewis. Its executive director is

Adam Umhoefer. Other AFER staffers rendered vital assistance, including Yusef Robb, Elizabeth Riel, and Shumway Marshall.

For the *Perry* case and its continuing efforts to achieve marriage equality throughout this nation, AFER has received financial support from many persons, associations, foundations, and corporations. If we were to list each of them individually, we would inevitably have to draw some lines and risk some omissions. We will instead simply say that each of them made the *Perry* case happen, and they are continuing to make marriage equality progress in places such as Virginia and elsewhere. They represent scores of deeply committed individuals who are doing everything they can to bring about justice and equality in this nation. They will never receive all the gratitude they deserve, but they have made and are making a huge difference, which is the motivation for their generosity. We thank them for their contributions to redeeming the dreams of so many individuals.

We set out to influence public opinion at the same time we sought to achieve victory in court. That effort was guided by the Griffin-Schake communications firm, including, of course, Chad Griffin and Kristina Schake, as well as their colleague Felix Schein. In addition to all the other things he did, Chad, along with Kristina, managed, orchestrated, and disciplined our public relations effort. Kristina was there from the beginning, providing her ideas, instincts, judgment, and charm, helping us assist and support the plaintiffs with her wisdom and kindness and in other ways too numerous to recite.

We were closely tracked throughout this case by the award-winning photographer Diana Walker. She recorded our planning, our preparation, and our moods, and exquisitely captured members of our legal team and our plaintiffs throughout the history of this case. She was always there, unobtrusive and always delightful to be around. Some of her marvelous photographs adorn these pages. Thousands more exist in her archives. We will always treasure her work and the memories it evokes.

Stan Pottinger first approached us about writing this book. He and our editor, Rick Kot, and the fantastic team at Viking—Nick Bromley,

Barbara Campo, Nancy Resnick, Roland Ottewell, and Jane Cavo-
lina—made skillful, indefatigable, and meticulous contributions that
guided this book to completion.

Ben Cotner and Ryan White filmed the development of this case
from start to finish, the participants and the action. They were with us
constantly, quietly recording the thinking, the stress, the emotions,
and the thrills. Their award-winning work became the HBO documentary *The Case Against 8*. We are enormously grateful for the incredible and extraordinarily professional contributions of Sheila
Nevins and her team at HBO for making this documentary into an
unforgettable masterpiece.

Among his many other contributions, Academy Award winner
Dustin Lance Black created the play *8*. When the Supreme Court prevented the broadcasting of the *Perry* trial, he took the written transcript and transformed it into a riveting play that has been performed
by the world's leading acting talent and theatrical groups everywhere.
The play brings audiences to their feet wherever it is performed.

Finally, but most importantly, our four plaintiffs, Kris Perry, Sandy
Stier, Paul Katami, and Jeff Zarrillo, provided inspiration and wisdom.
We constantly reminded ourselves that this case was and is all about
them. We have loved every minute of our lives with them.

Index